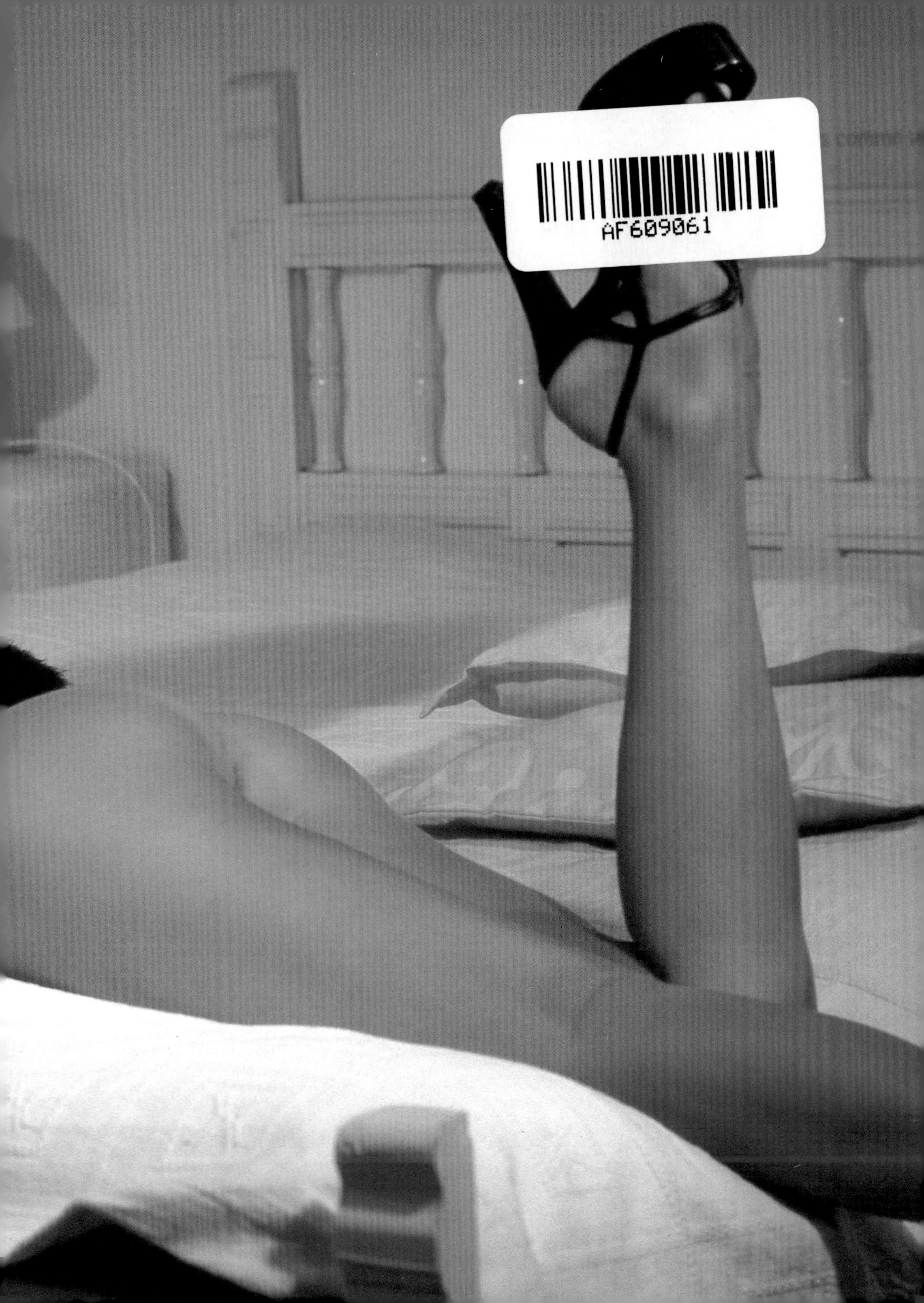

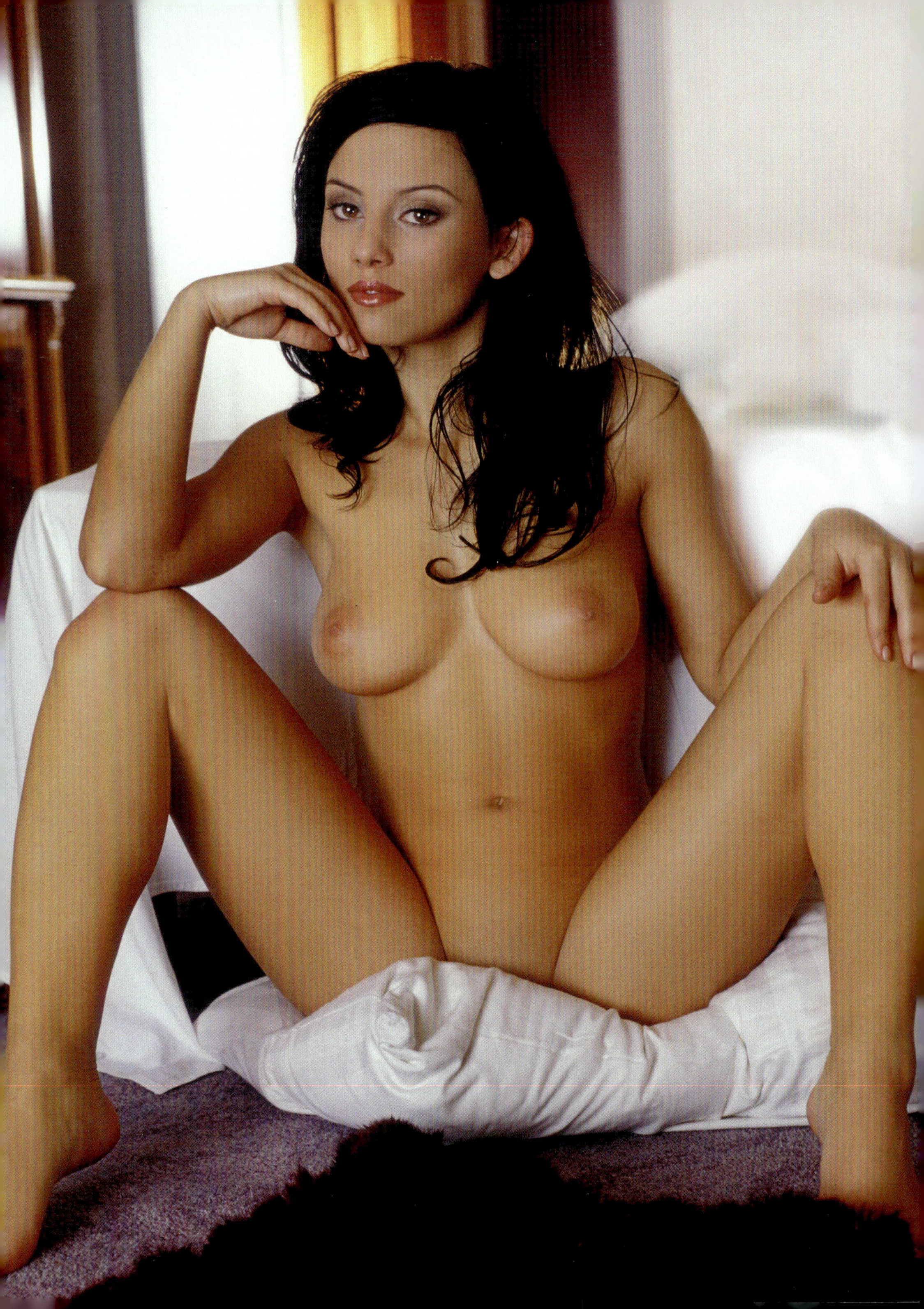

HOT 19

Emmanuel D. Fouquet

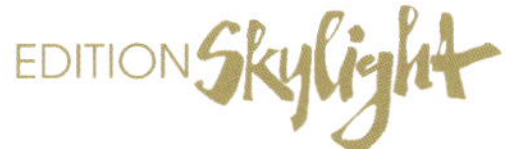

1st Edition 2012

EDITION SKYLIGHT
Willikonerstr. 10
CH-8618 Oetwil am See/Zürich
Switzerland
Mail: info@edition-skylight.com
Web: www.edition-skylight.com

ISBN 978-3-03766-632-6

Bibliographic information published by Die Deutsche Bibliothek
Die Deutsche Bibliothek lists this publication in the Deutsche Nationalbibliografie; detailed bibliographic data are available in the Internet at http://dnb.ddb.de.

Design: WGB
Printed in Italy

PREFACE

Many people ask me why I work with girls of between 18 and 20, i.e. quite young. I freely admit I prefer taking pictures of young girls than older women. Girls aged between 18 and 20 have everything you need to excite a man's imagination such as the age restrictions, the crossing of borderlines…

Of course, these young women consciously play with the need to look naïve, with its innocent, natural qualities. The same look can be seen everywhere today, in songs, fashion and the cinema.

In this day and age, women all want to preserve their youthfulness right up to old age. And let's not forget that today's generation of young girls is far from innocent. This kind of photography is not new and will always have its place in society. And I am not thinking of morbid perversions such as paedophilia, etc.

Of course, my photography is a "turn-on", a sort of Viagra, because, let's face it, it is extremely exciting for a man to view young girls in provocative poses. The aspects of forbidden love, past memories, one's first love, all this and related fantasies are triggered by these very young girls, who attract them like a magnet.

If he has the chance to get to know a much younger one, what man in his mid-life crisis would find women of a comparable age attractive, if they only remind him of why he left home in the first place?

It's the youngest and most beautiful girls who do the nastiest things…

Emmanuel D. Fouquet

VORWORT

Viele Leute haben mich gefragt, weshalb ich speziell mit solchen Mädchen Aufnahmen mache, mit Lolitas, kindlichen Frauen und Püppchen. Es war einfach für mich den Männerfantasien nach der „Kind-Frau" mittels Kamera nachzukommen, mit Bildern. Das war schon immer so, obwohl ich nicht nur Aufnahmen mit Lolitas mache, gebe ich gerne zu, dass ich persönlich lieber junge Frauen fotografiere als reifere. Junge Frauen zwischen 18 und 20 haben all das, was die Fantasien der Männer reizt – die Verbote, die Grenzüberschreitungen …

Natürlich spielen diese jungen Frauen bewusst mit der Vorgabe der Naivität (Jungfräulichkeit) und ihrer Natürlichkeit. Das zeigt sich überall, in den Liedern, in der Mode, im Kino etc.

In der heutigen Zeit wollen alle Frauen ihre Jugendlichkeit bewahren bis ins hohe Alter. Und vergessen wir nicht, dass die heutige Generation dieser jungen Mädchen weit davon entfernt ist, unschuldig zu sein.

Diese Art der Fotografie ist nicht neu und wird immer ihren Platz in der Gesellschaft haben. Dabei denke ich nicht an die krankhaften Auswüchse wie Pädophilie usw.

Meine Fotografie ist natürlich eine „Scharfmacherei", sozusagen ein Viagra, denn seien wir ehrlich, es ist für einen Mann äusserst erregend, diese aufreizenden Posen der sehr jungen Mädchen zu betrachten. Die Seite der verbotenen Liebe, Erinnerungen an Vergangenes, erste Jugendliebe, all das gegen diese sehr jungen Mädchen, das zieht magnetisch an.

Welcher Mann in seiner Midlifekrise wird sich an eine gleichaltrige Frau wenden, wenn er die Möglichkeit einer jüngeren hat, die ihn daran erinnert, warum er von zu Hause ausgezogen ist?

Es sind die schönsten und jüngsten Mädchen, die die schlimmsten Dinge tun …

Emmanuel D. Fouquet

avant PROPOS

Beaucoup de gens m'ont demandé pourquoi je travaille justement avec des jeunes filles de 18 – 20 ans. J'avoue préférer shooter une petite NANA qu'une femme mûre, c'est personnel! Les jeunes filles de 18 – 20 ans font fantasmées parce qu'elles portent en elles tout les interdits de la limite acceptable ...

Bien sûr c'est tendancieux parce qu'elles jongle souvent avec la notion de virginité et de fraicheur. Ces attitudes marchent dans la chanson, dans la mode, et dans le cinéma.

Aujourd'hui, toutes les femmes veulent rester jeunes, très longtemps. Et n'oublions pas que cette génération de jeunes filles est loin d'être innocente. Ce style de photo n'est pas nouveau et trouvera toujours sa place dans notre société. Bien sûr, je ne parle pas de ces vicieux pathologiques comme les pédophiles, etc.

Ma photographie est bien entendu une « pilule excitante », car, soyons honnêtes, c'est très excitant pour un homme de contempler les poses attirantes de ces jeunes femmes. Le côté amour interdit, réminiscence du passé, première amour d'enfance, l'attire comme un aimant vers ces très jeunes femmes.

Quel homme en pleine crise de la quarantaine se tournera vers une femme de son âge s'il a la possibilité d'en avoir une plus jeune qui lui rappelle pourquoi il est parti ?

Ce sont les filles les plus belles et les plus jeunes qui font les choses les plus sales ...

Emmanuel D. Fouquet

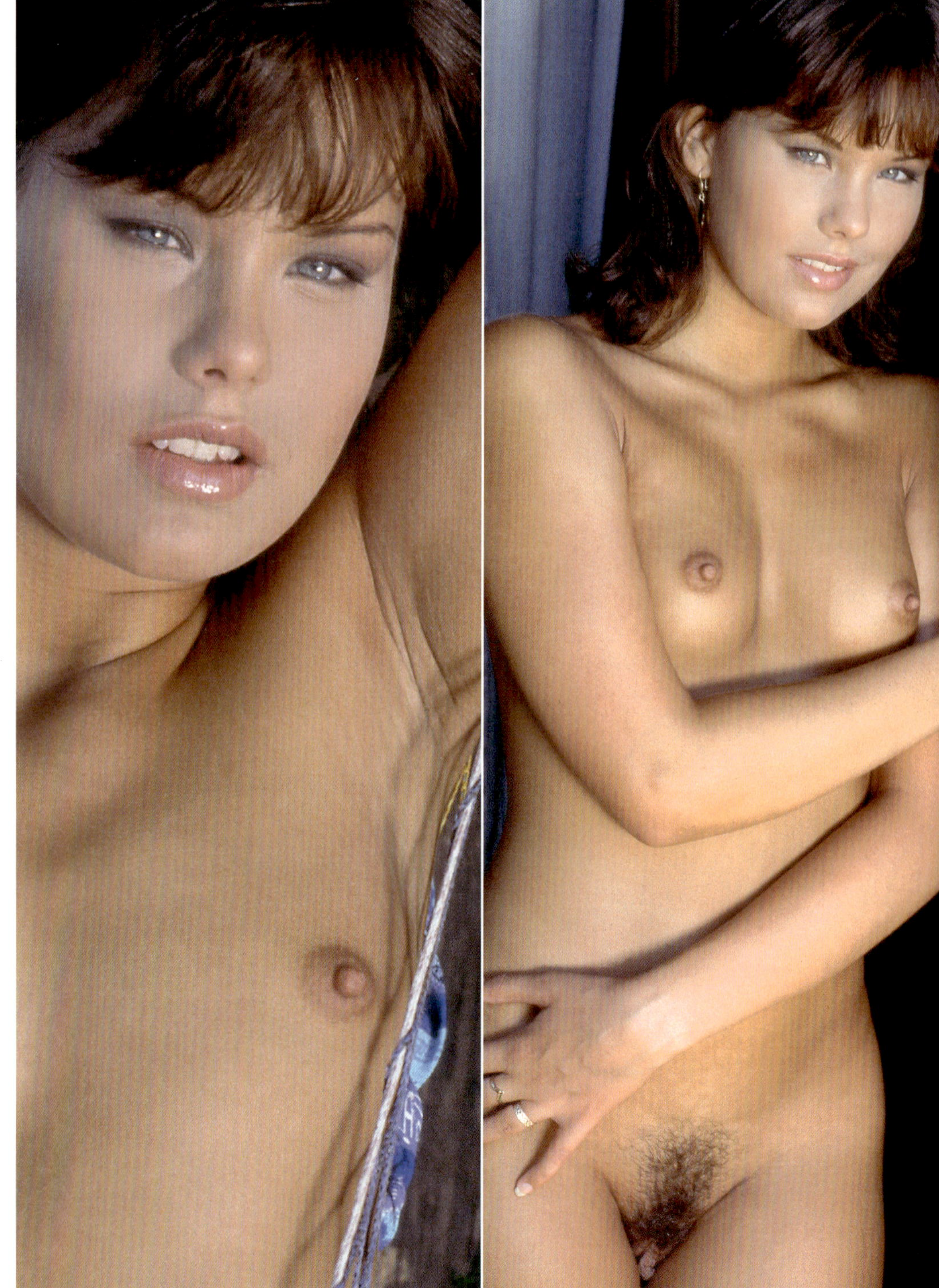

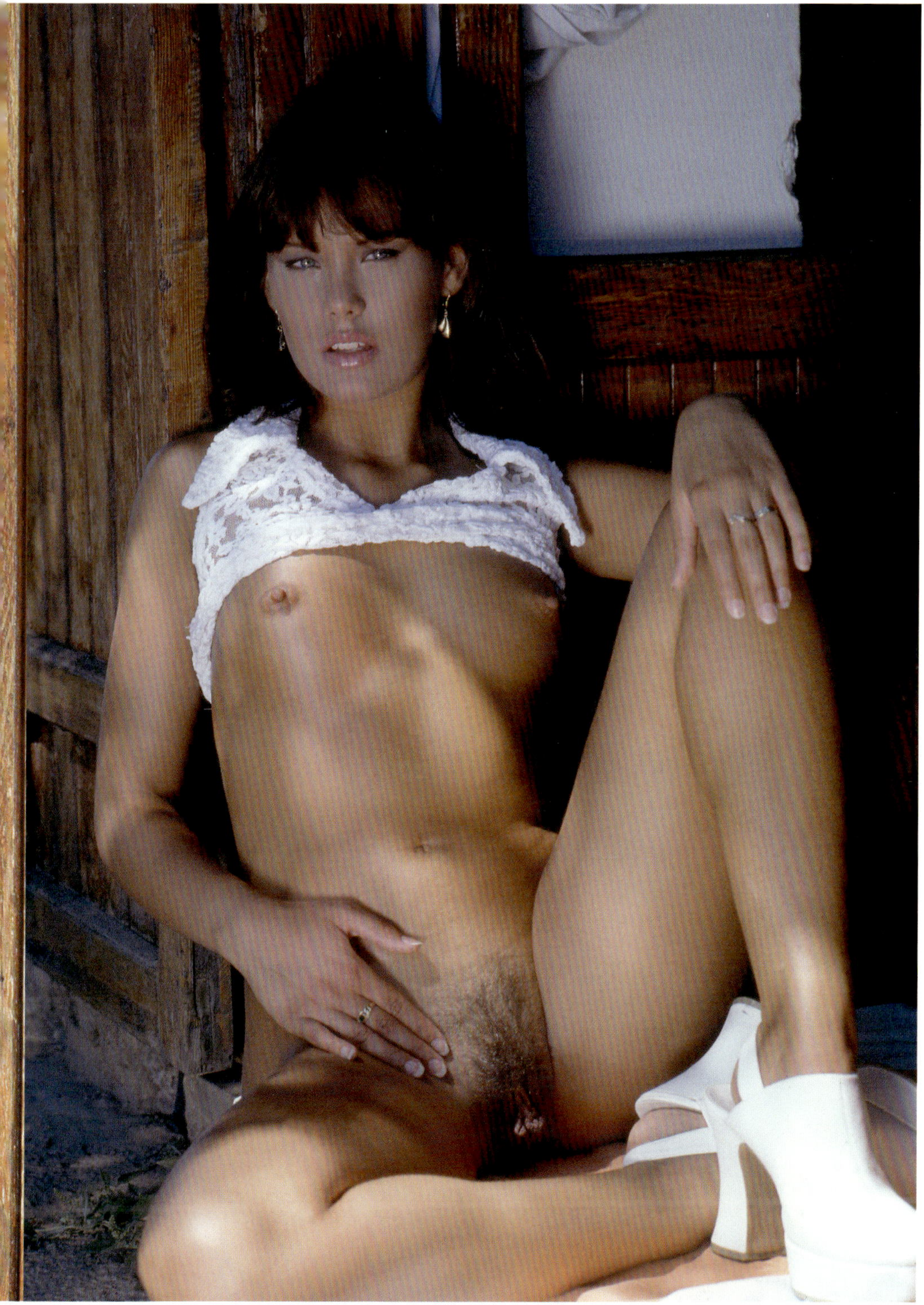

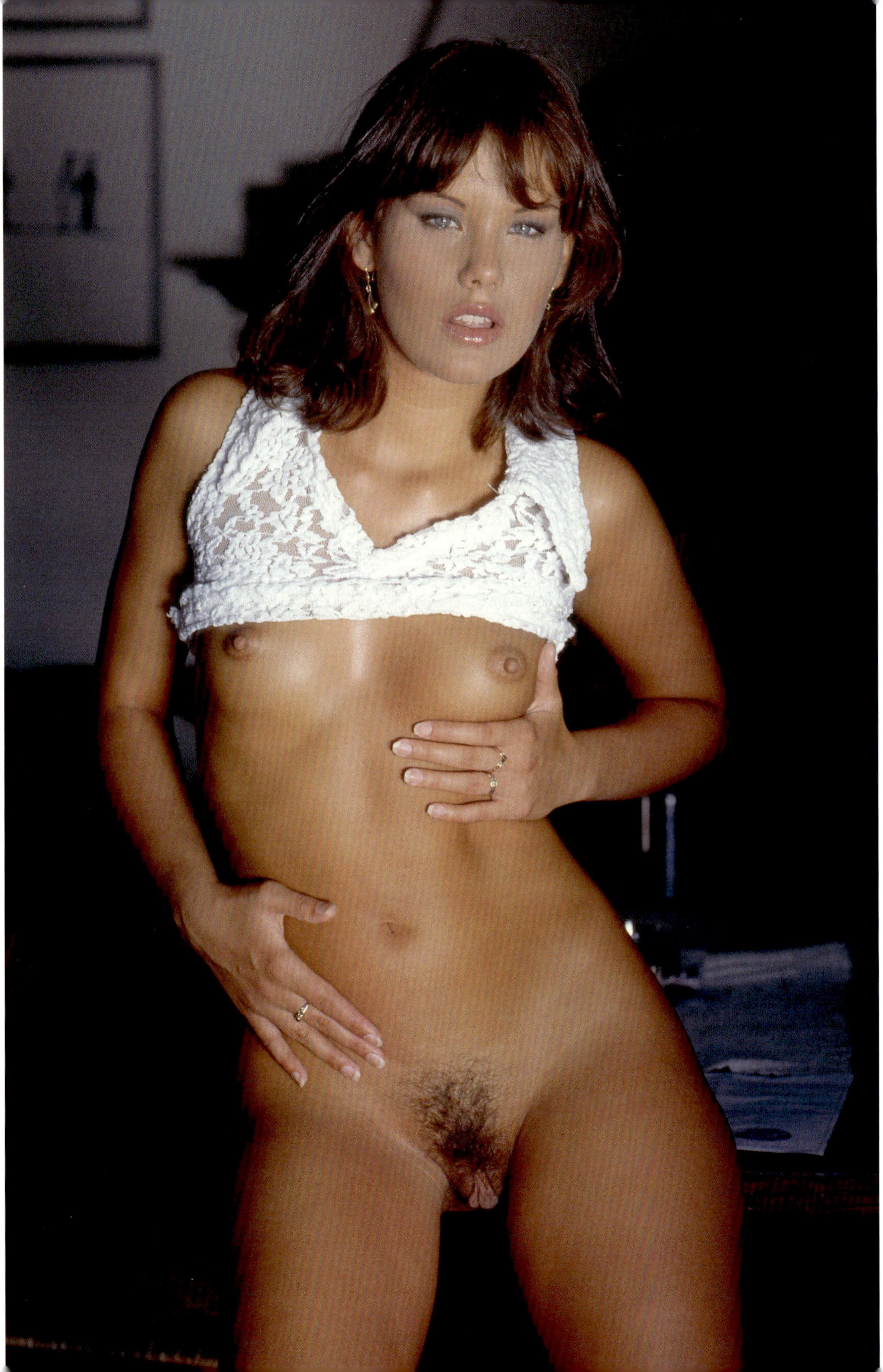

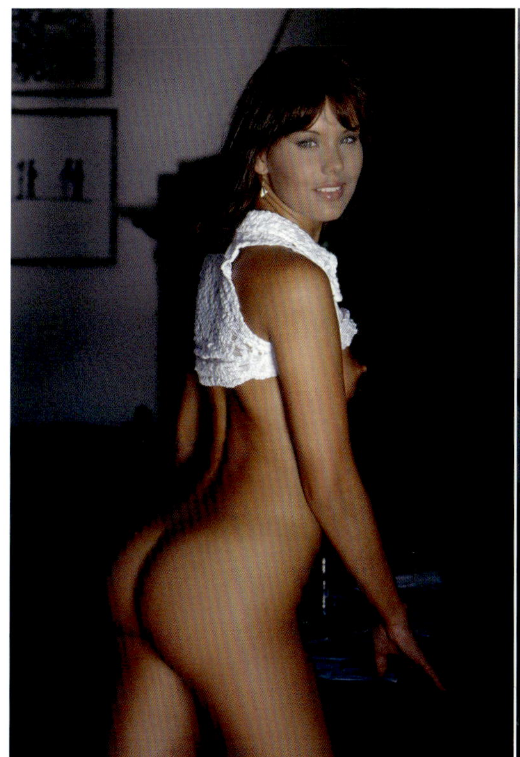

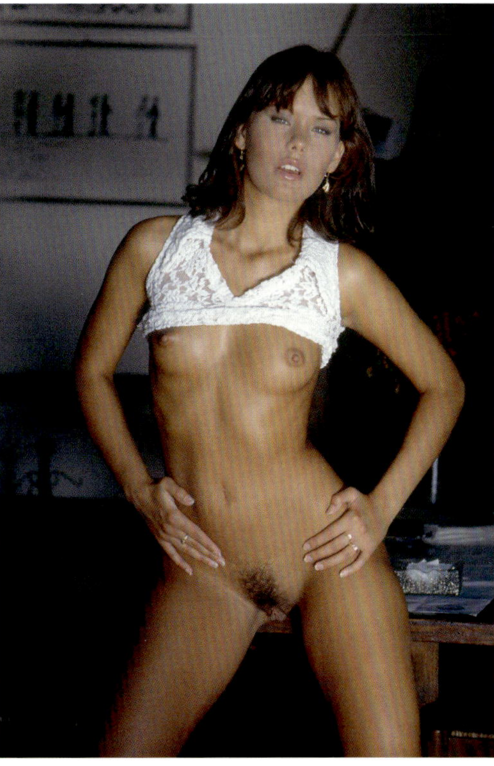

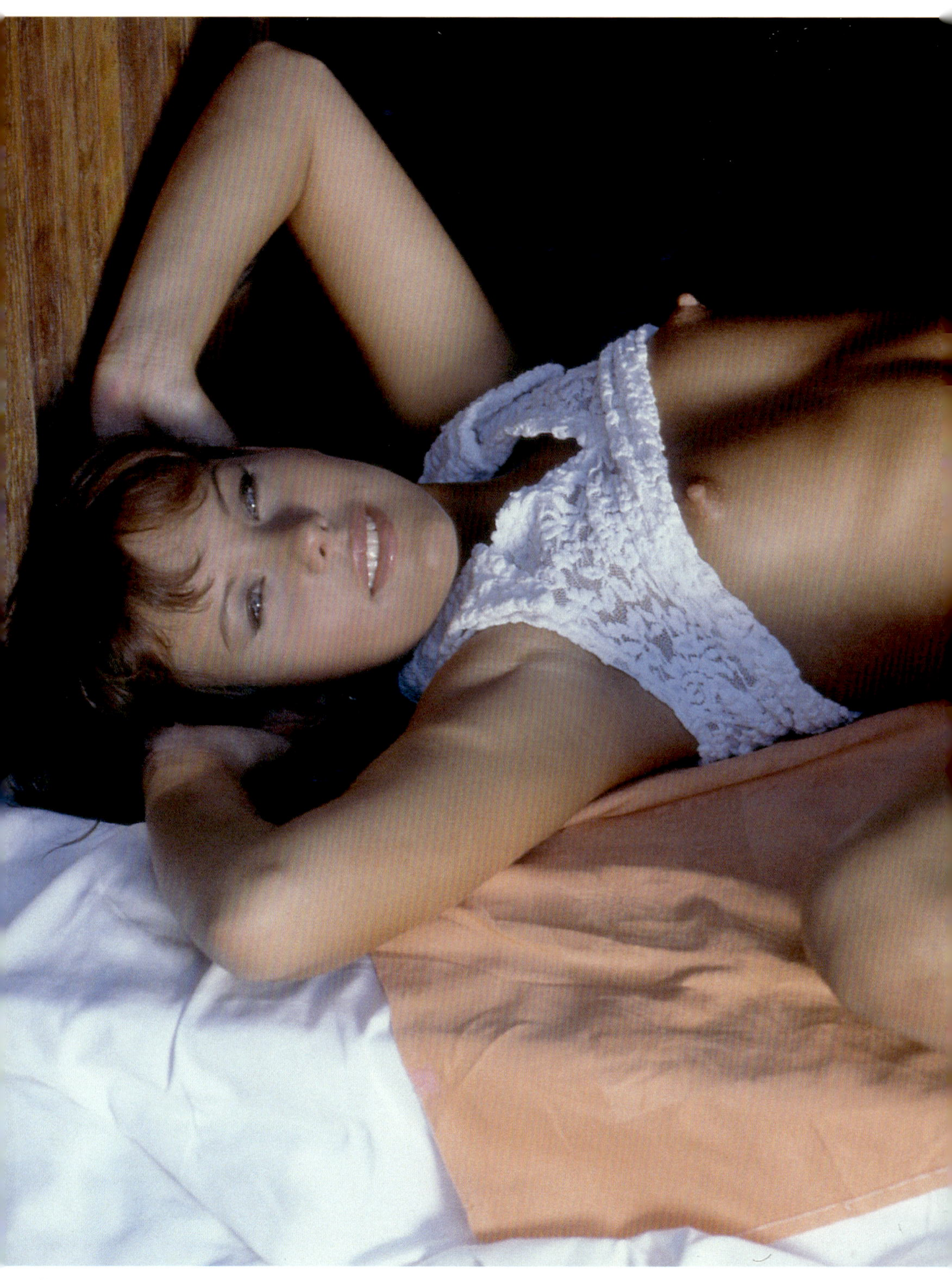

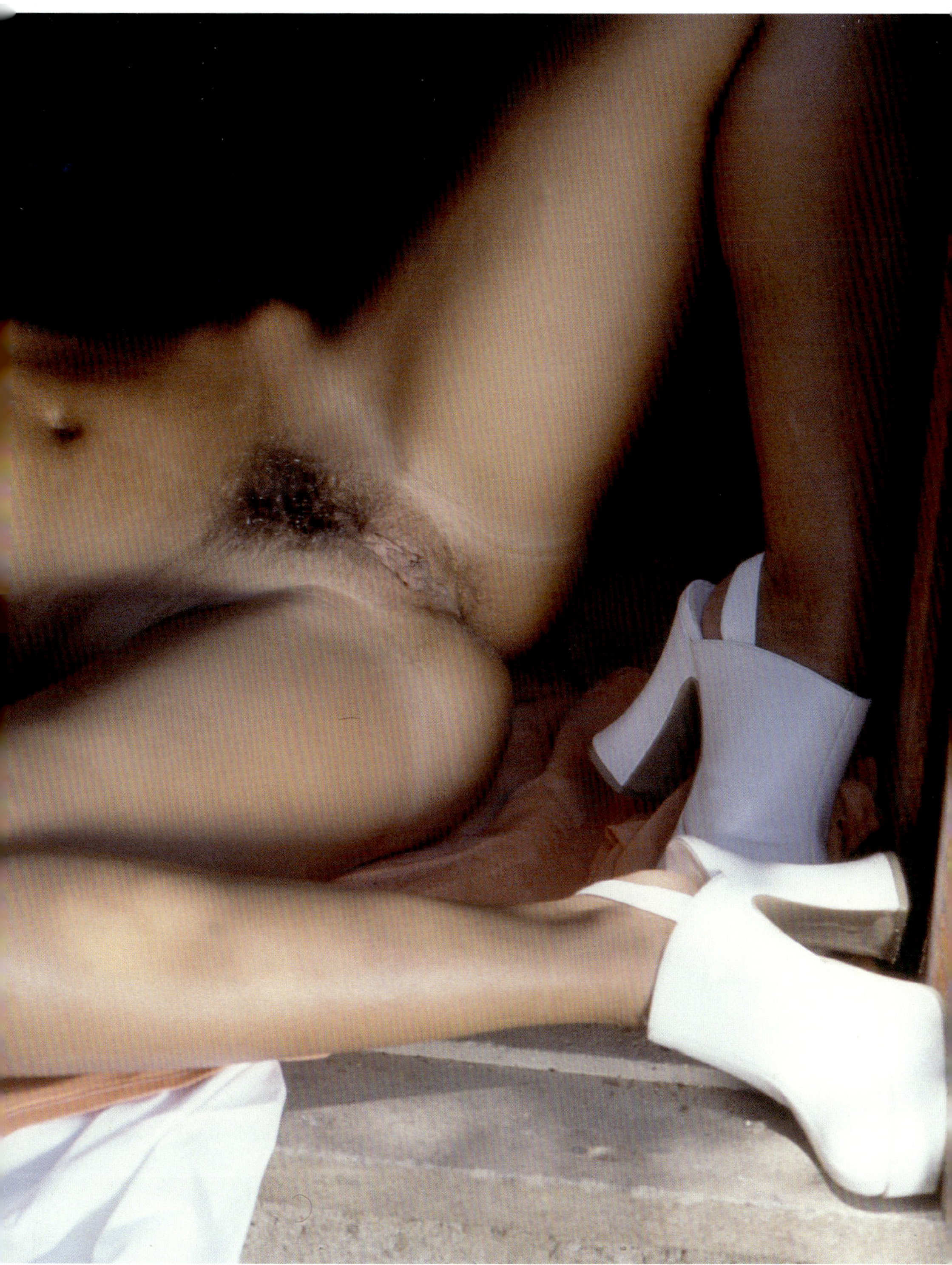

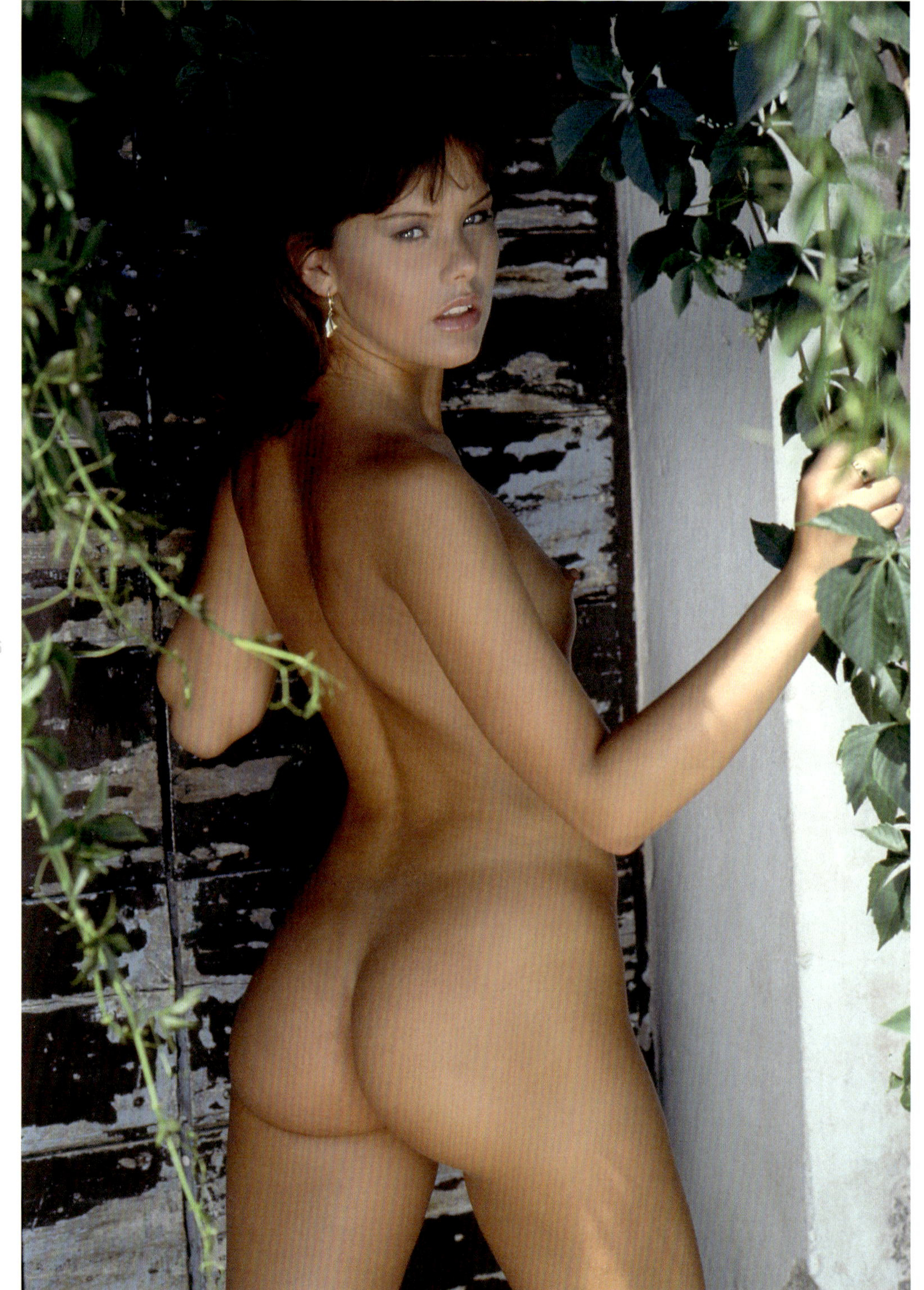

ava

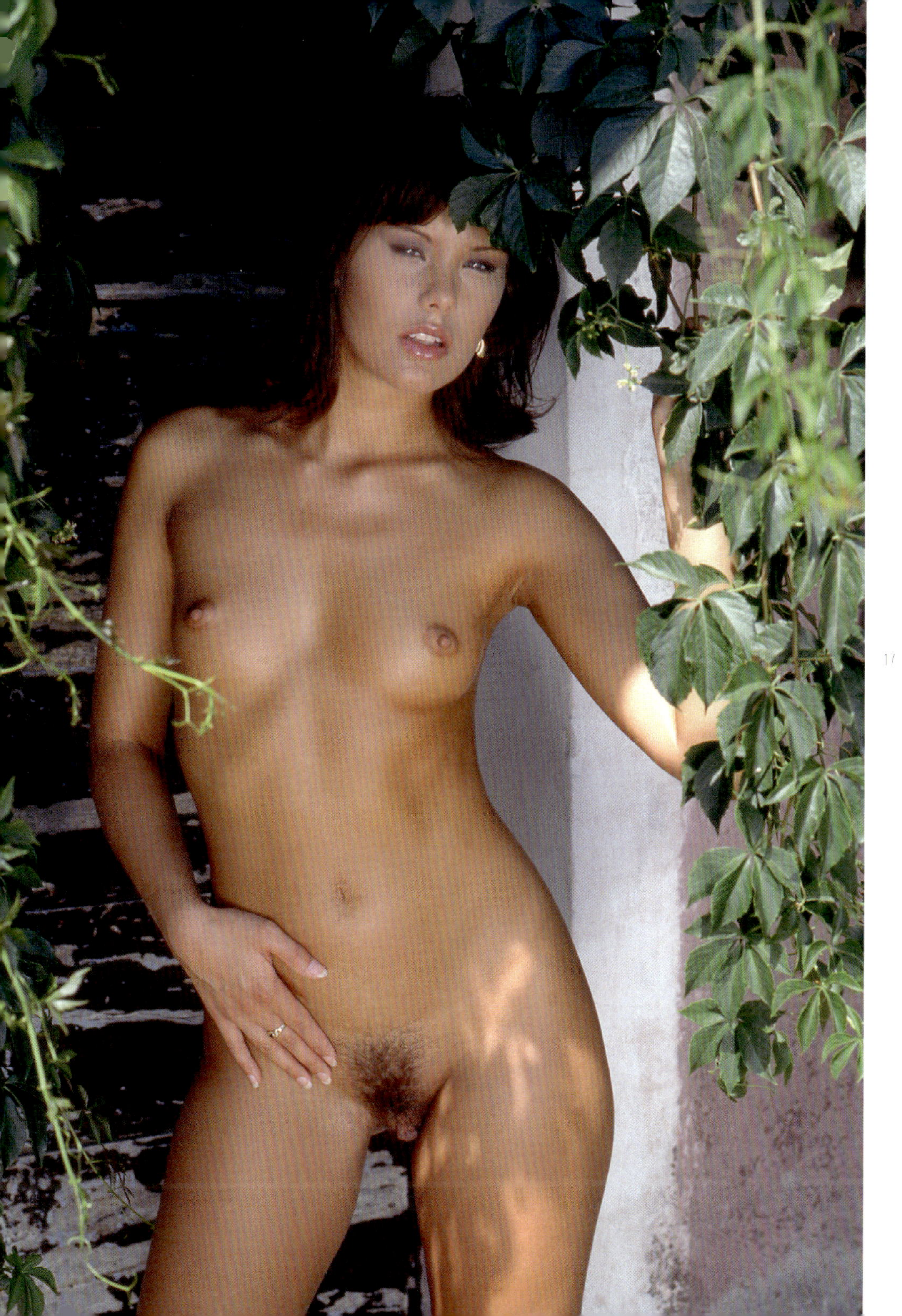

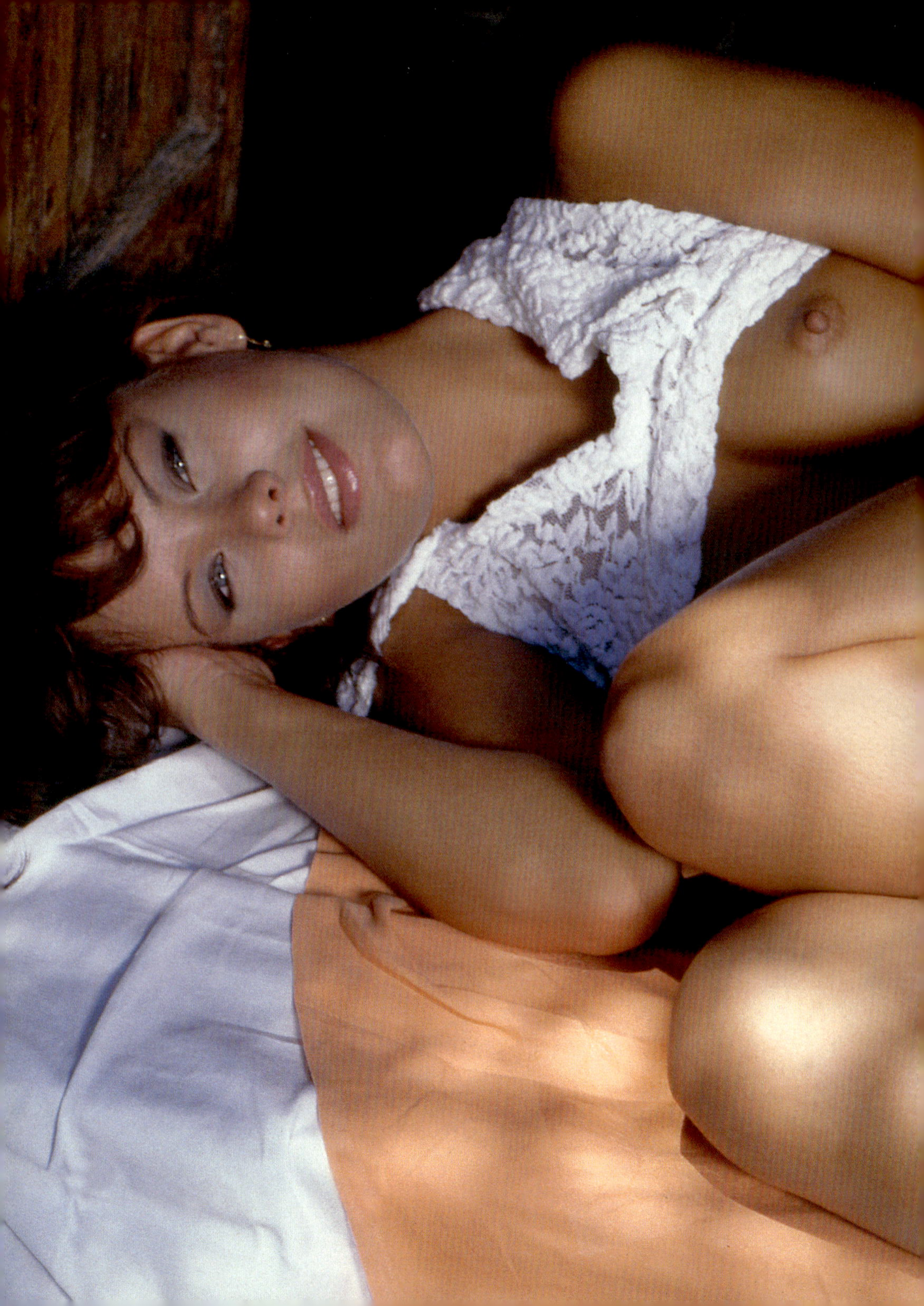

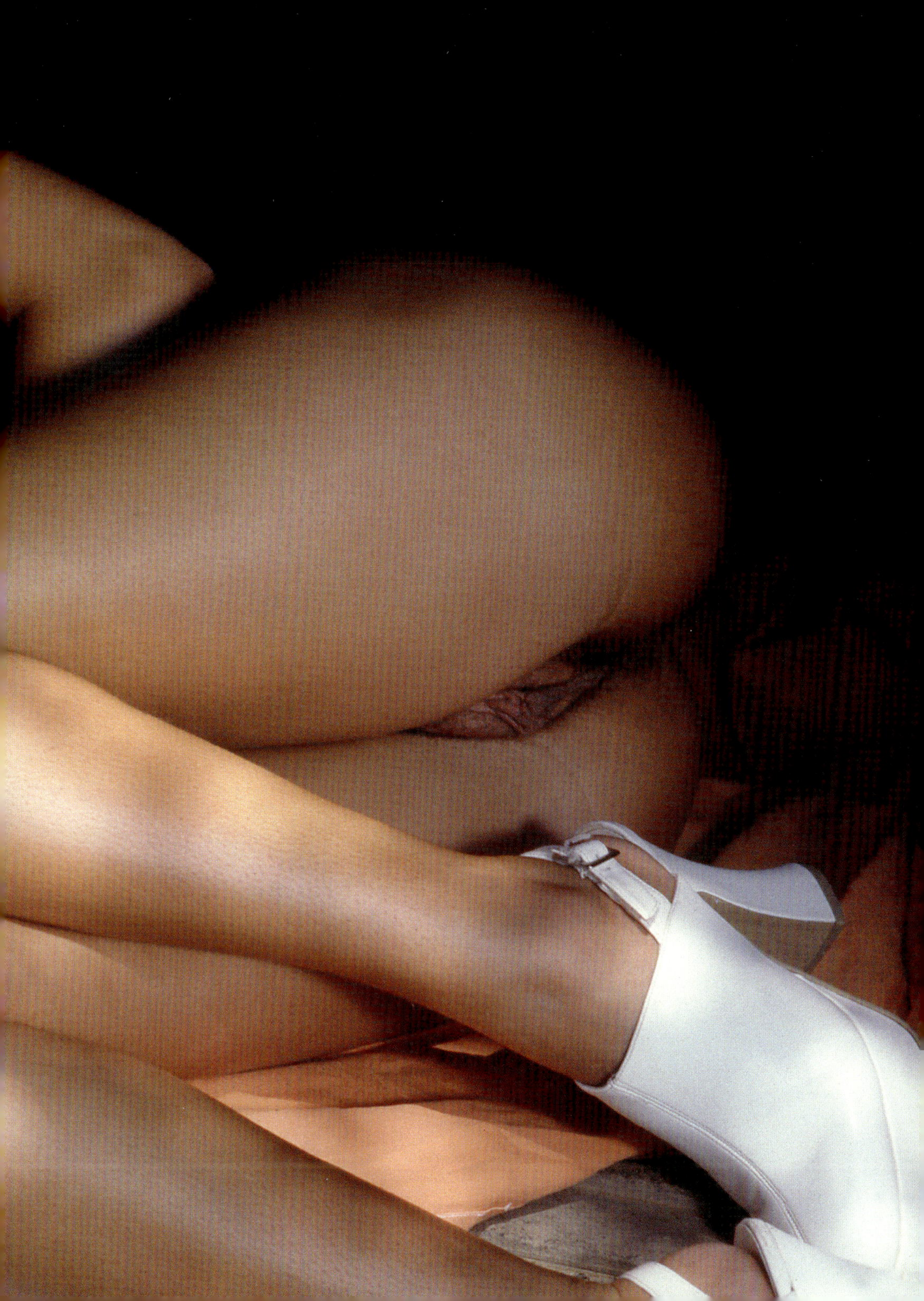

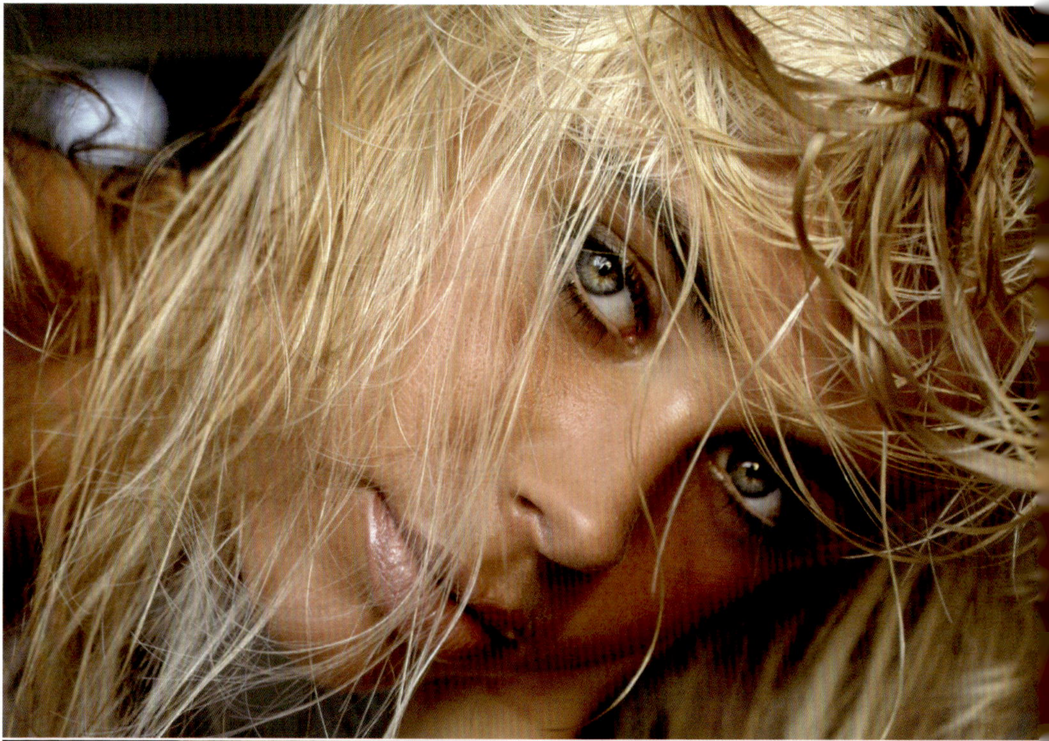

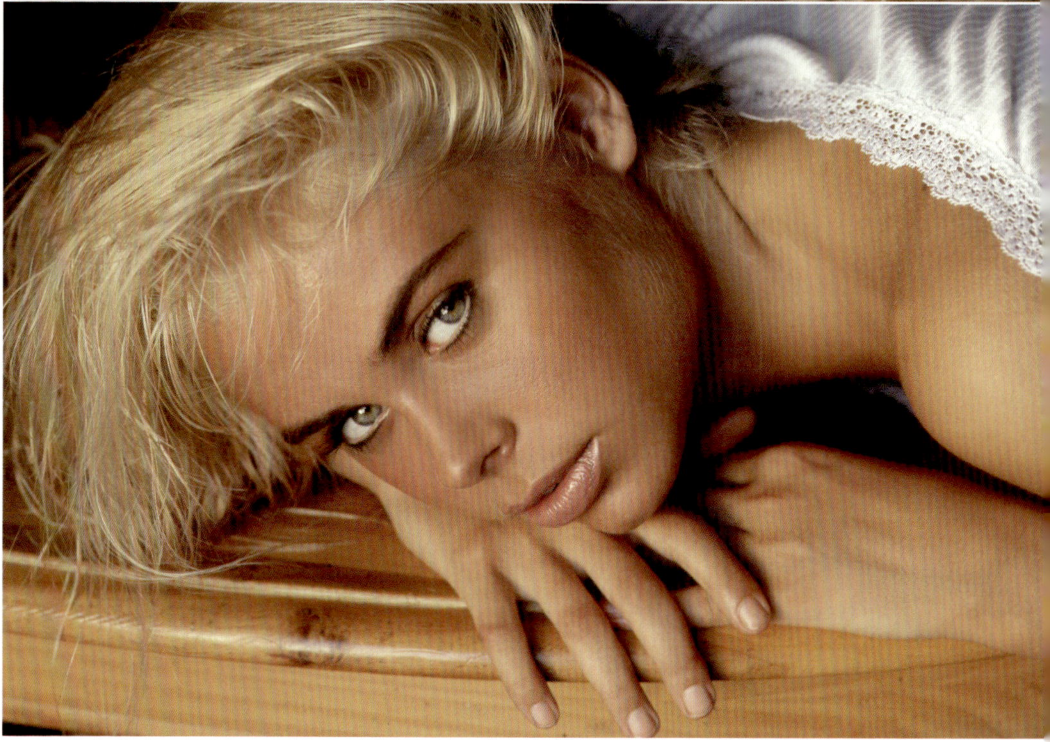

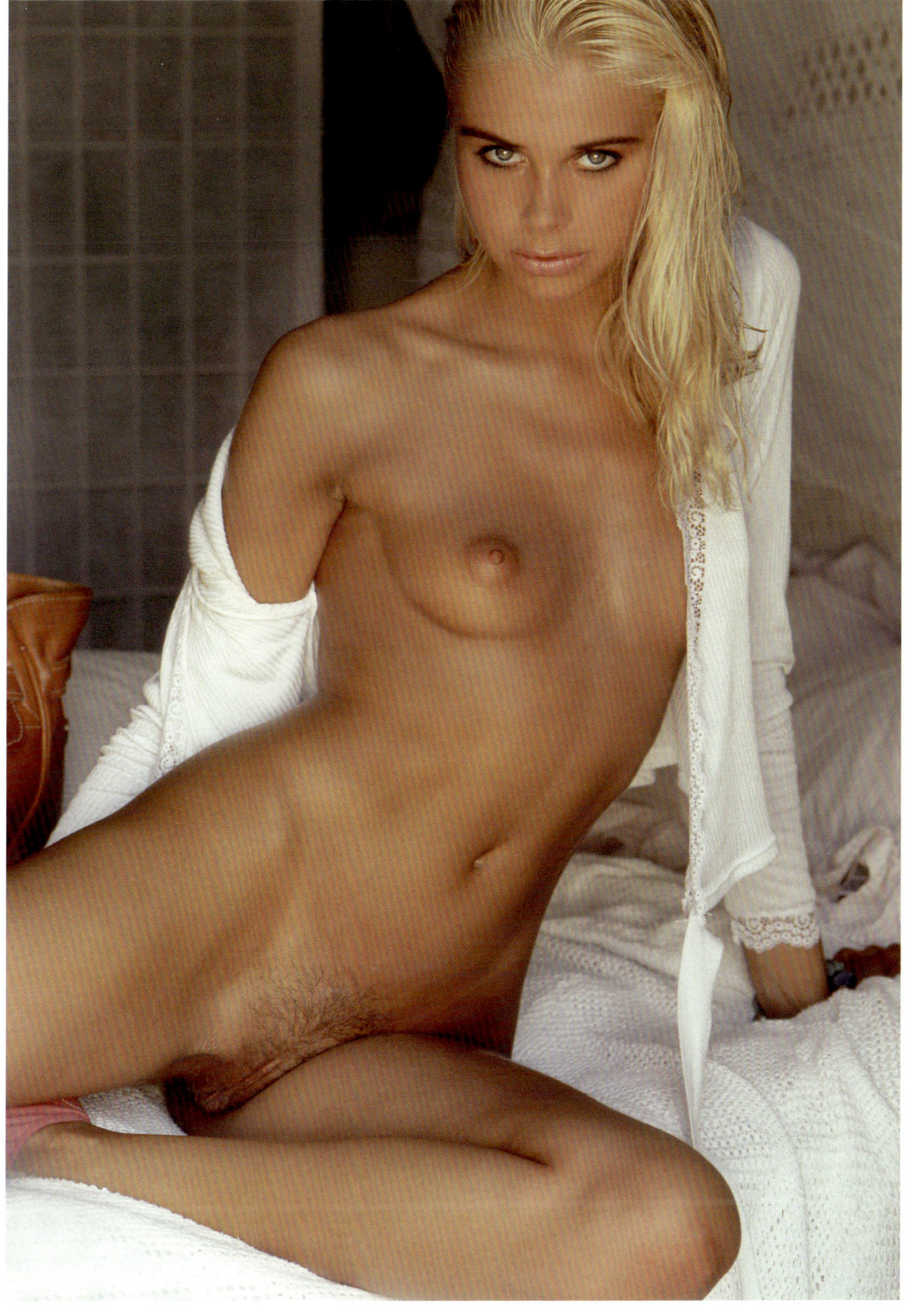

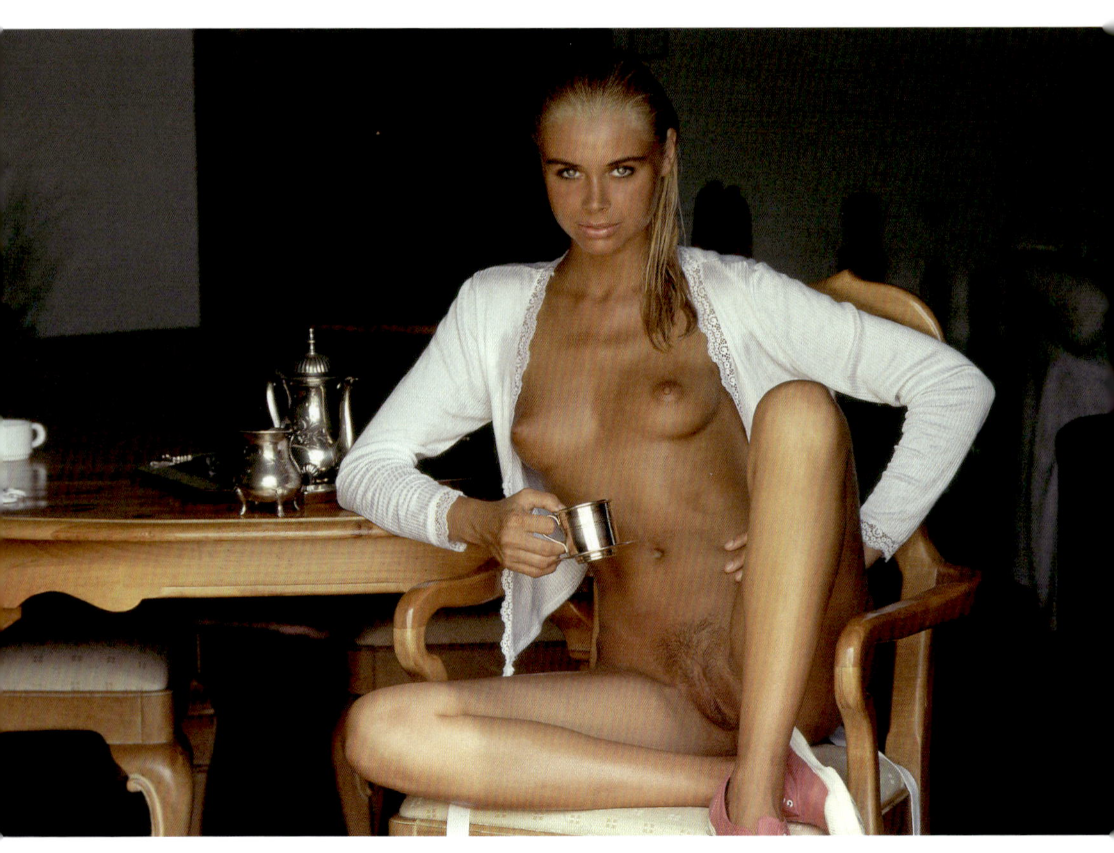

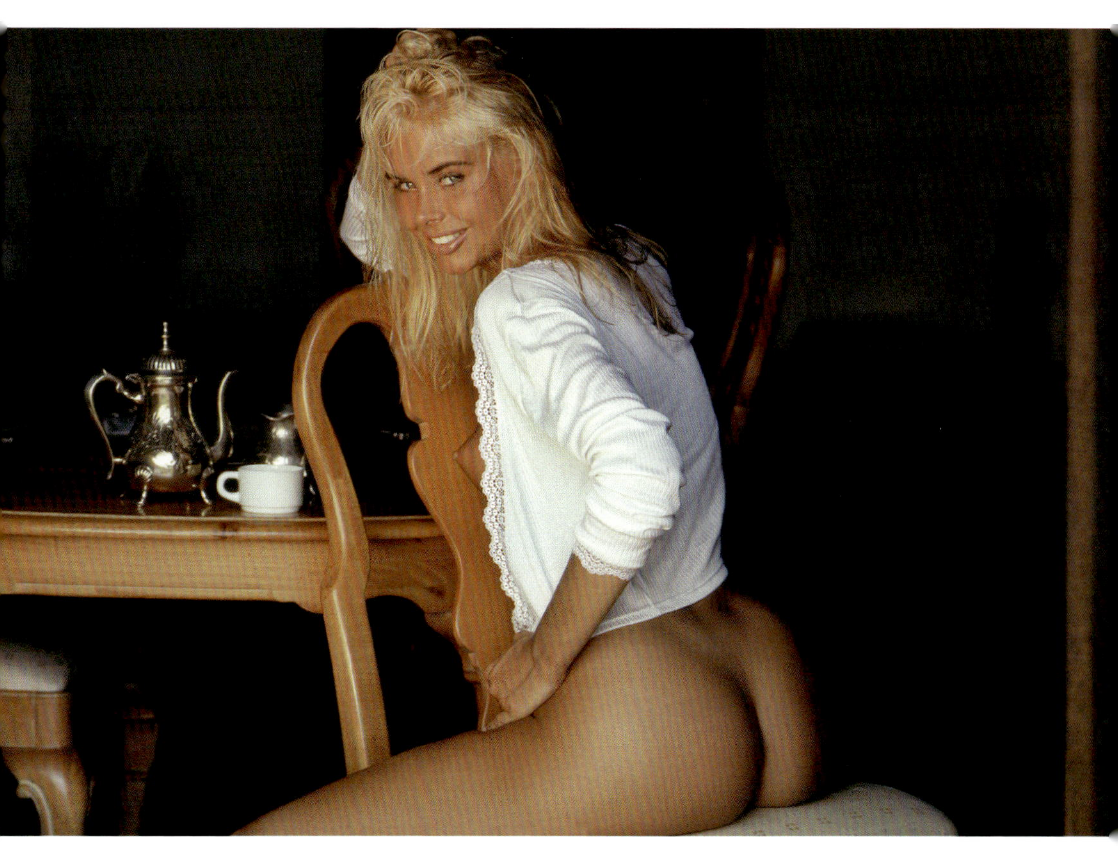

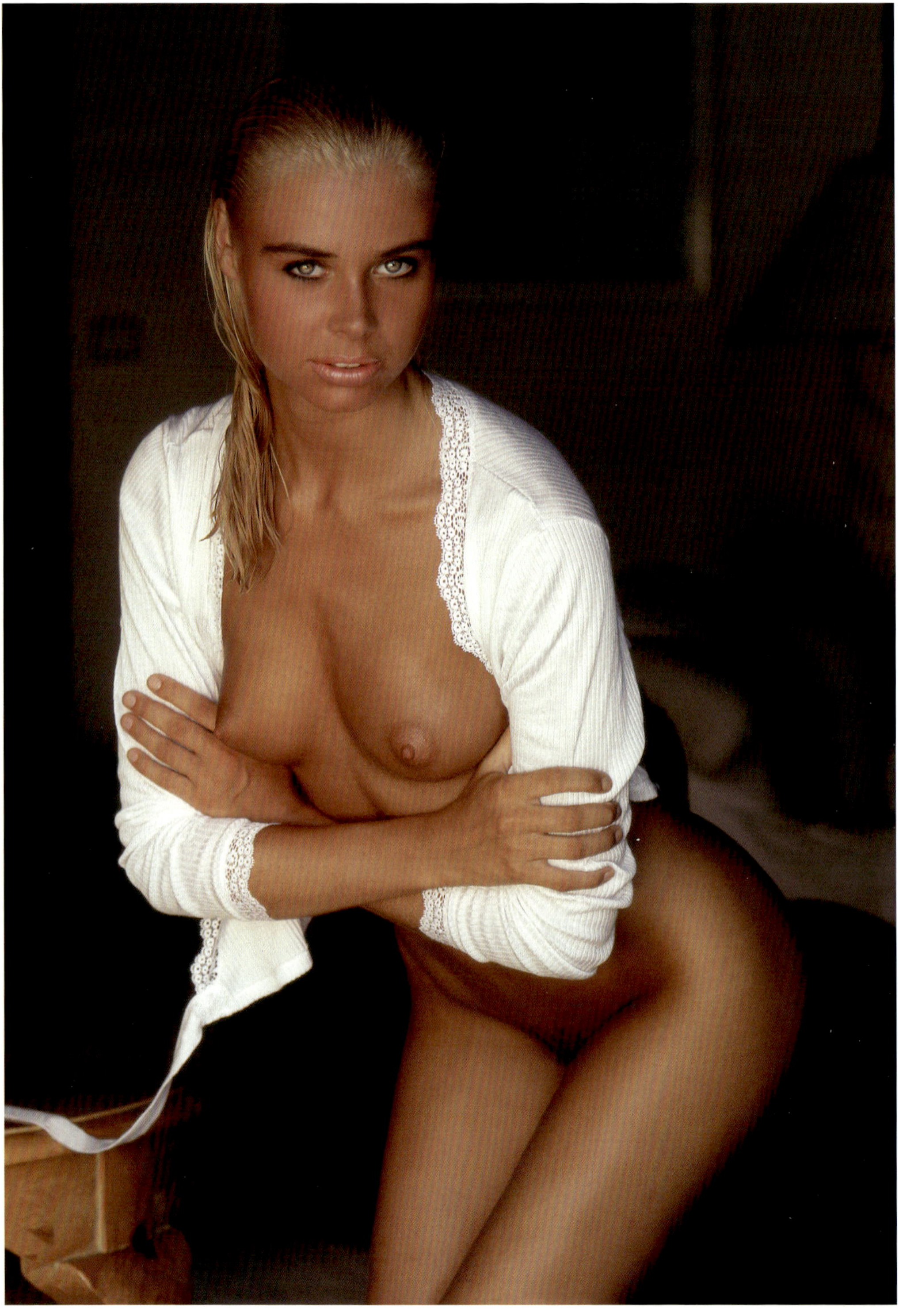

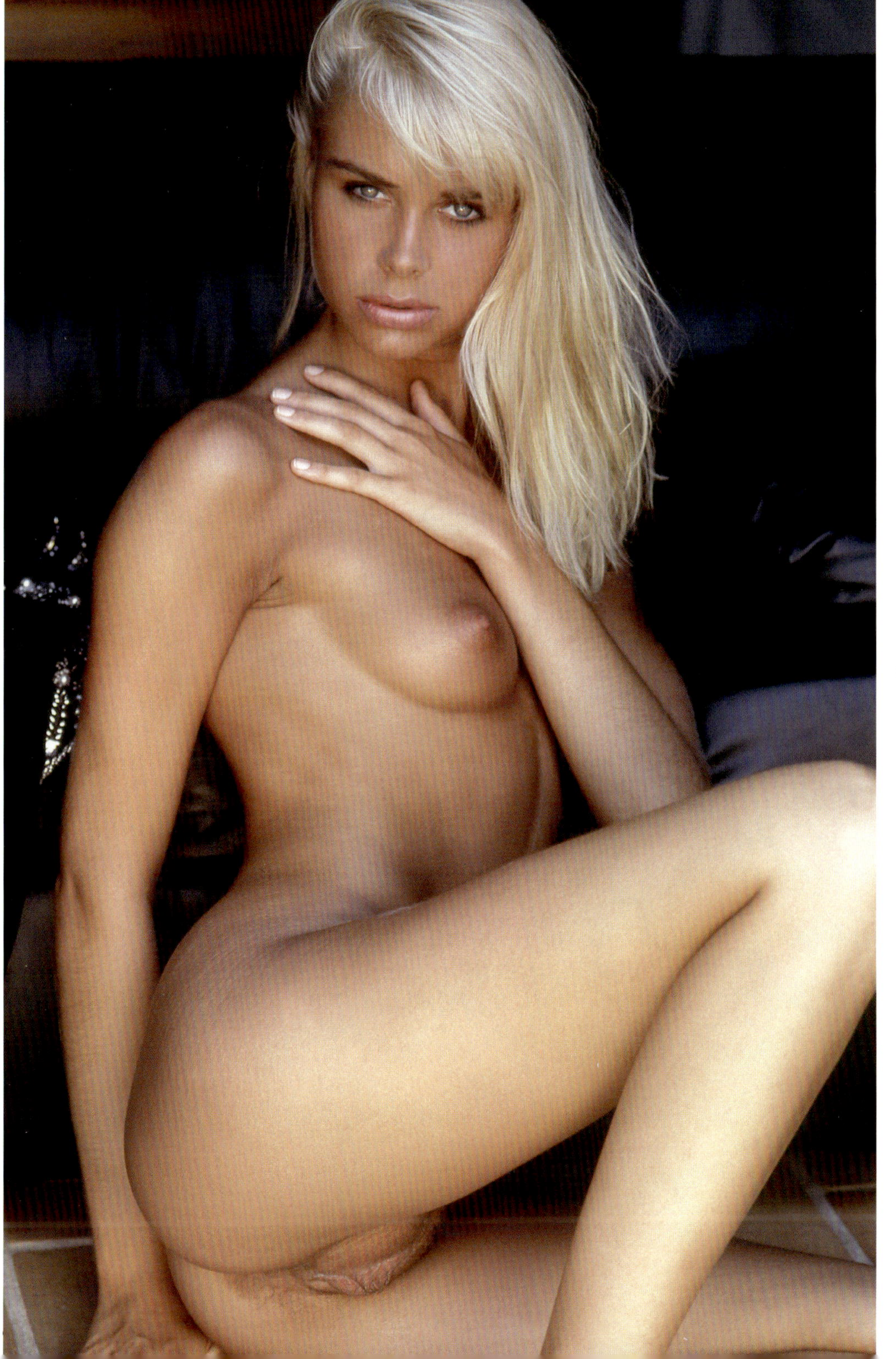

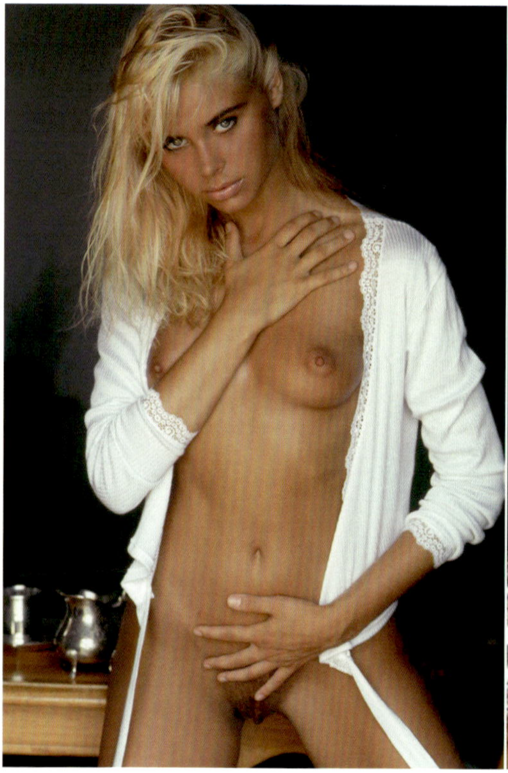

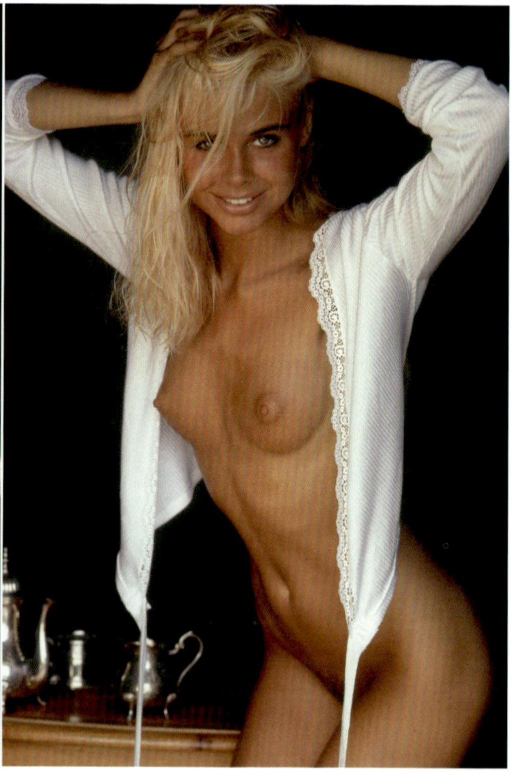

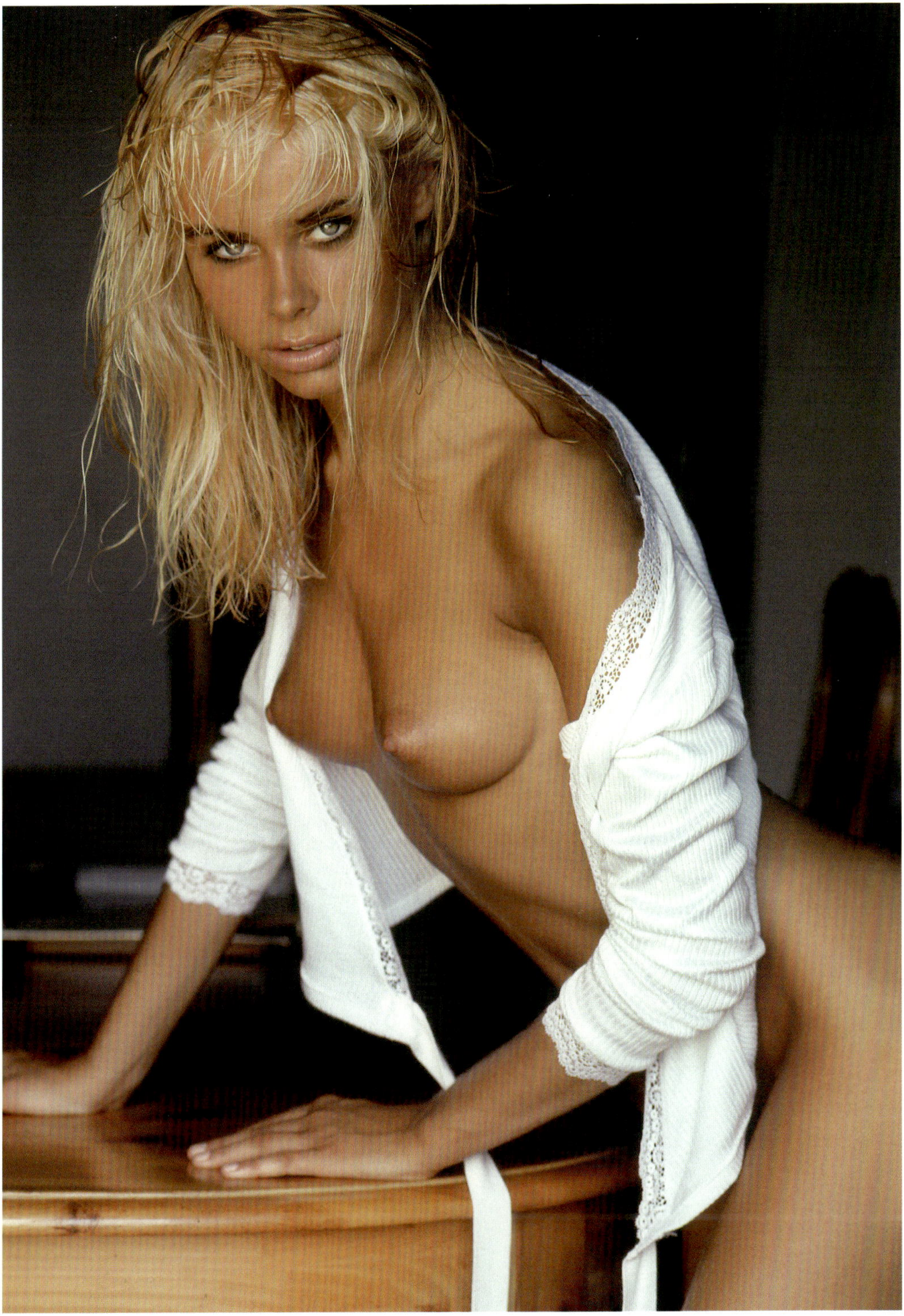

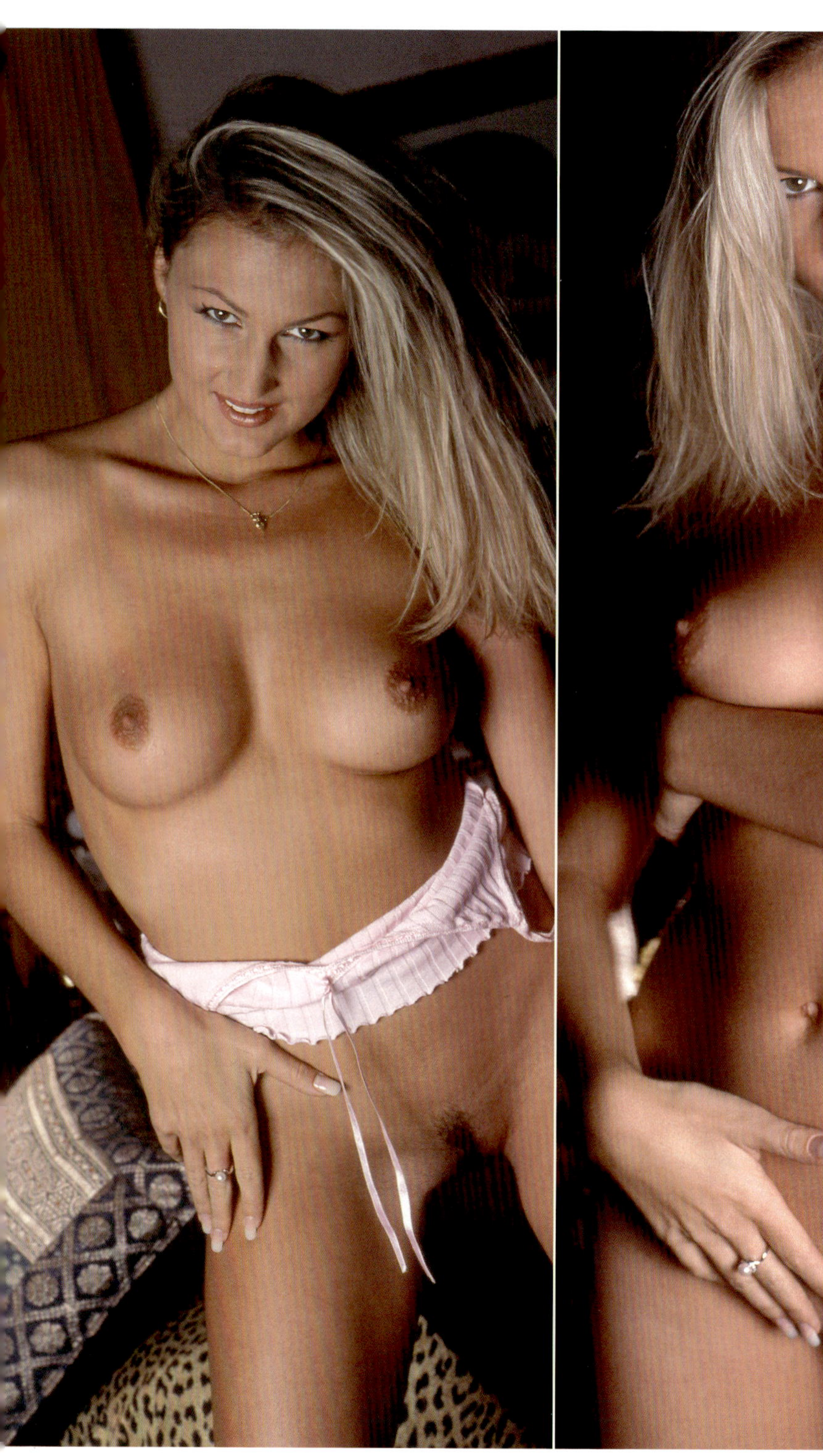

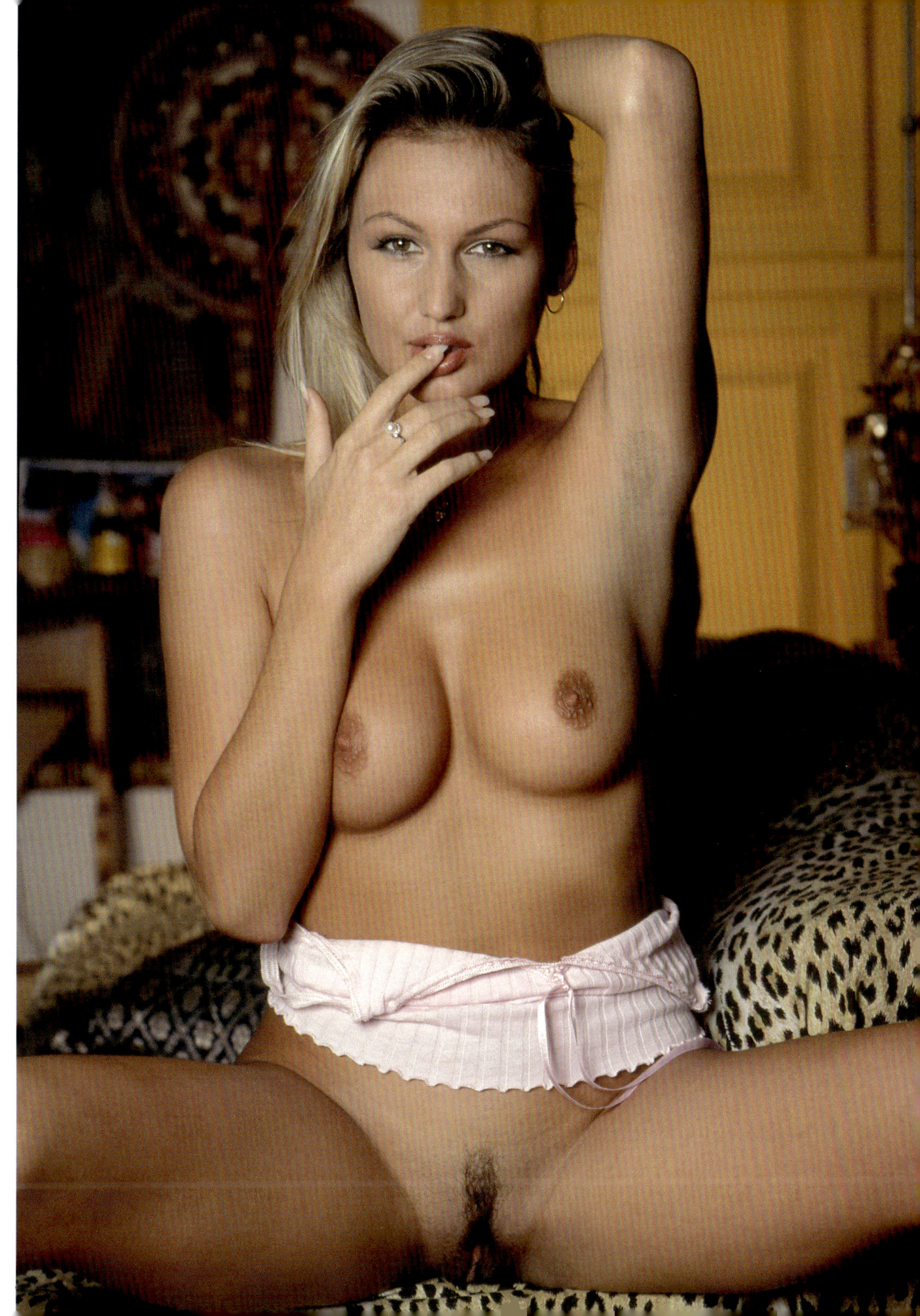

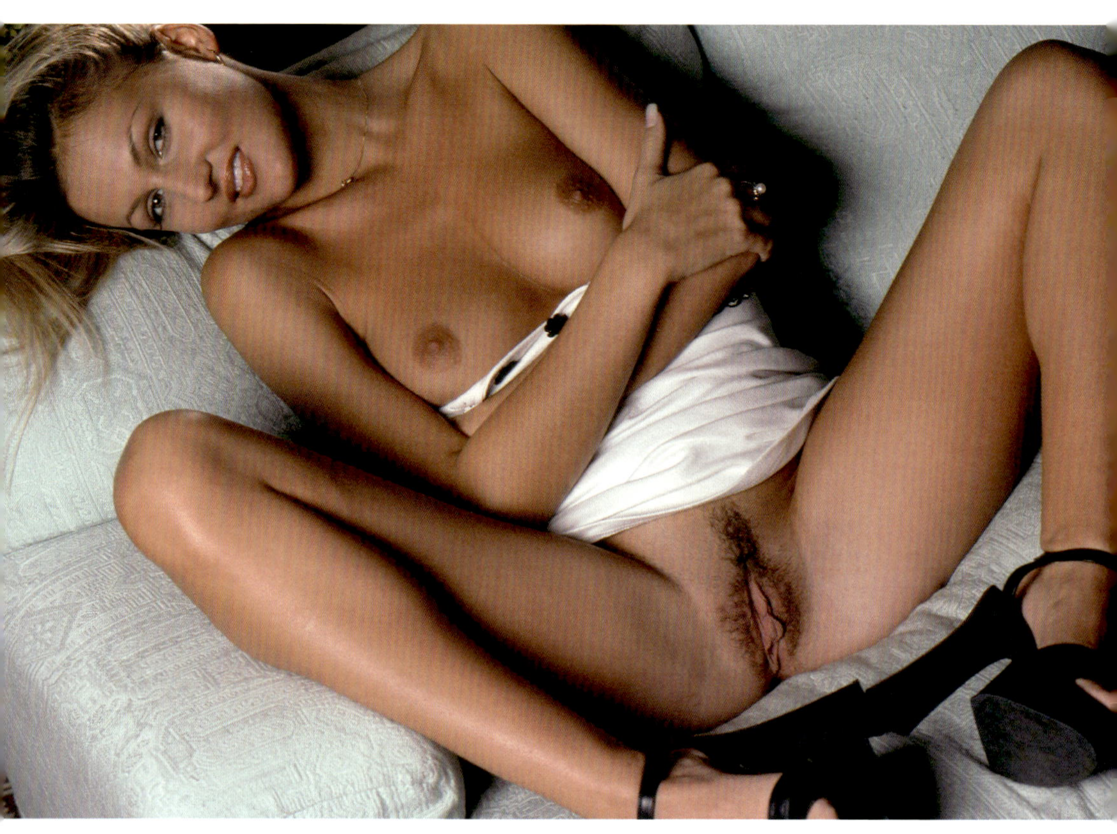

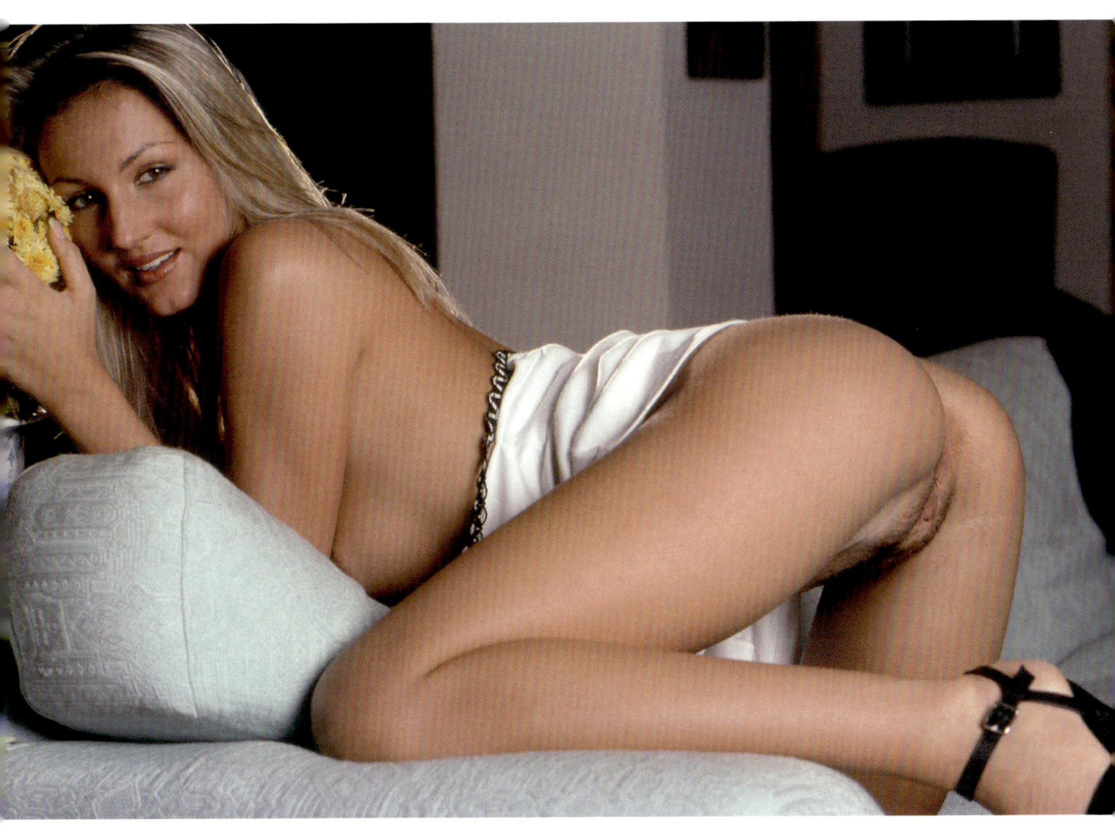

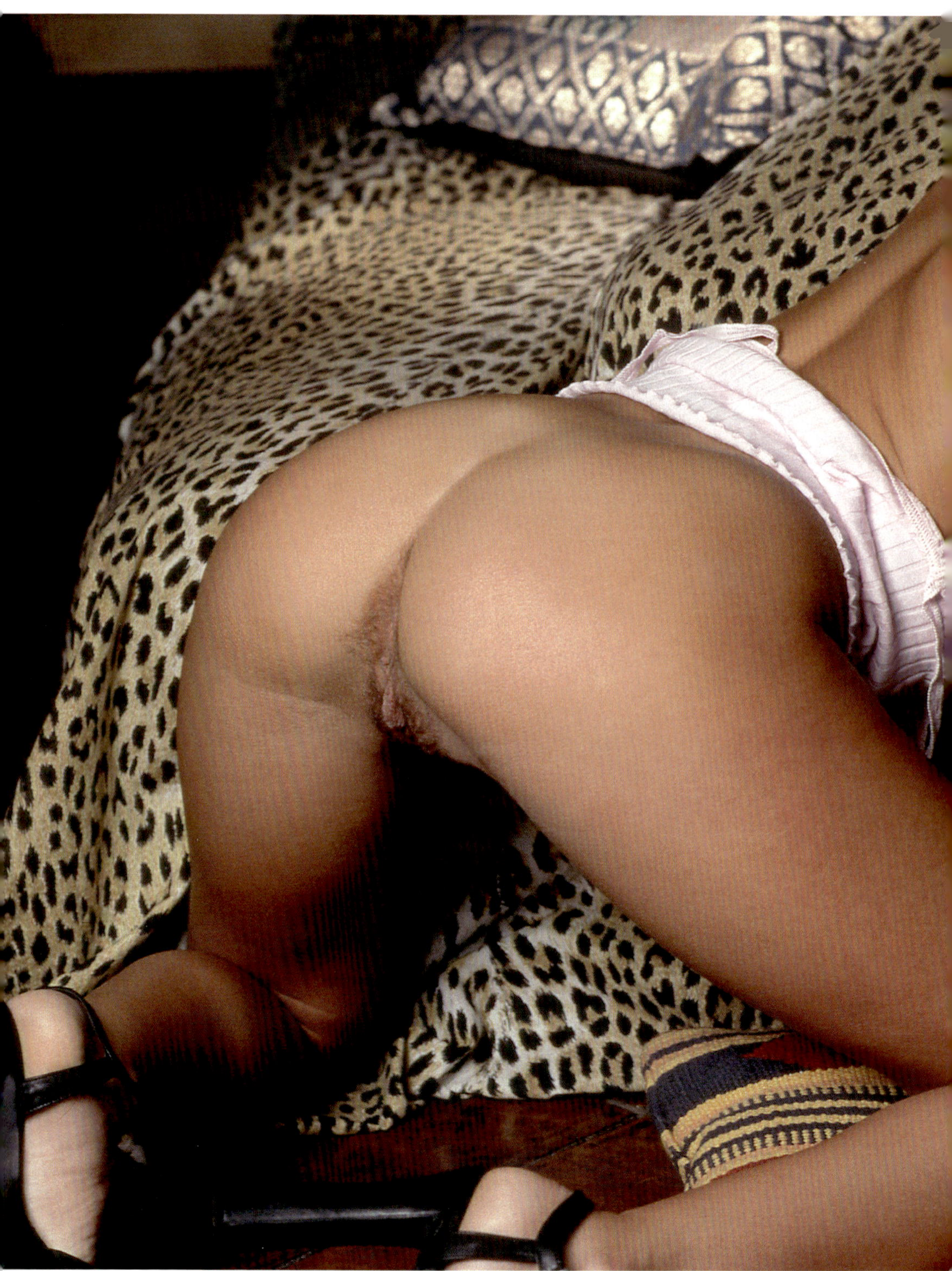

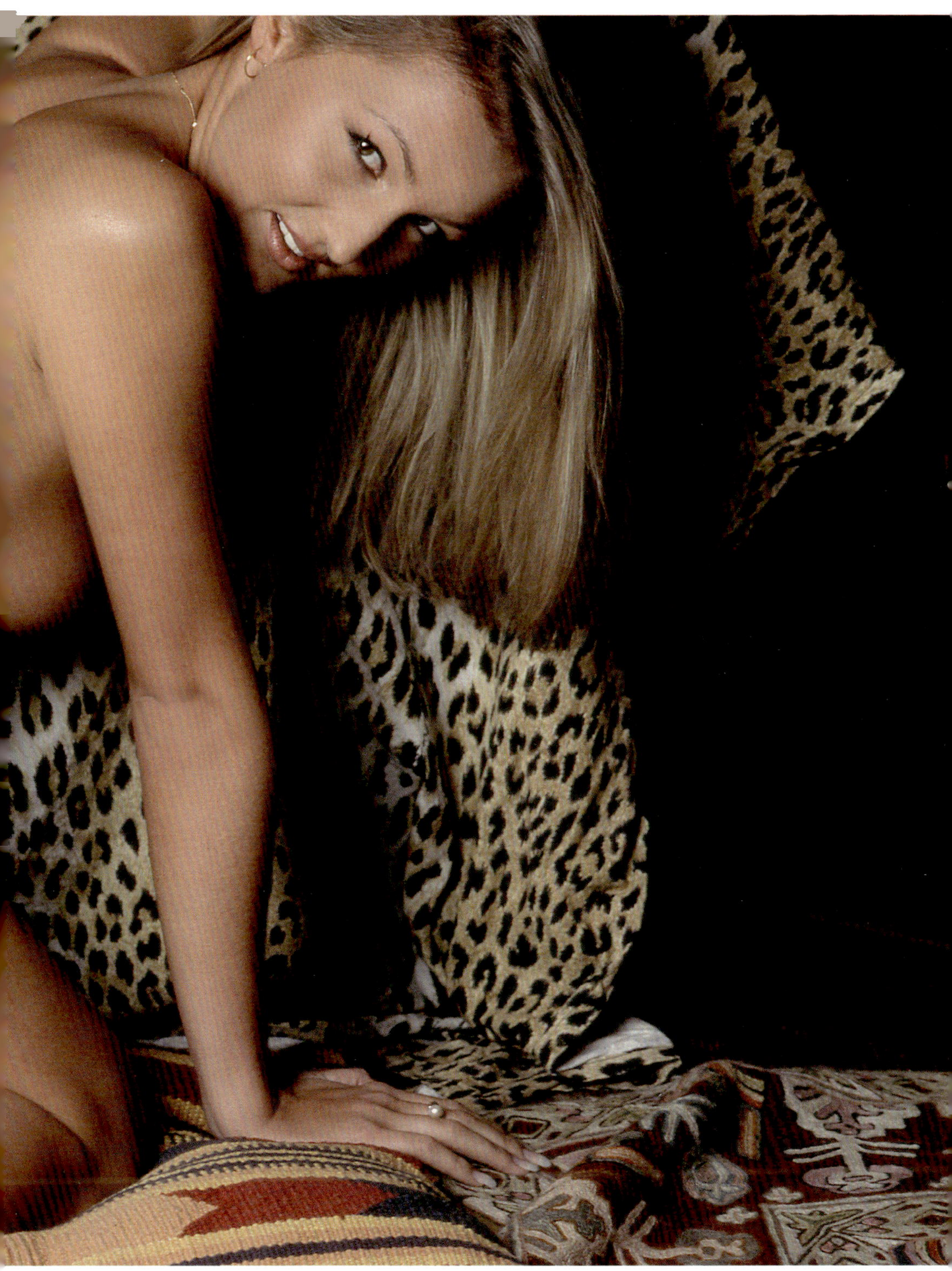

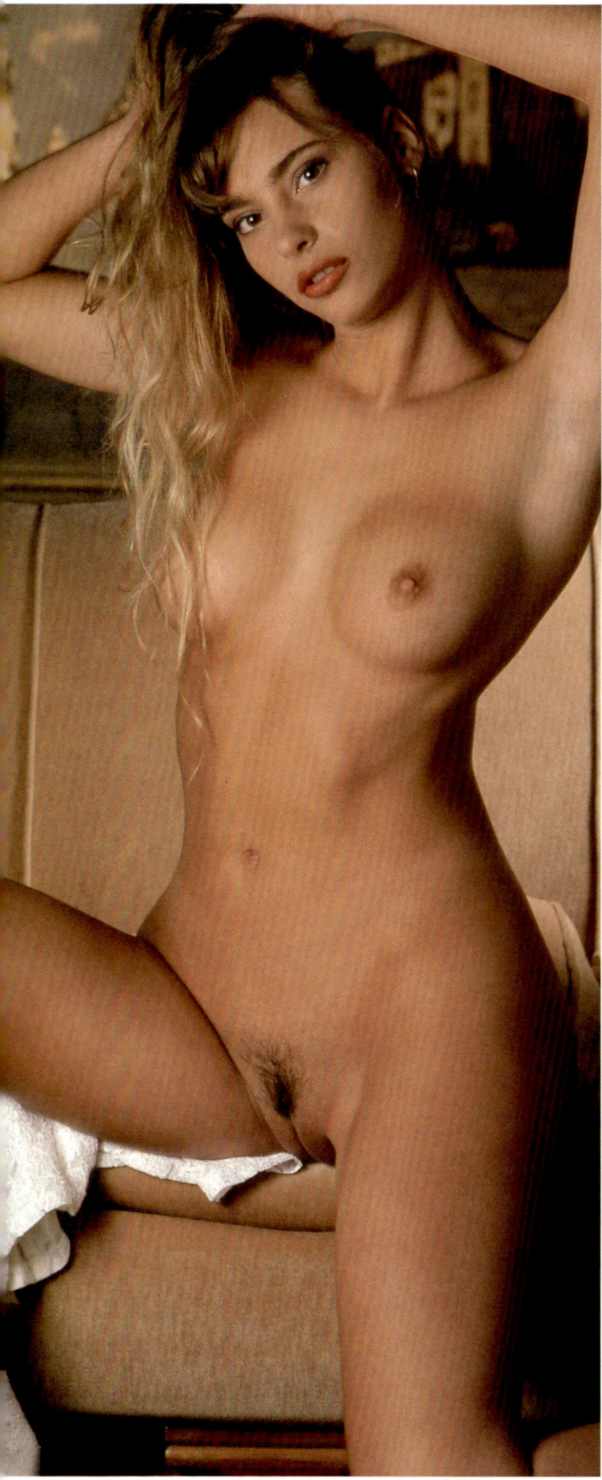

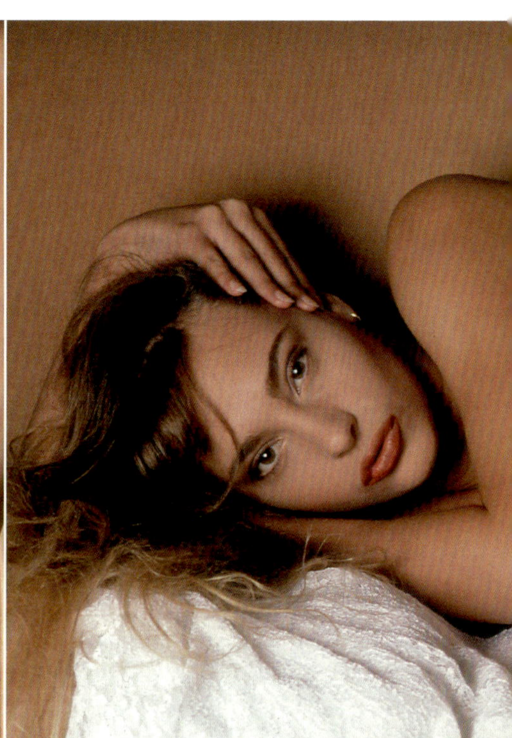

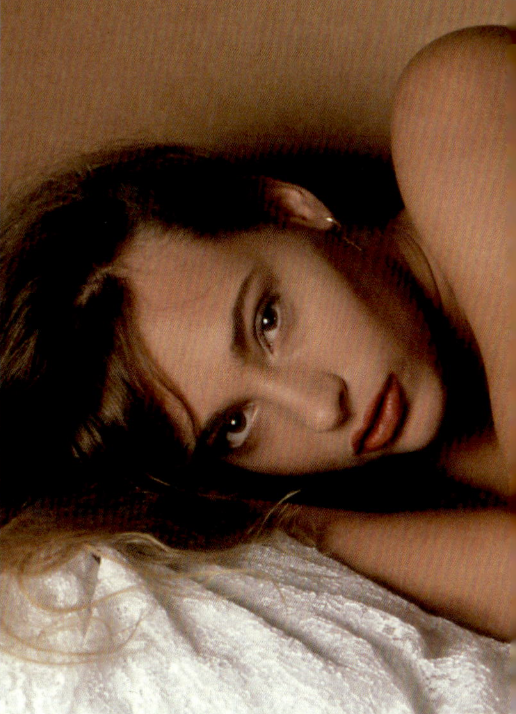

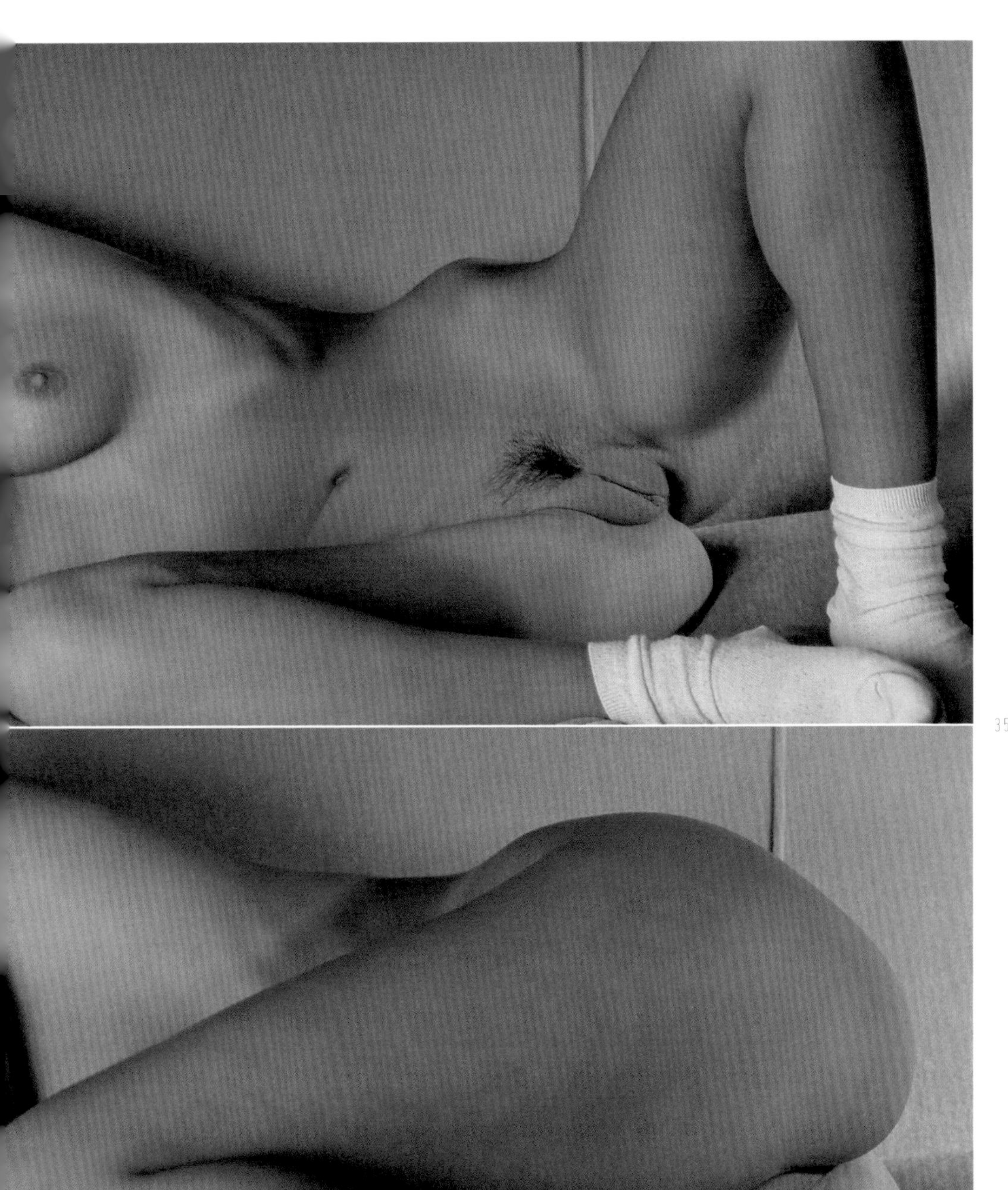

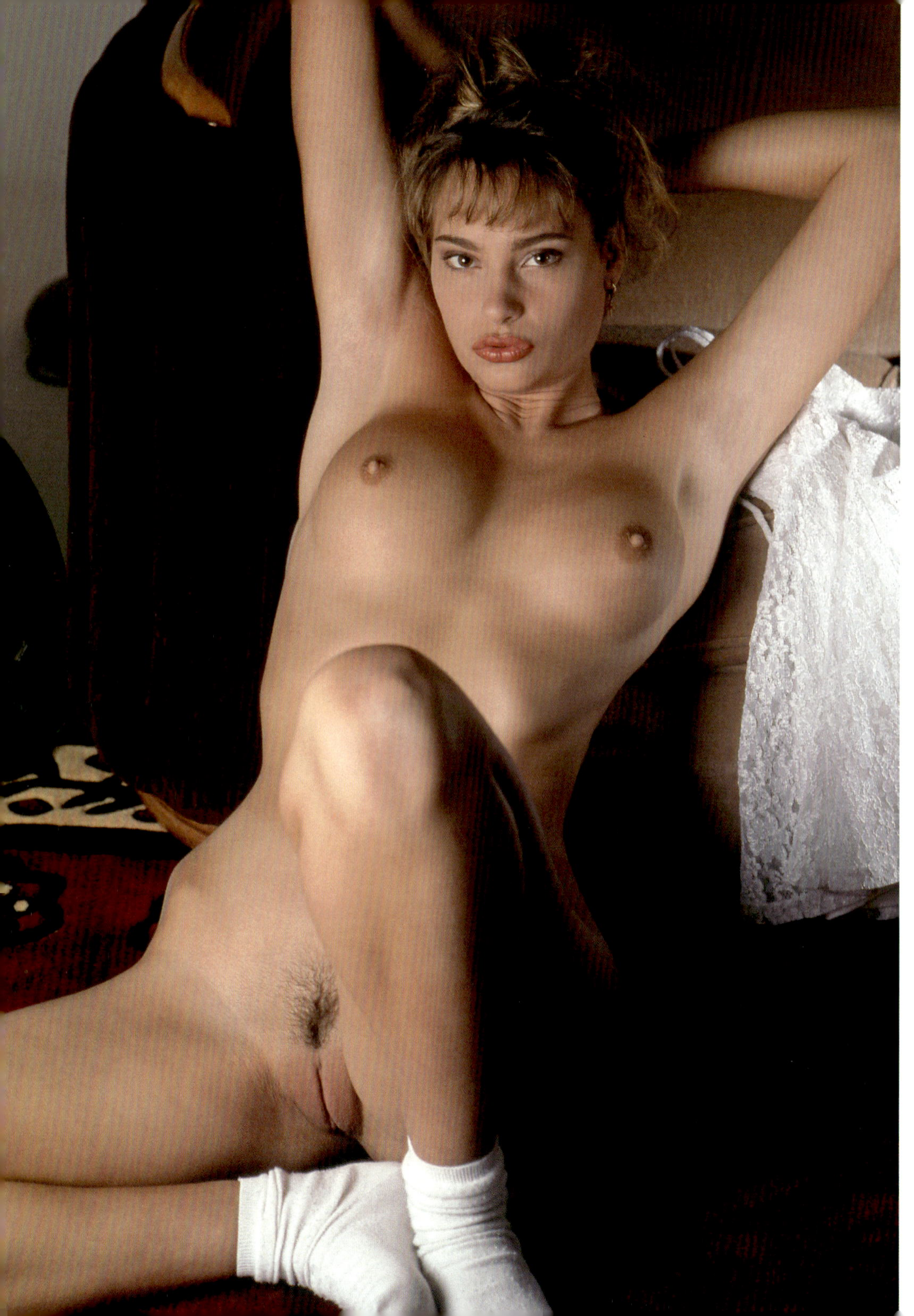

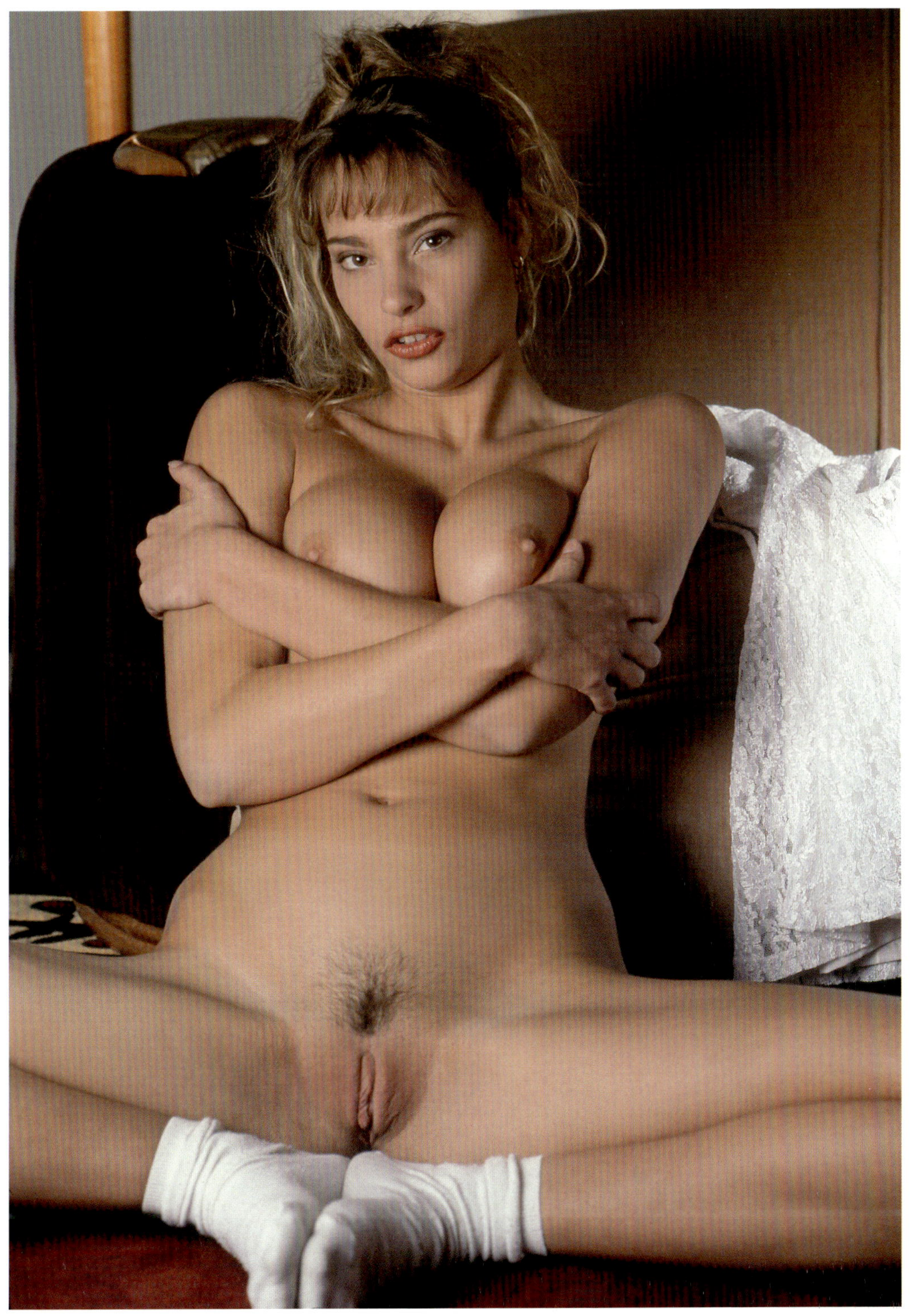

JULIA

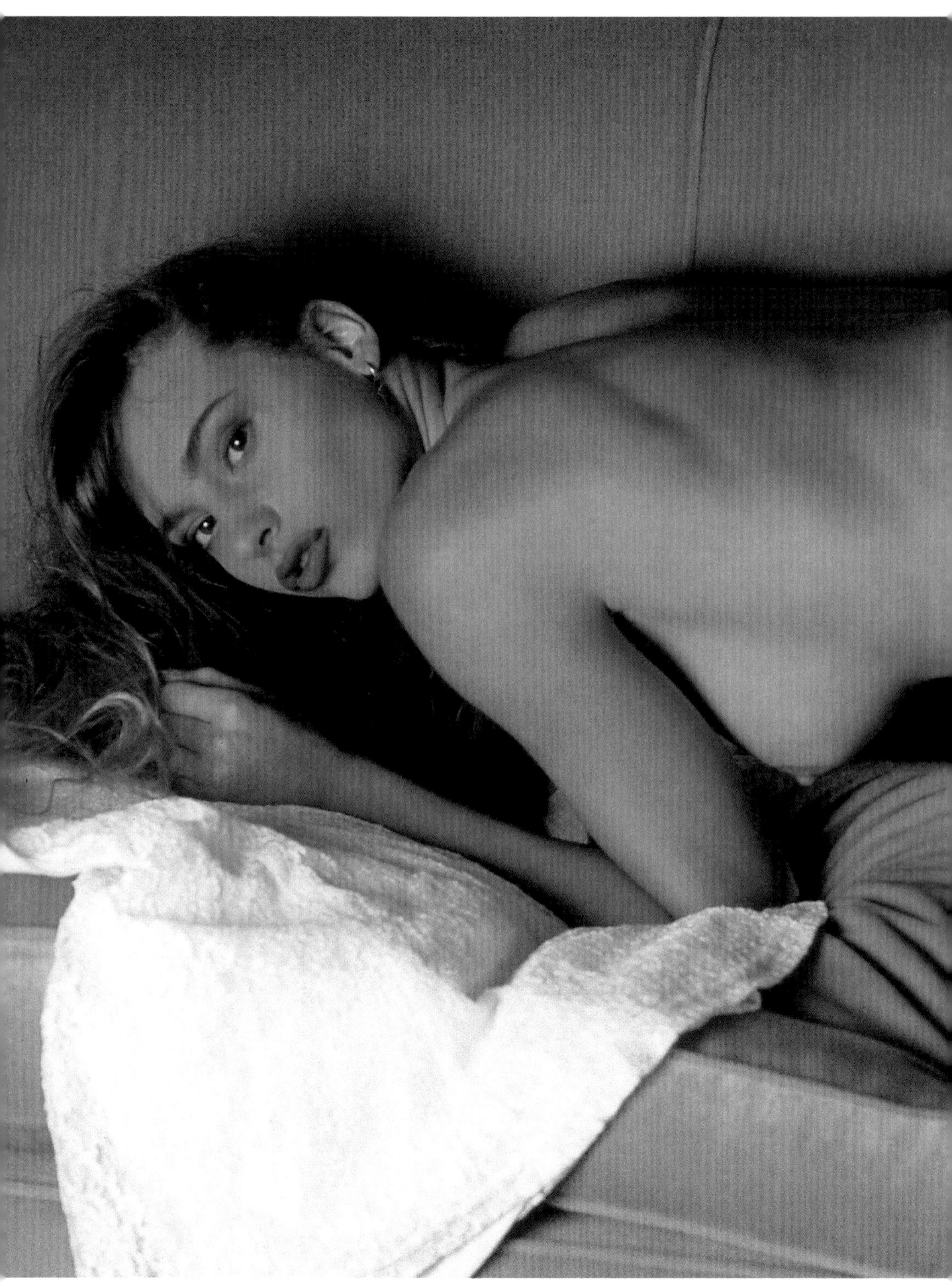

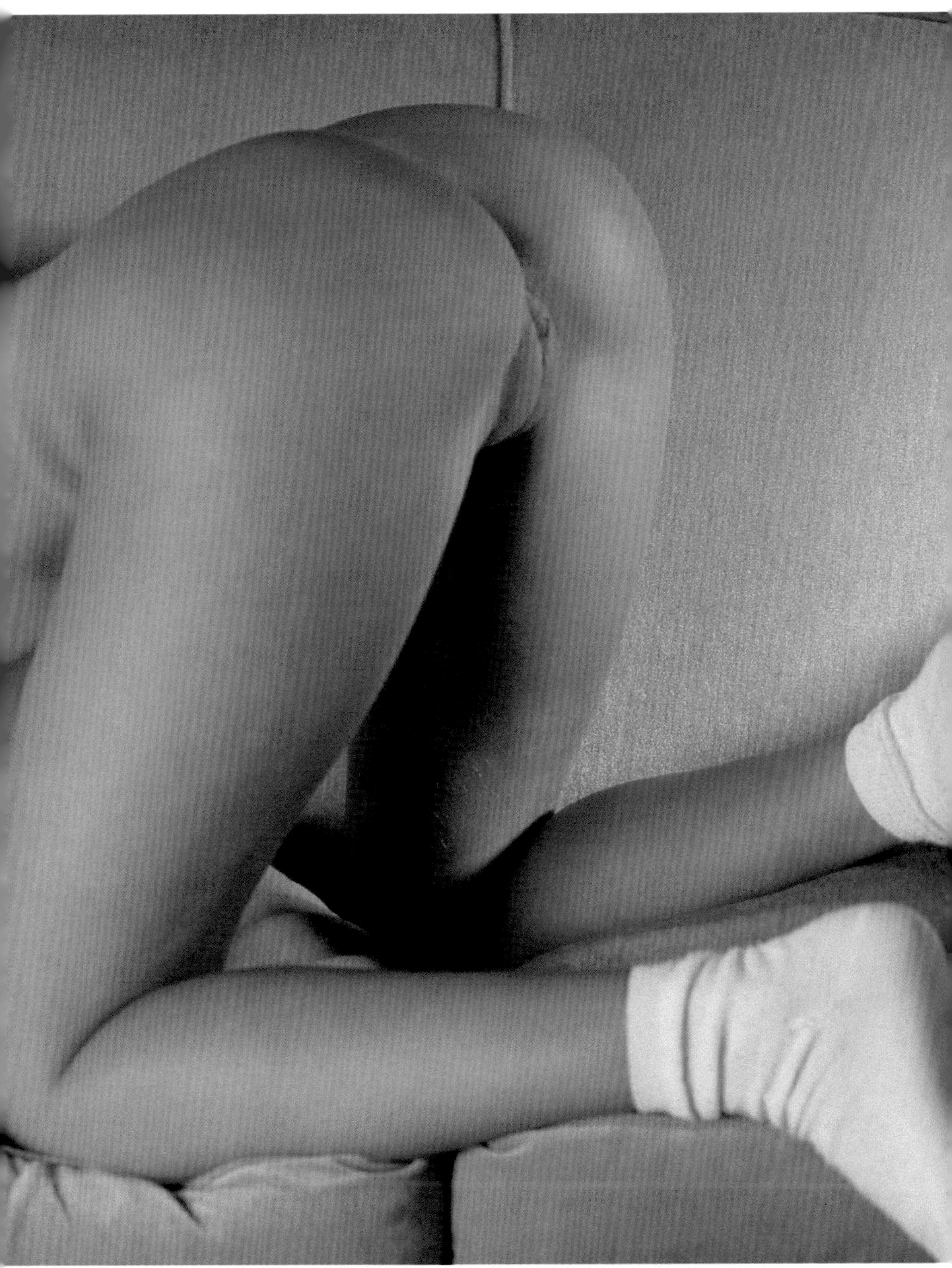

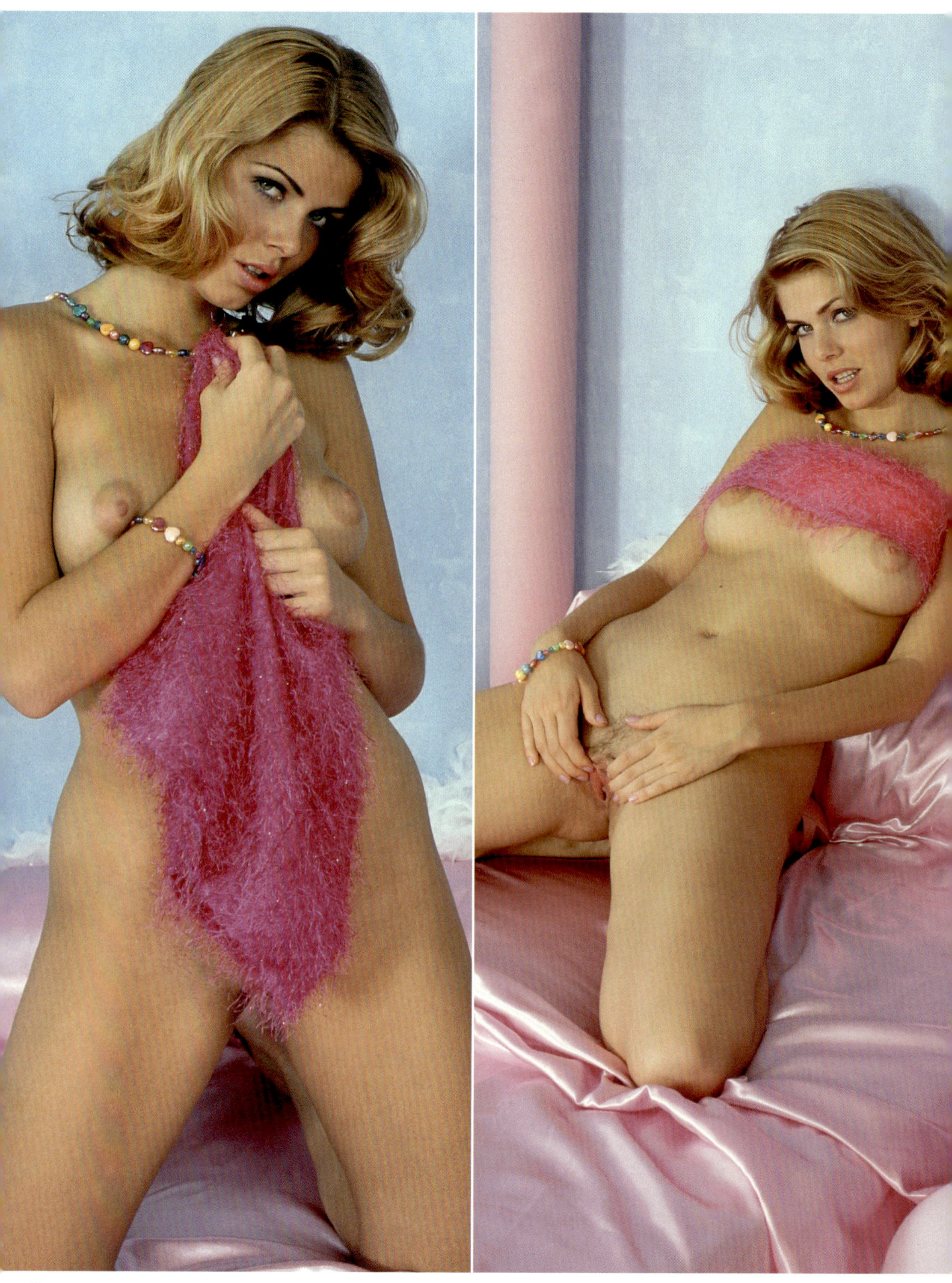

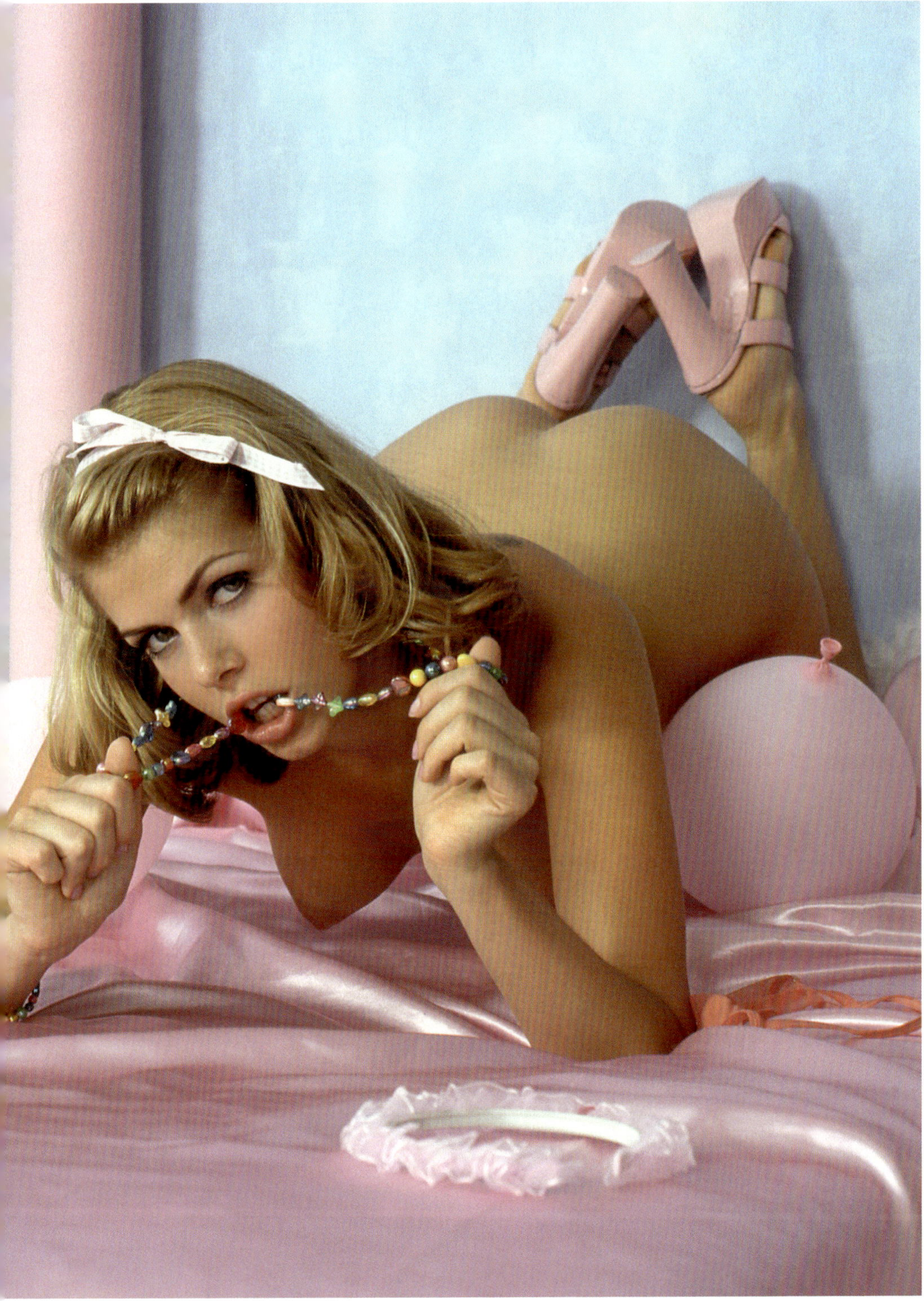

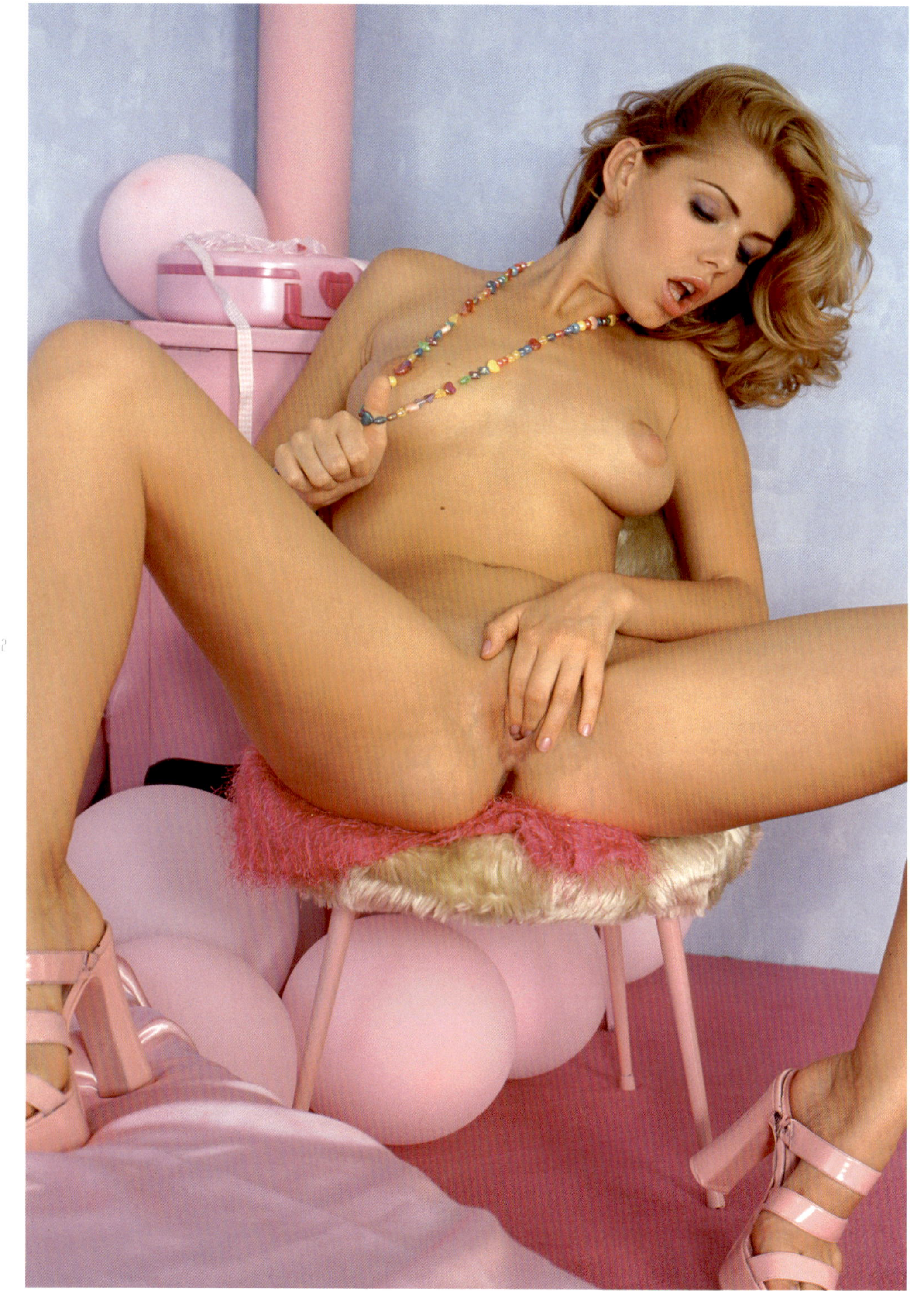

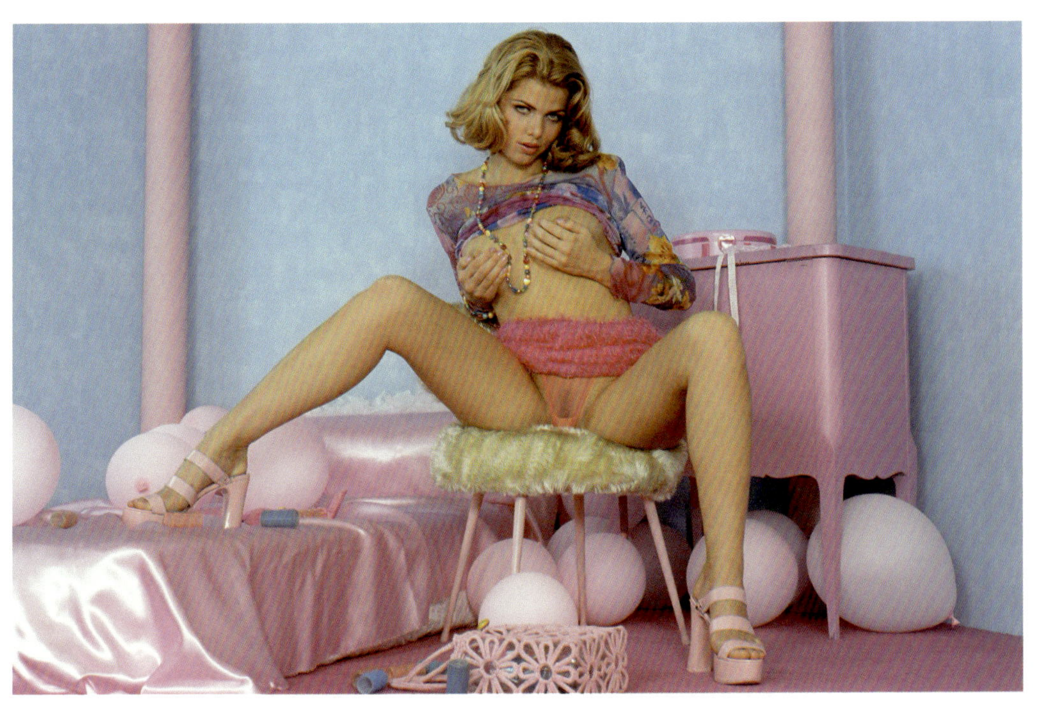

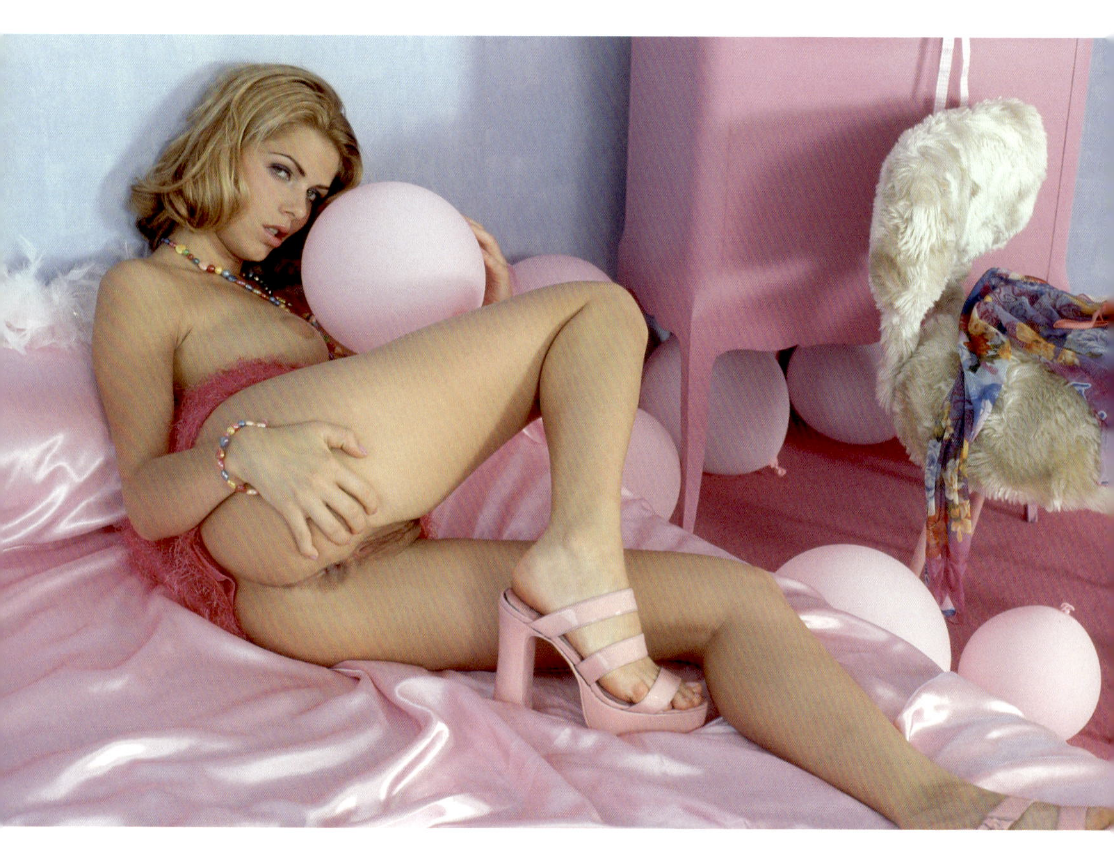

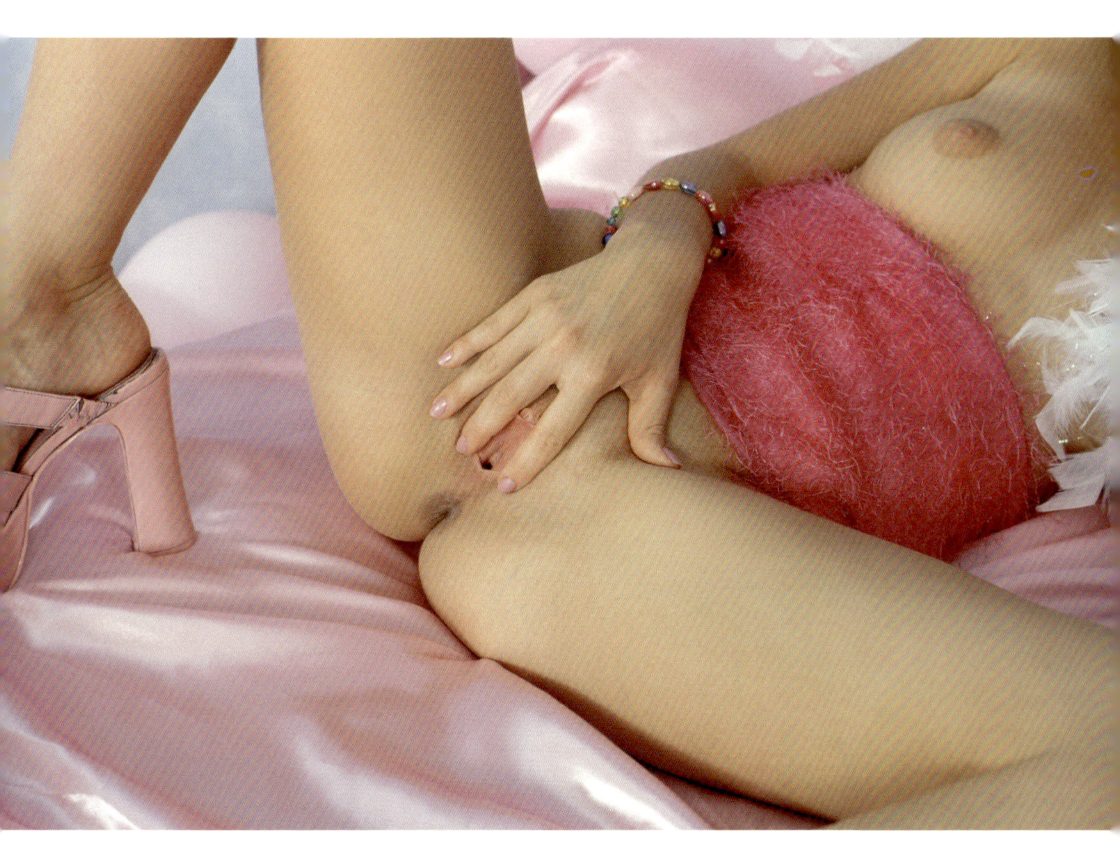

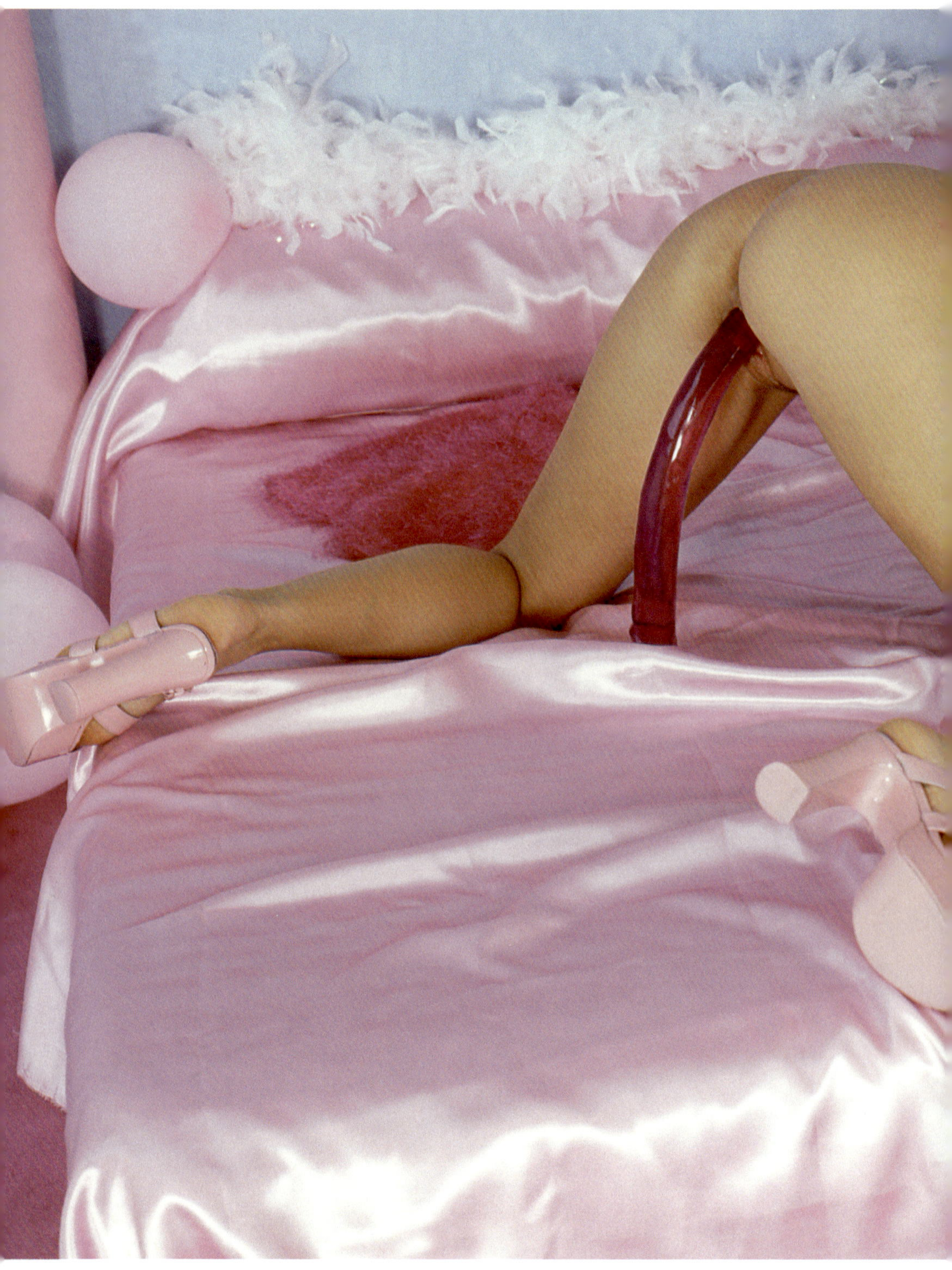

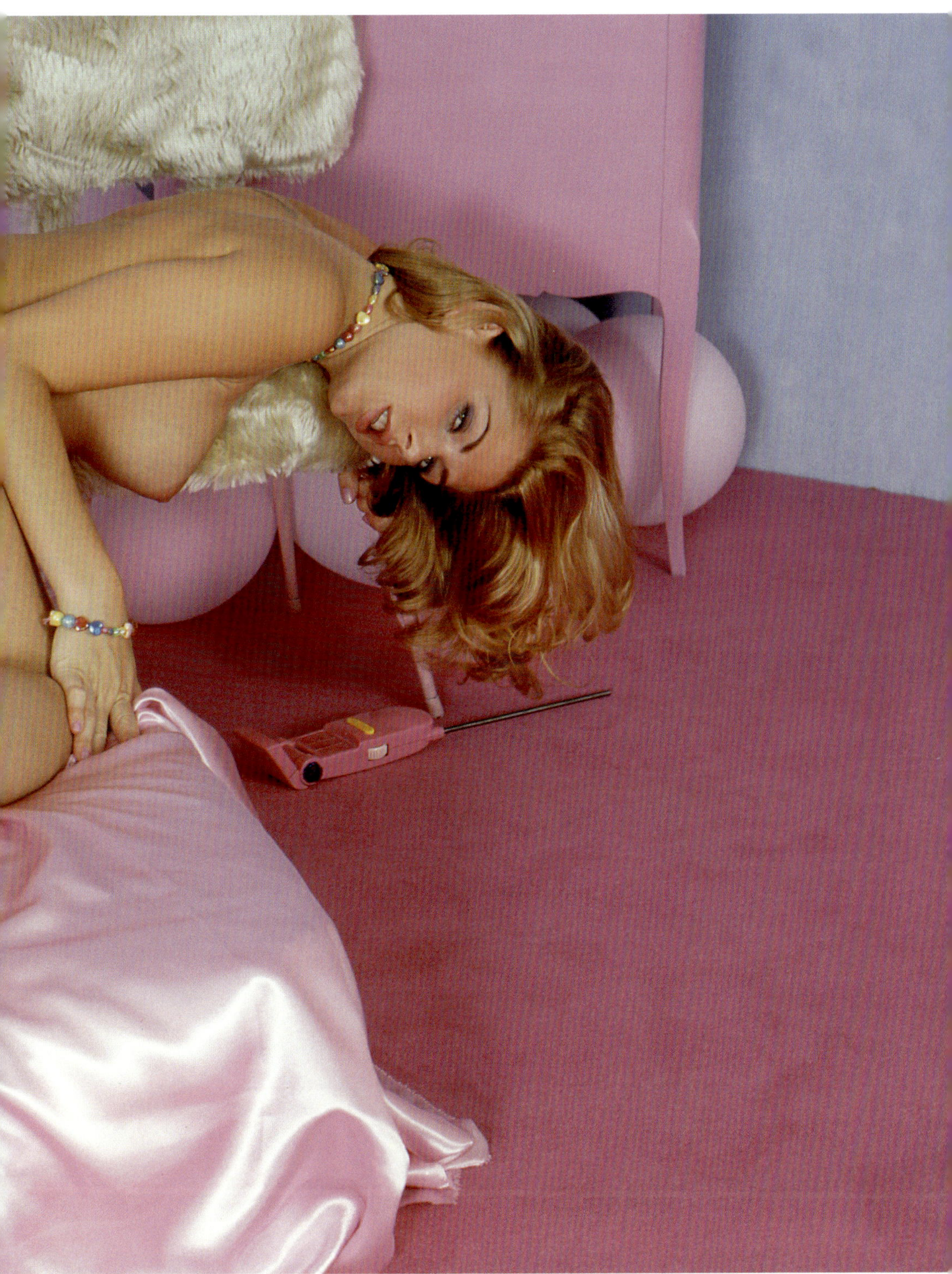

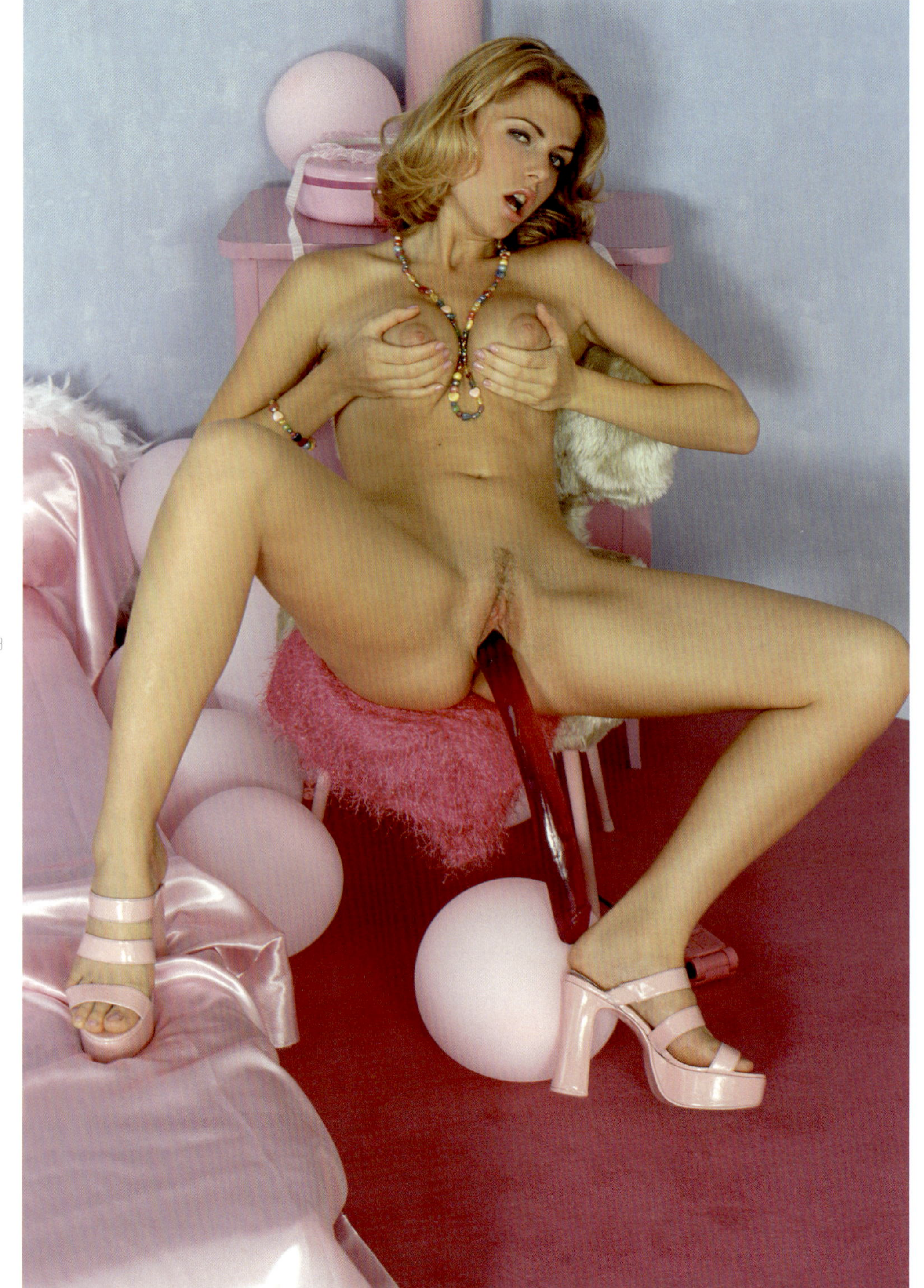

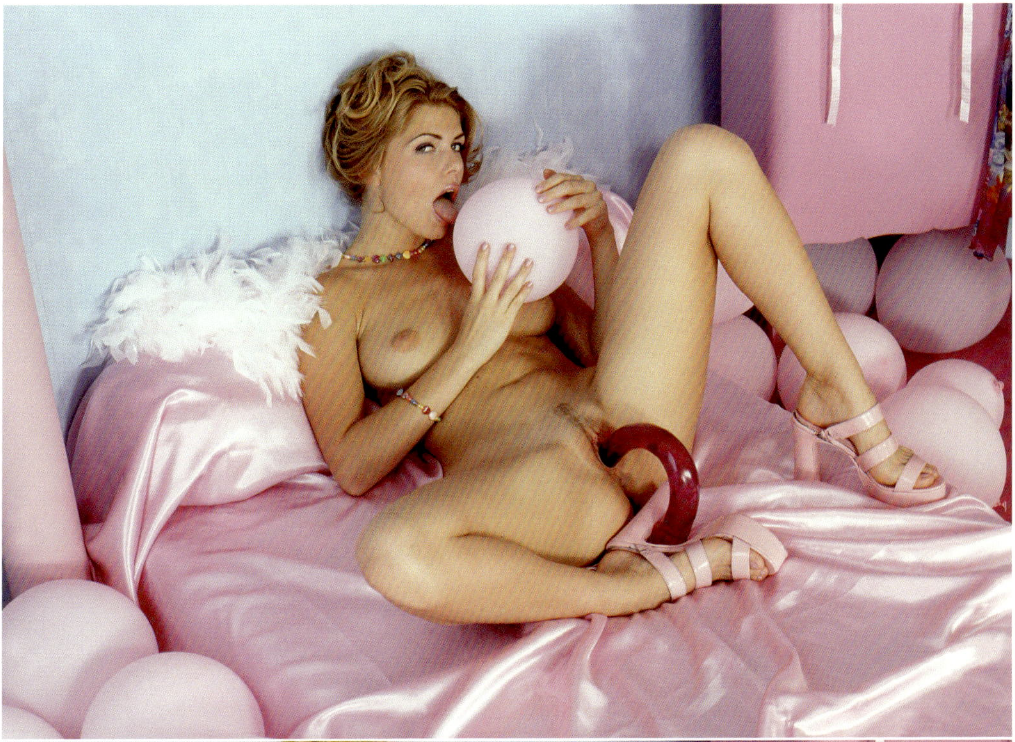

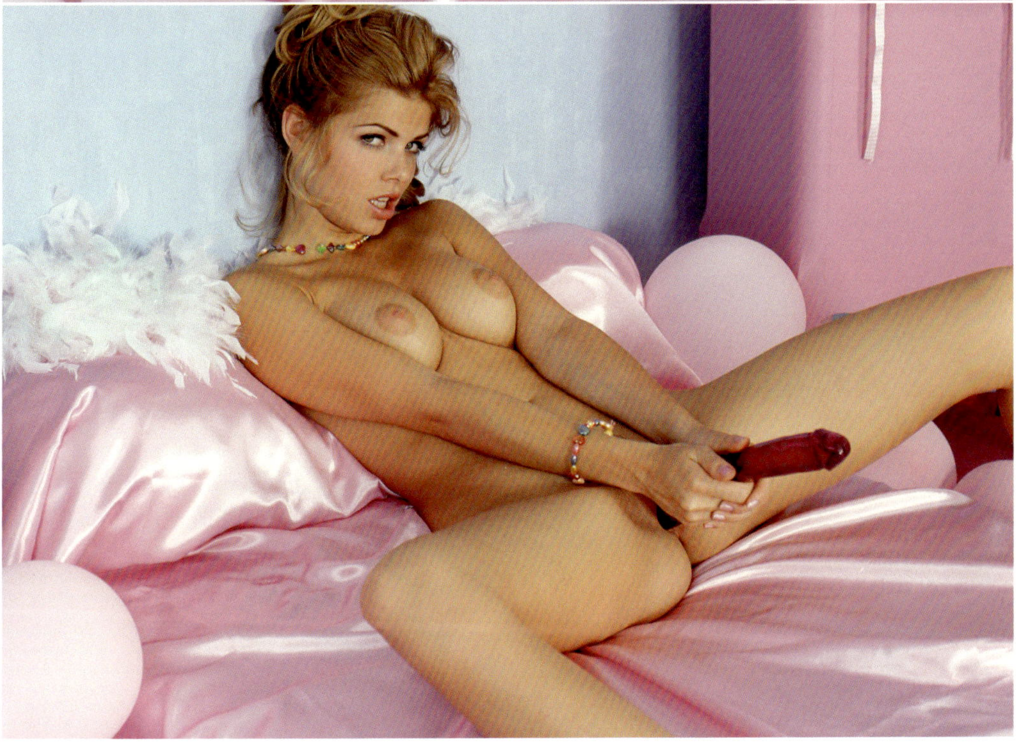

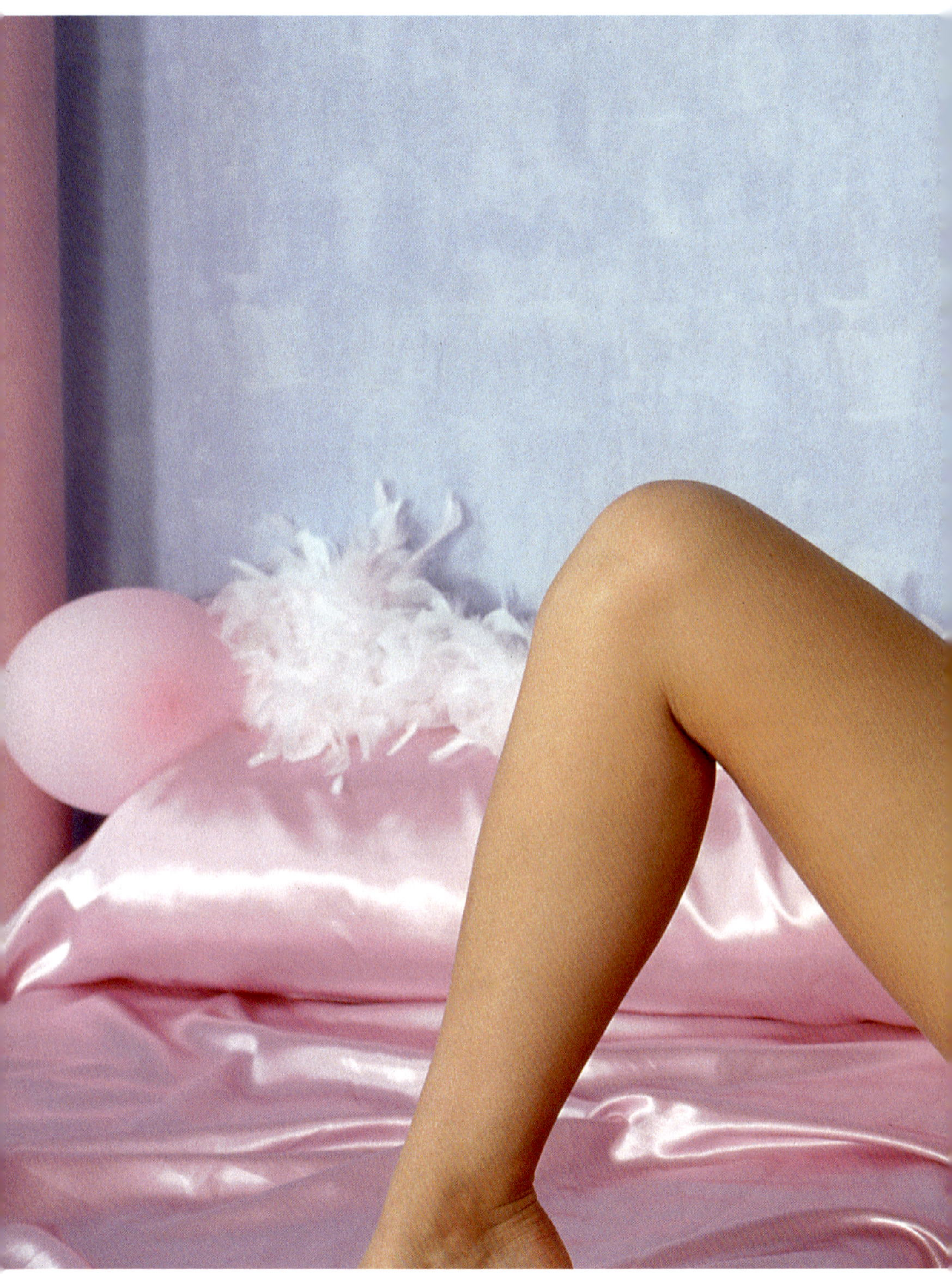

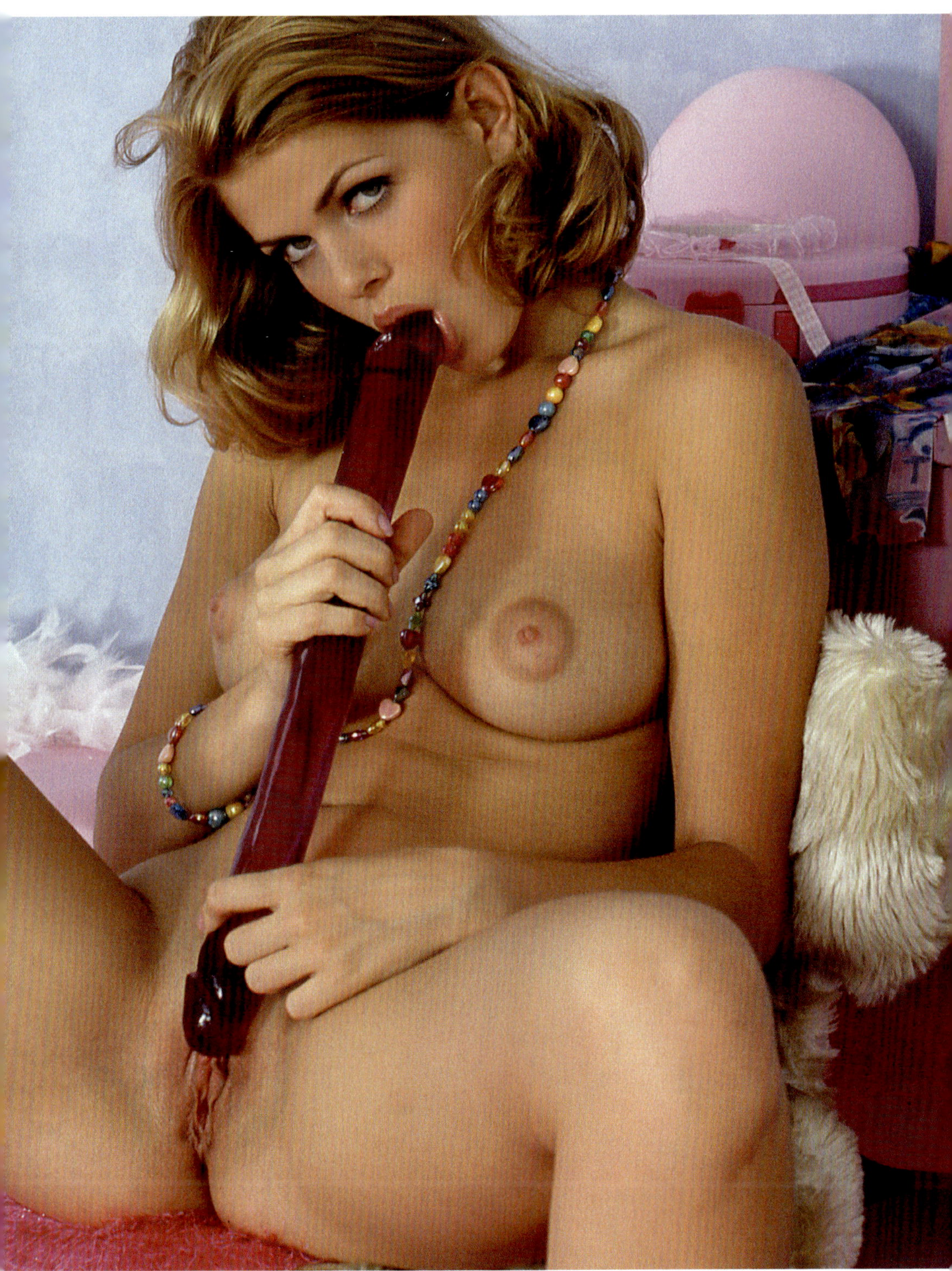

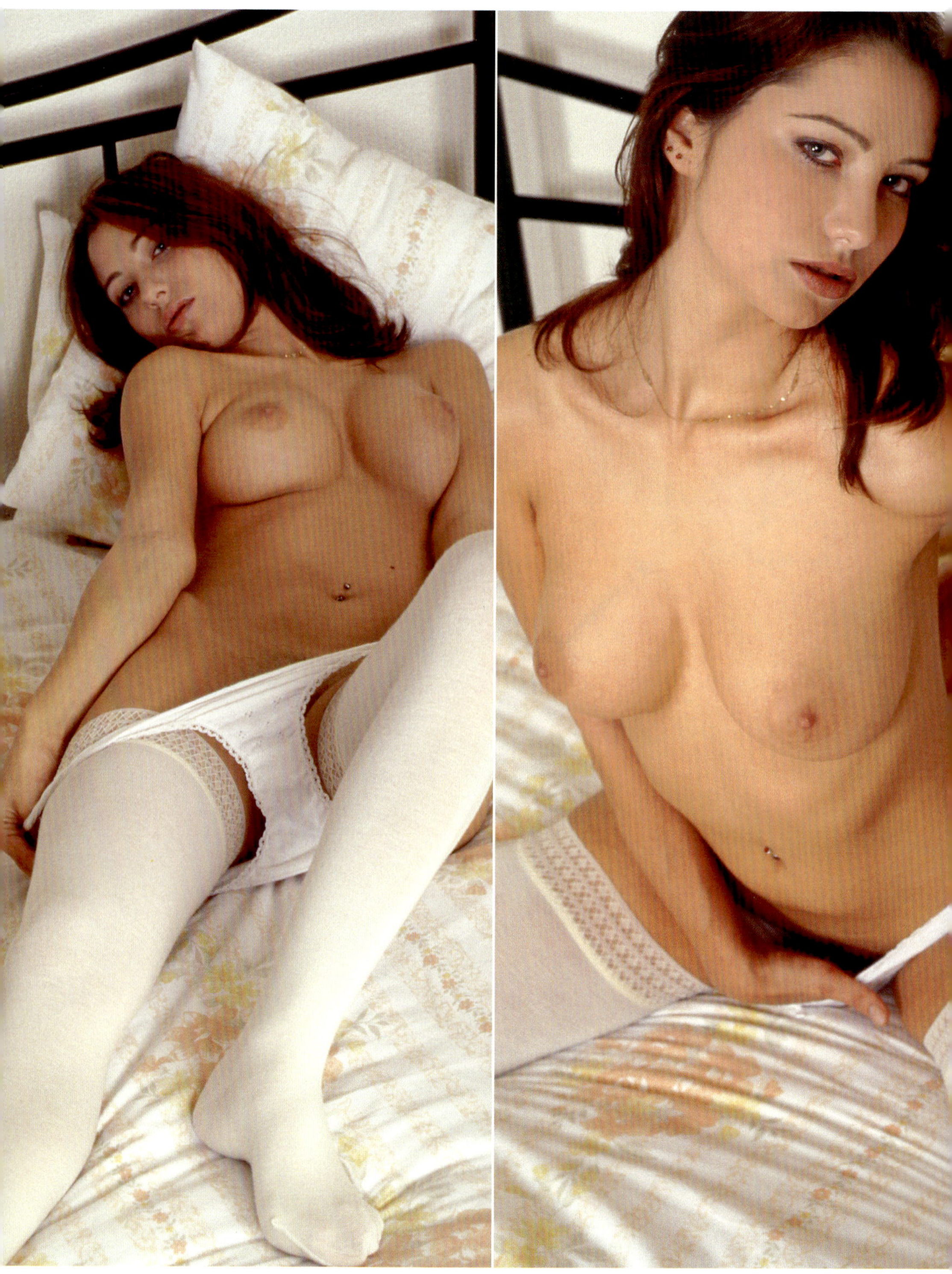

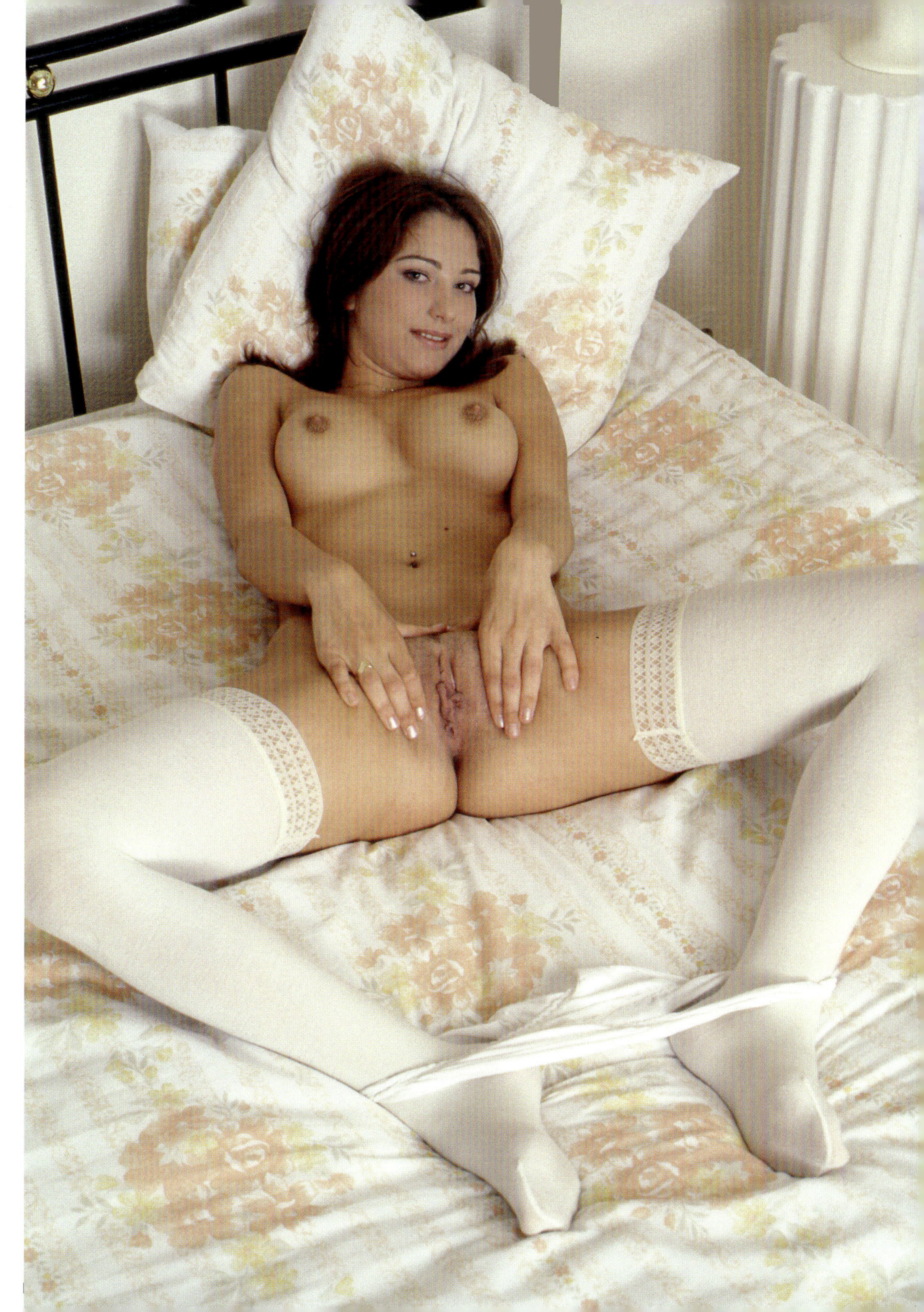

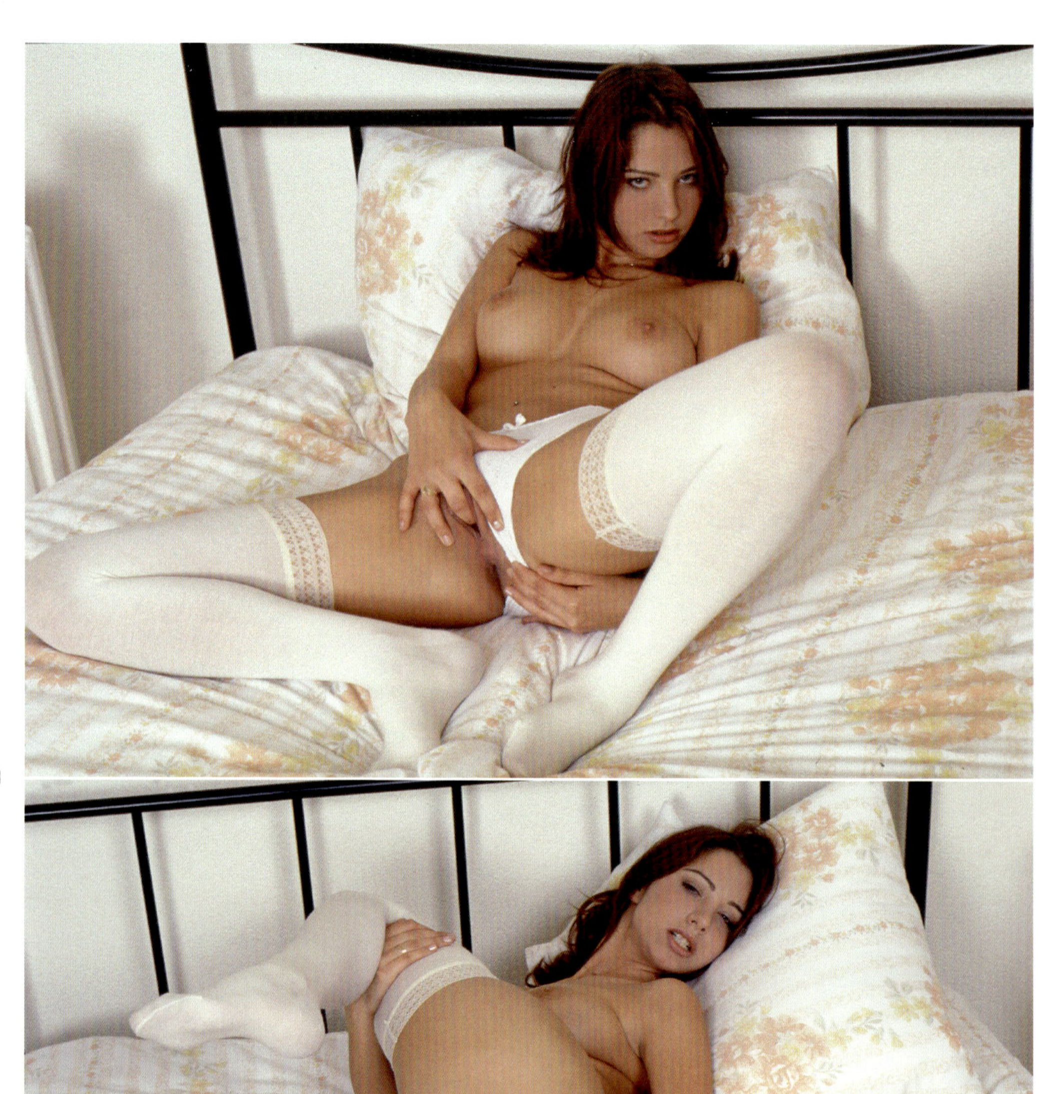

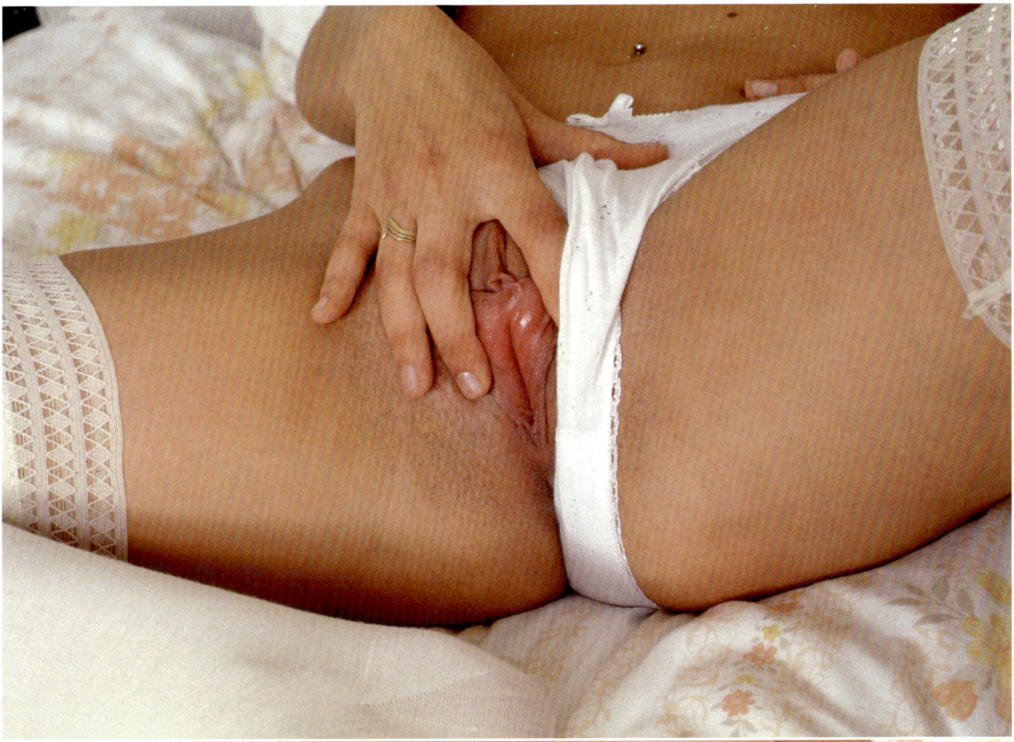

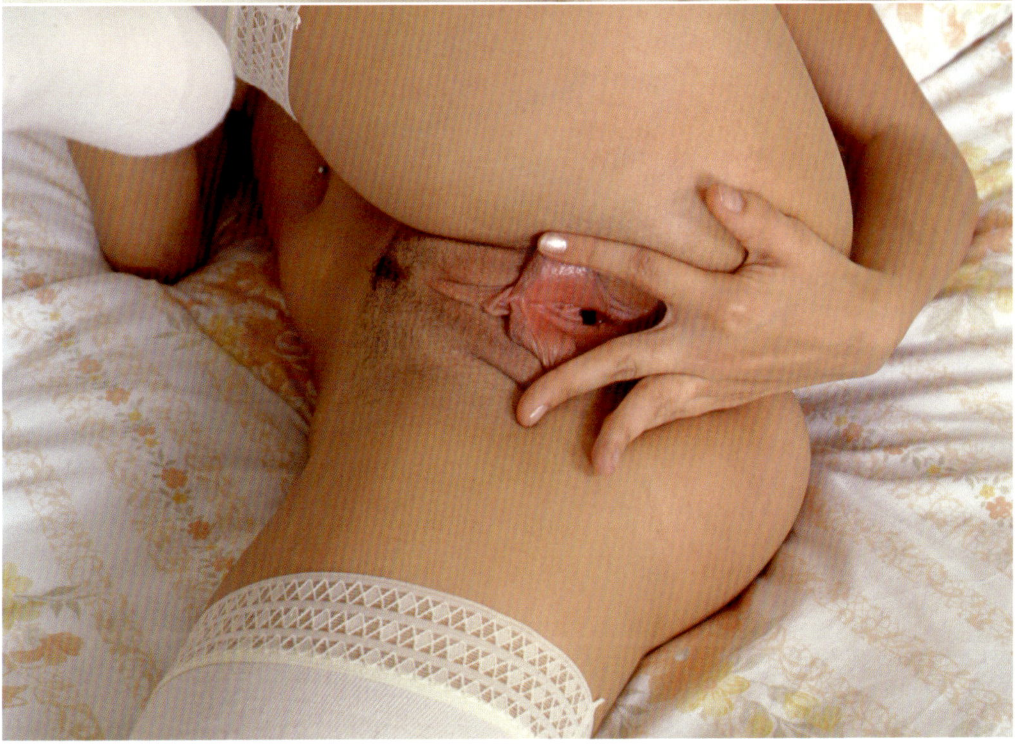

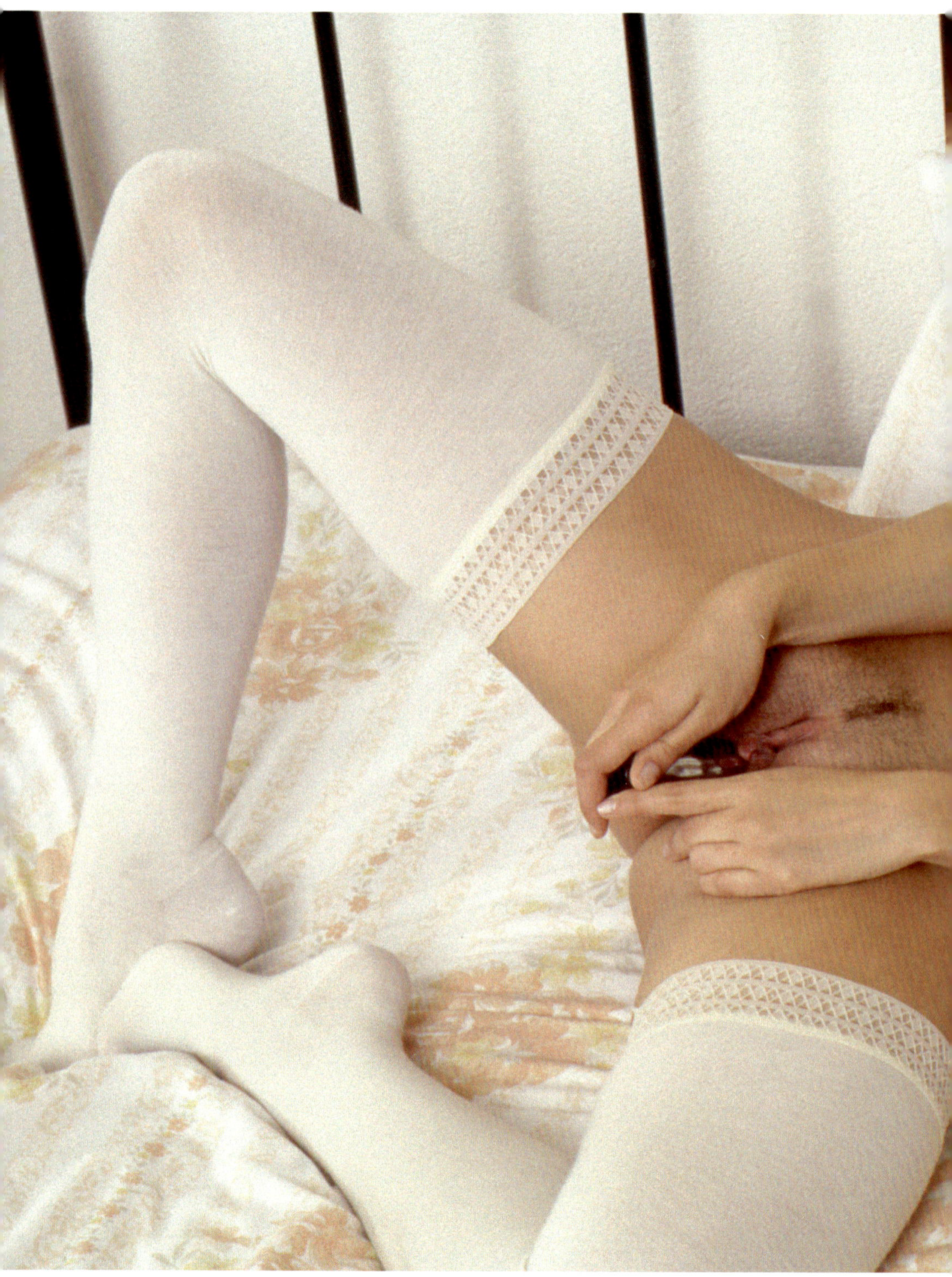

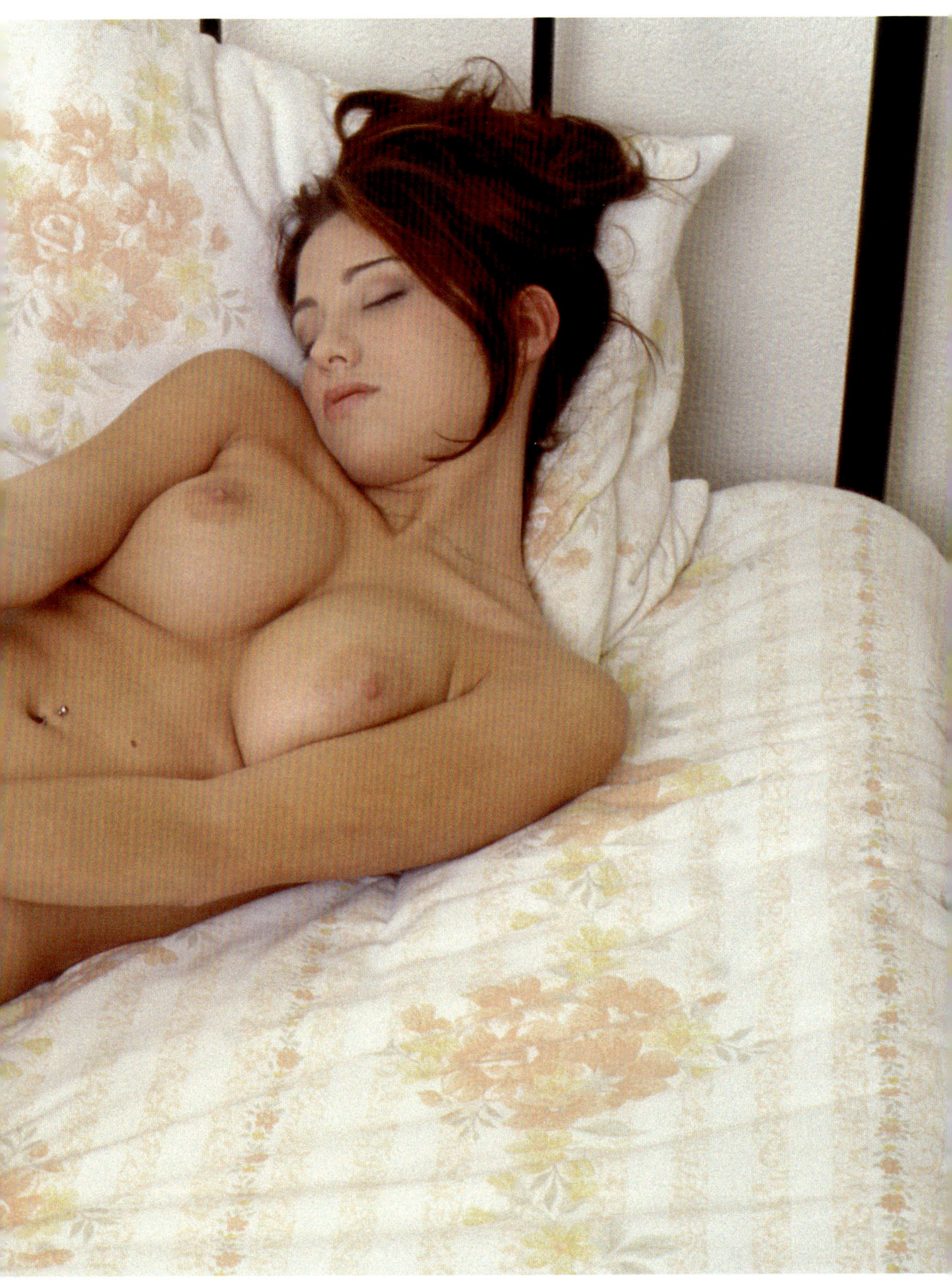

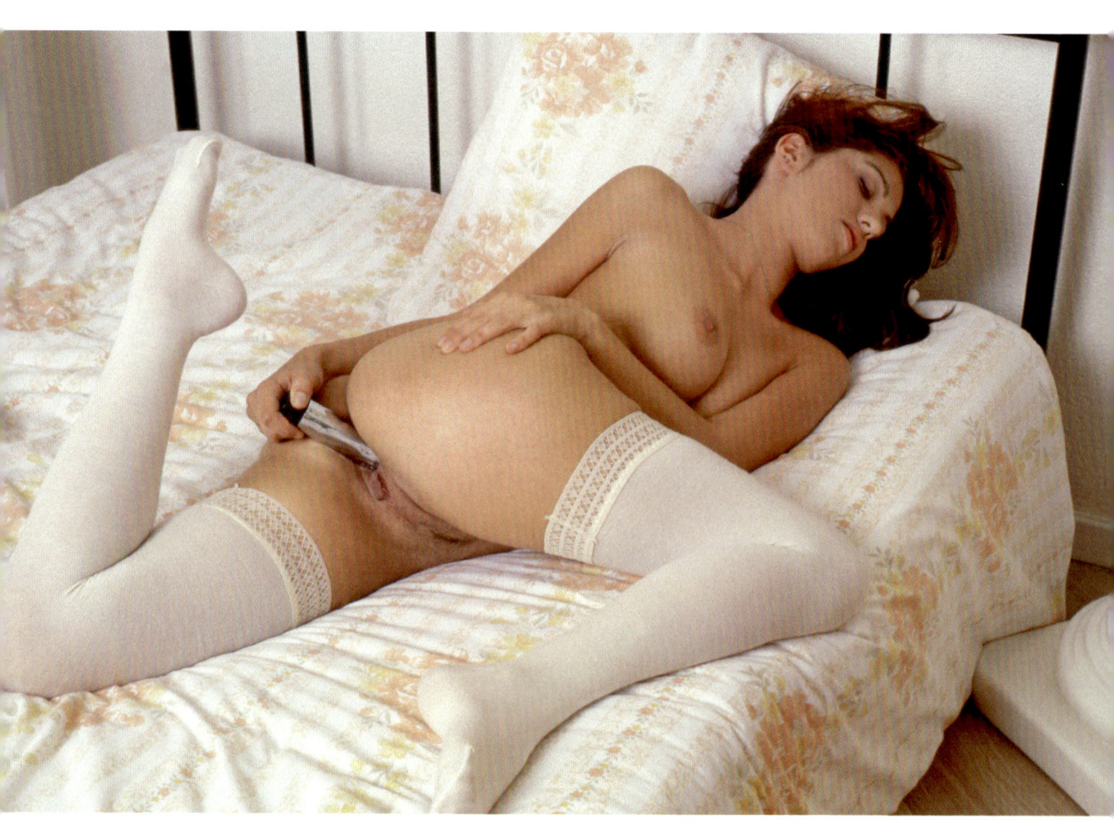

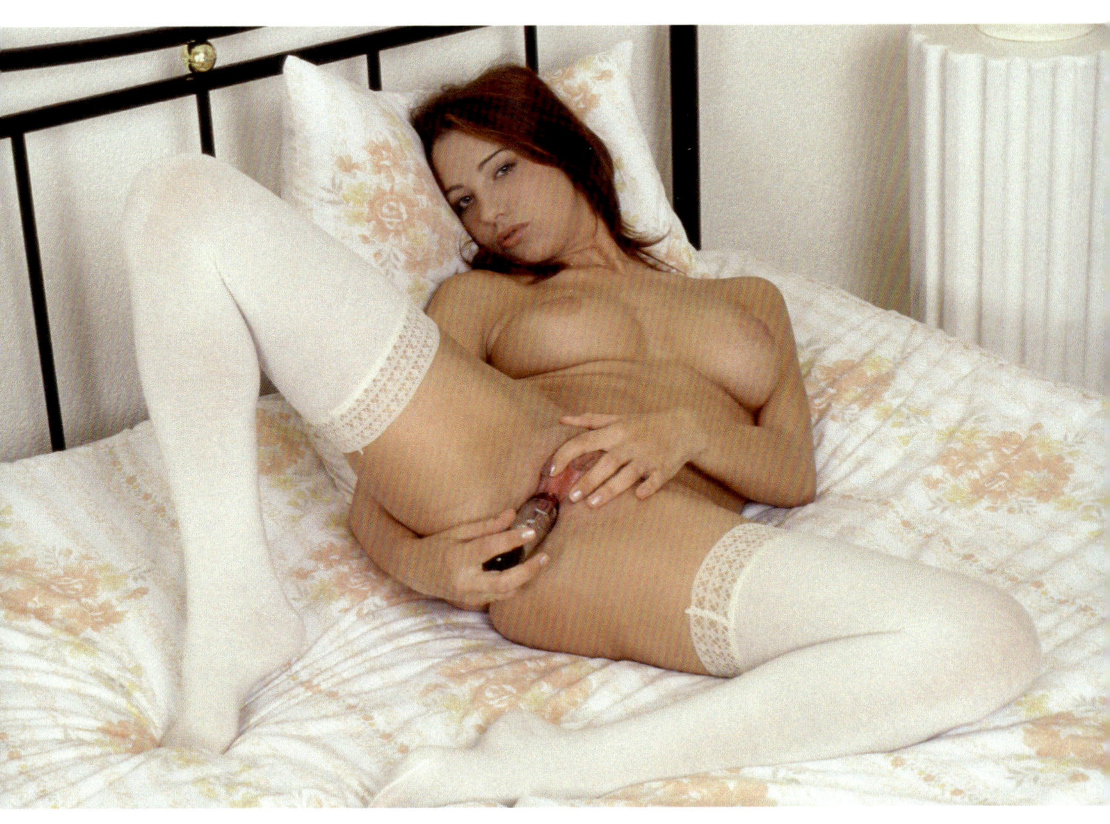

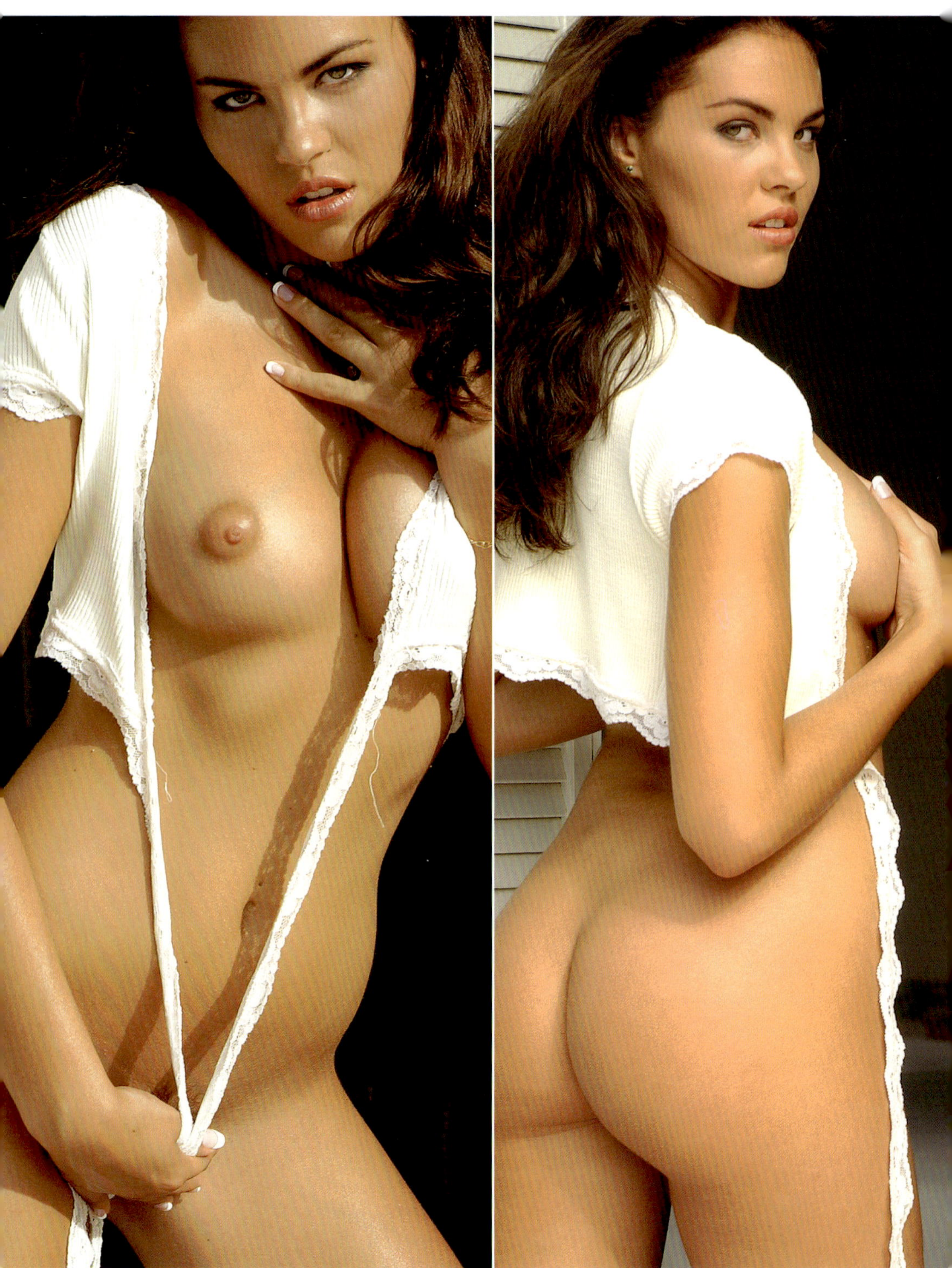

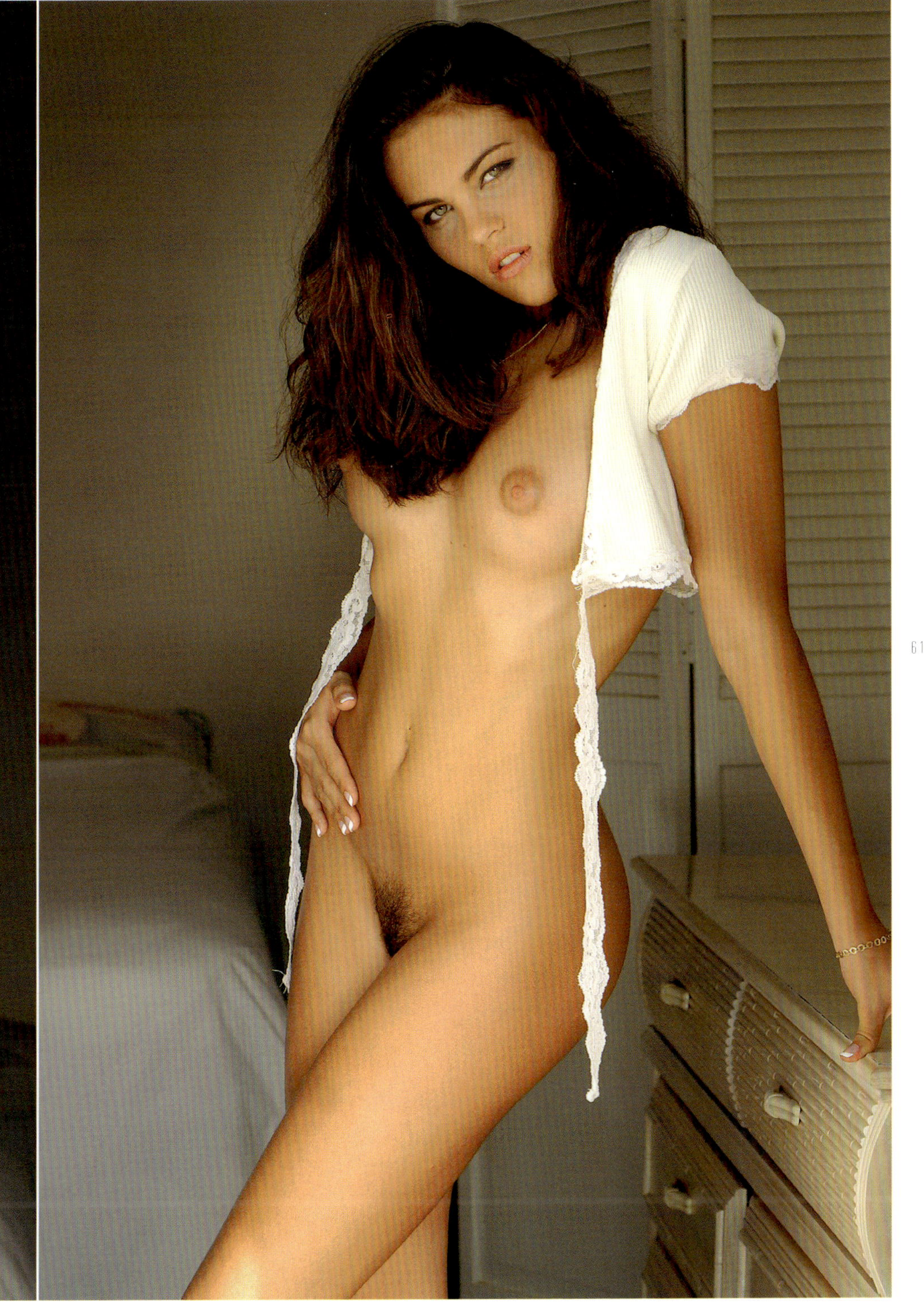

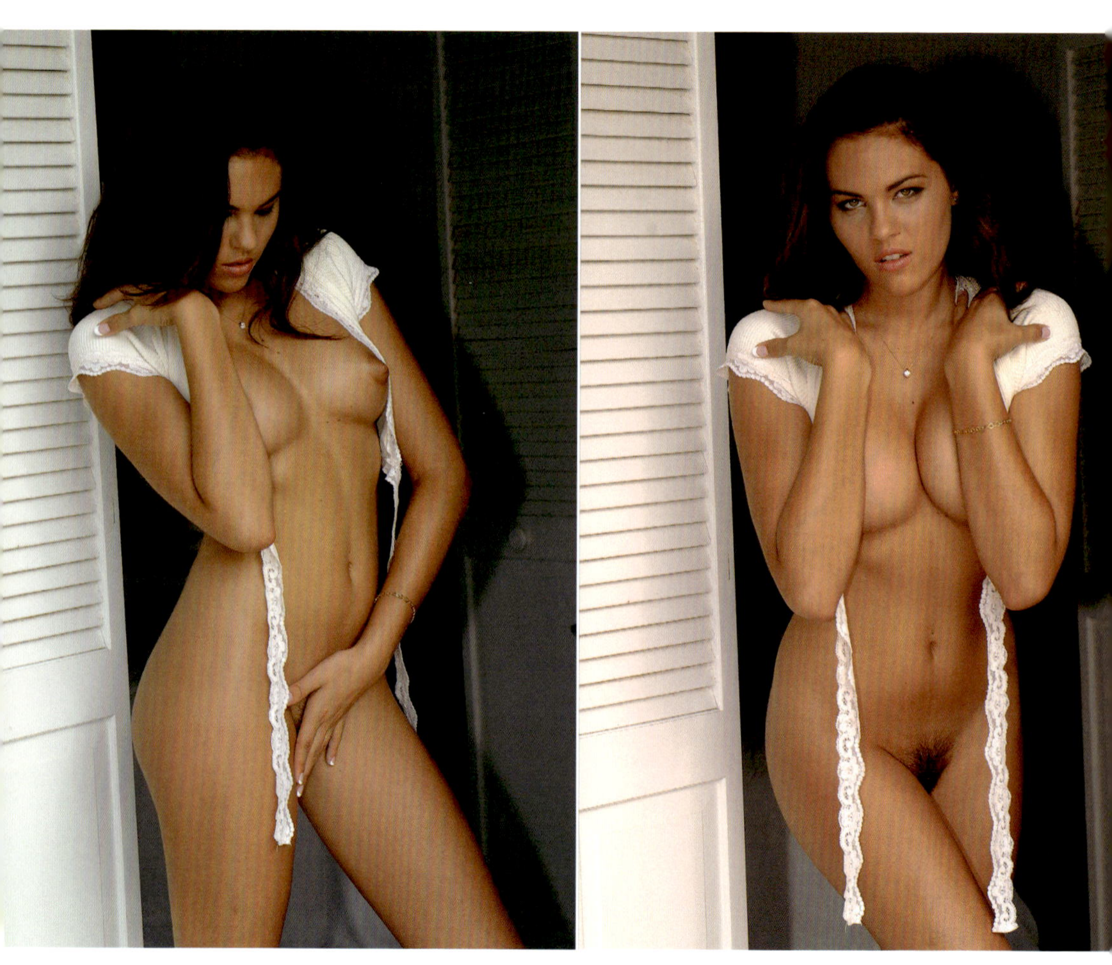

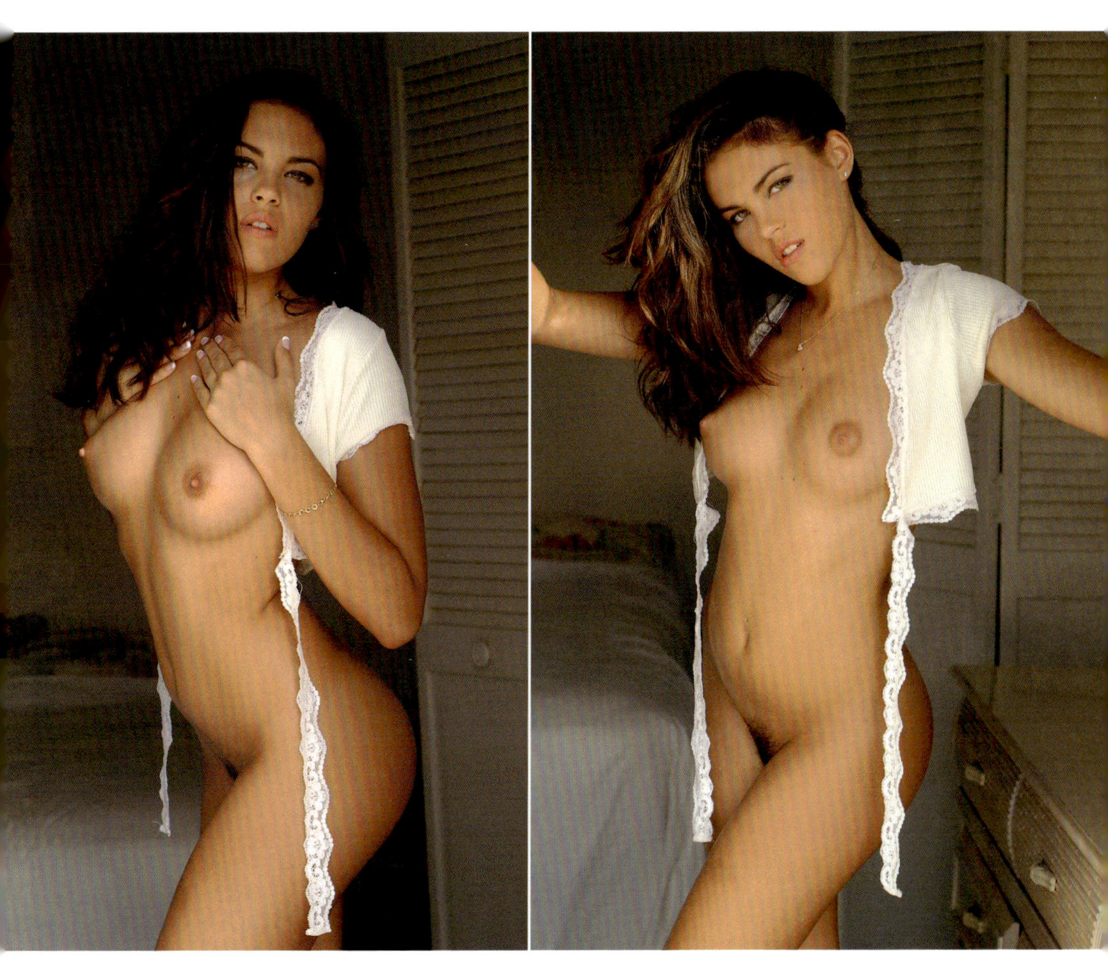

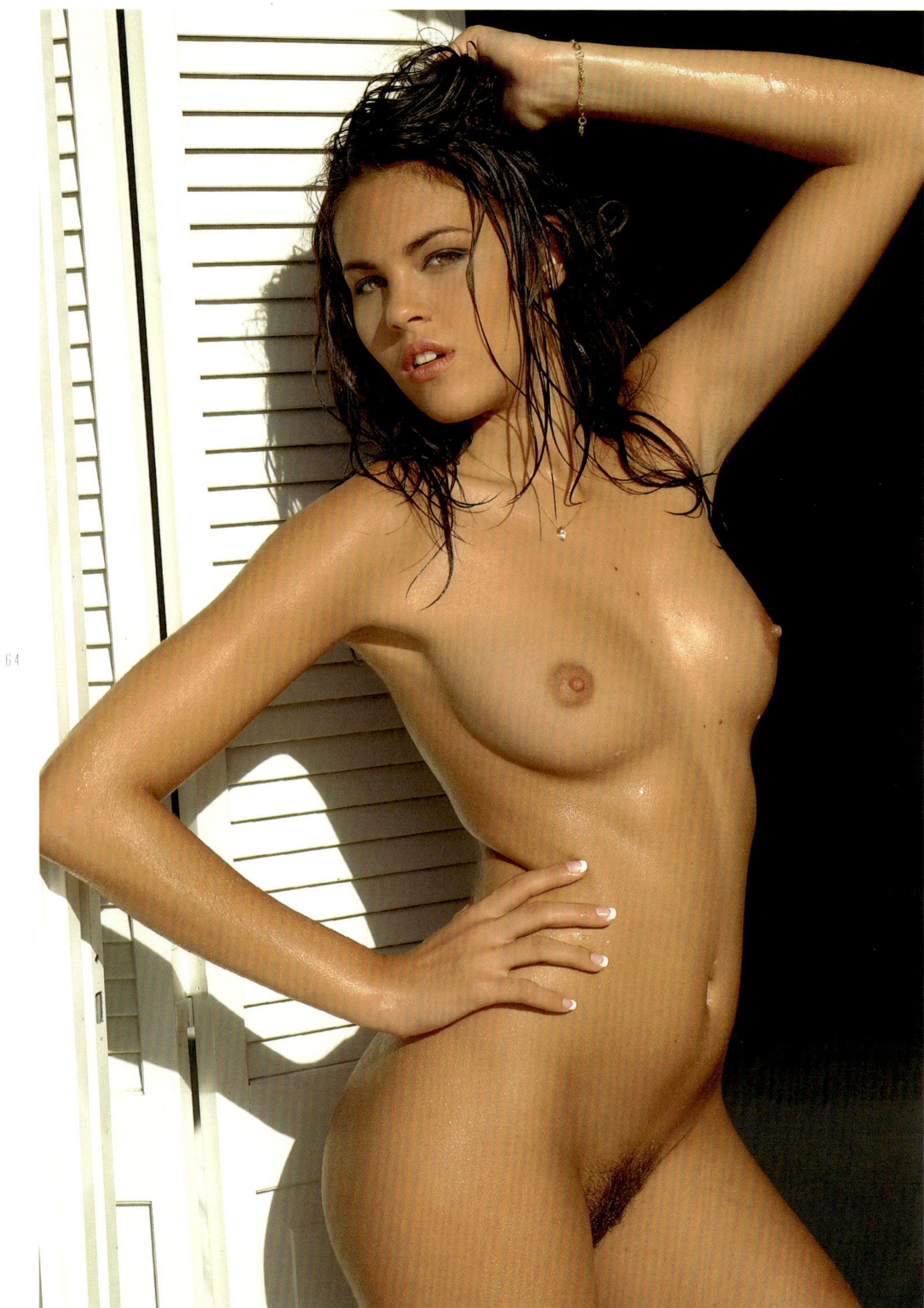

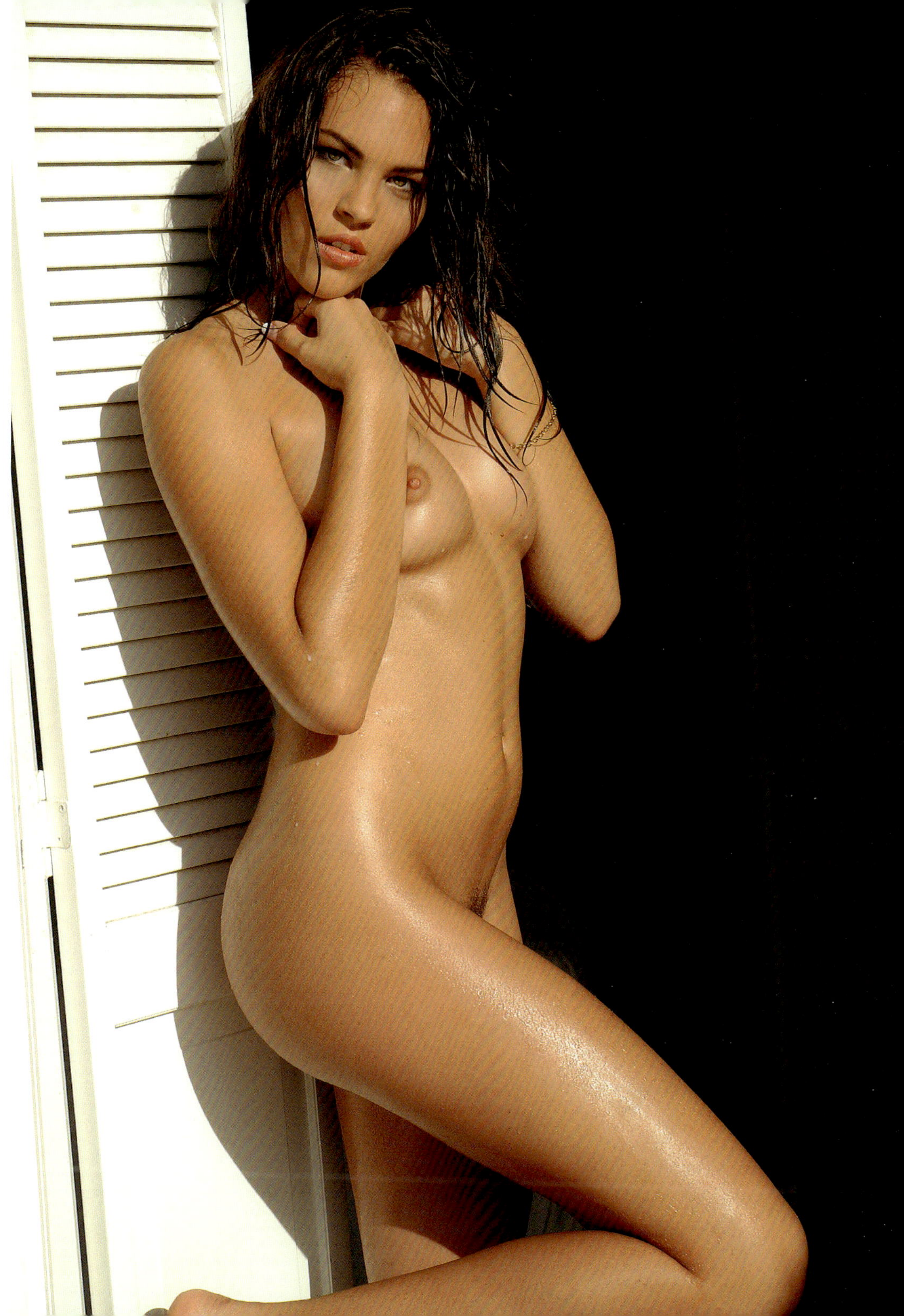

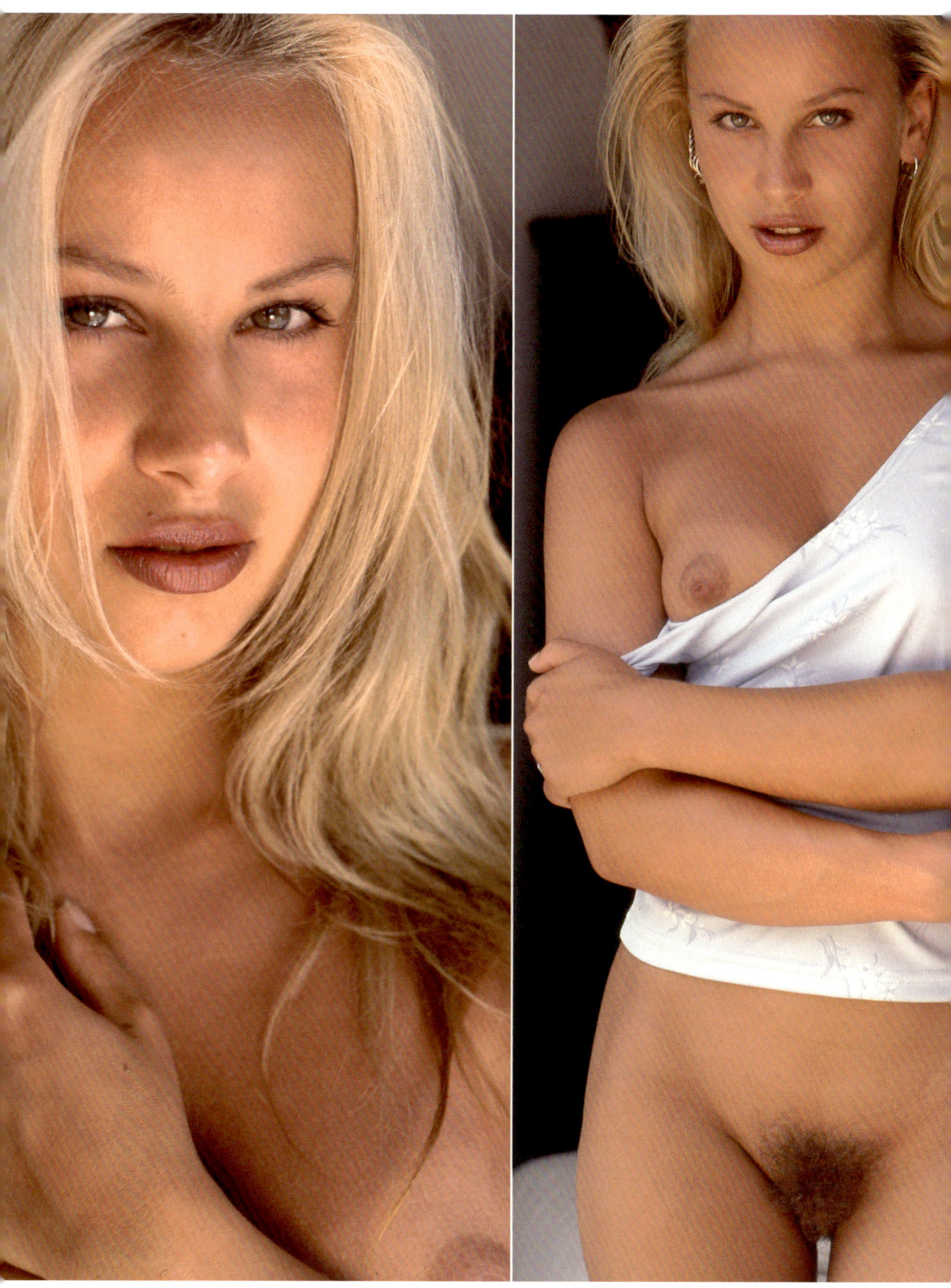

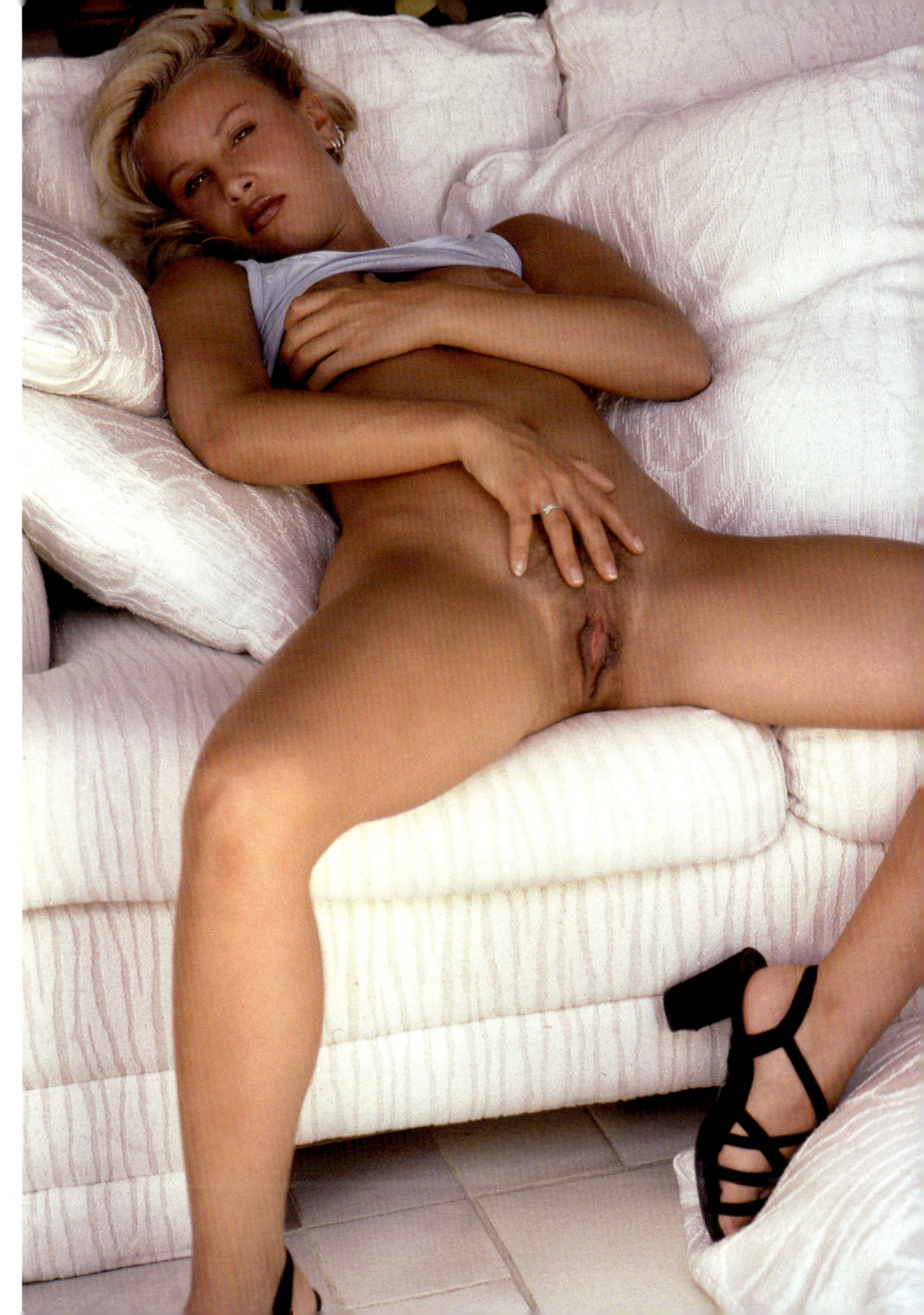

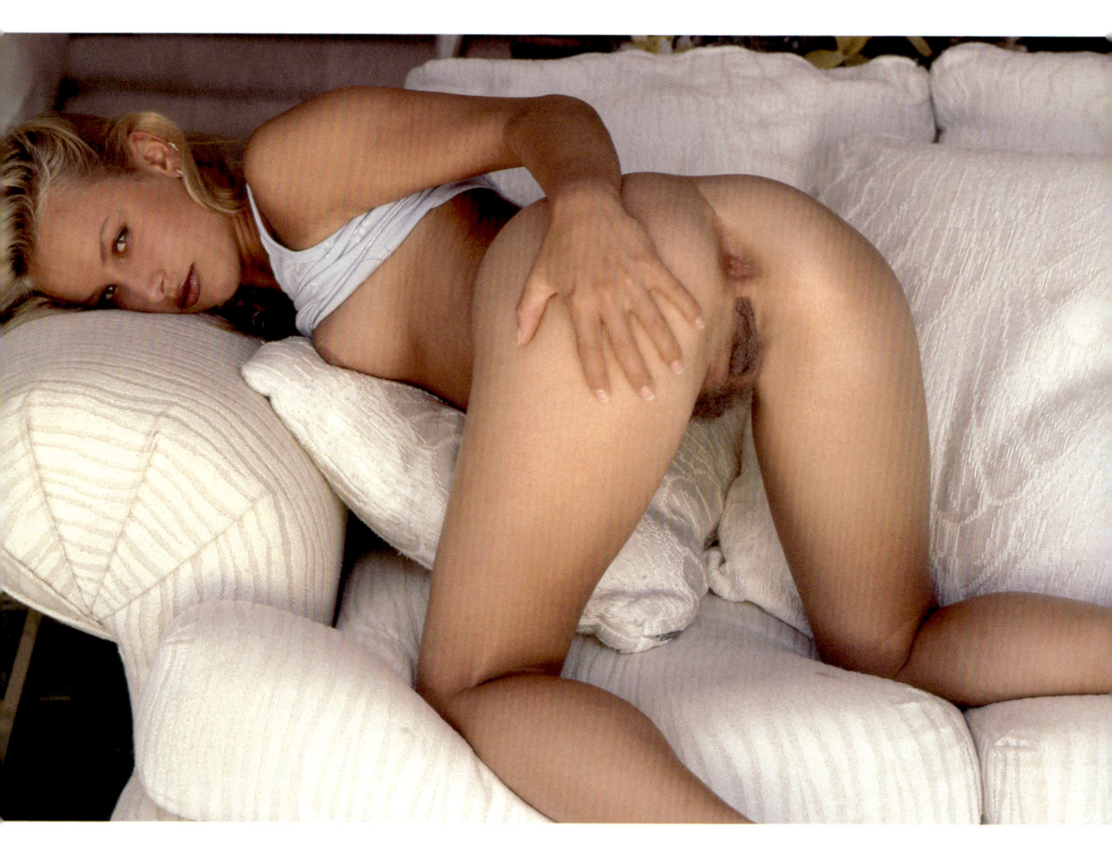

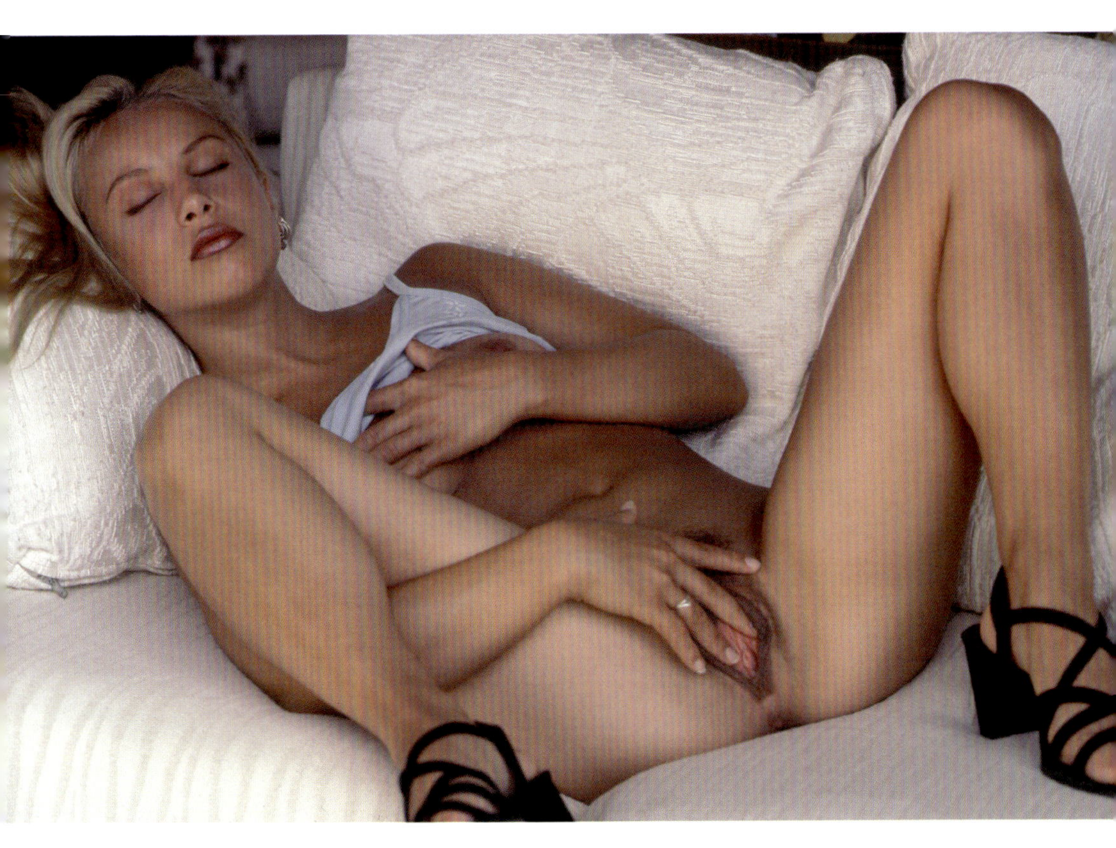

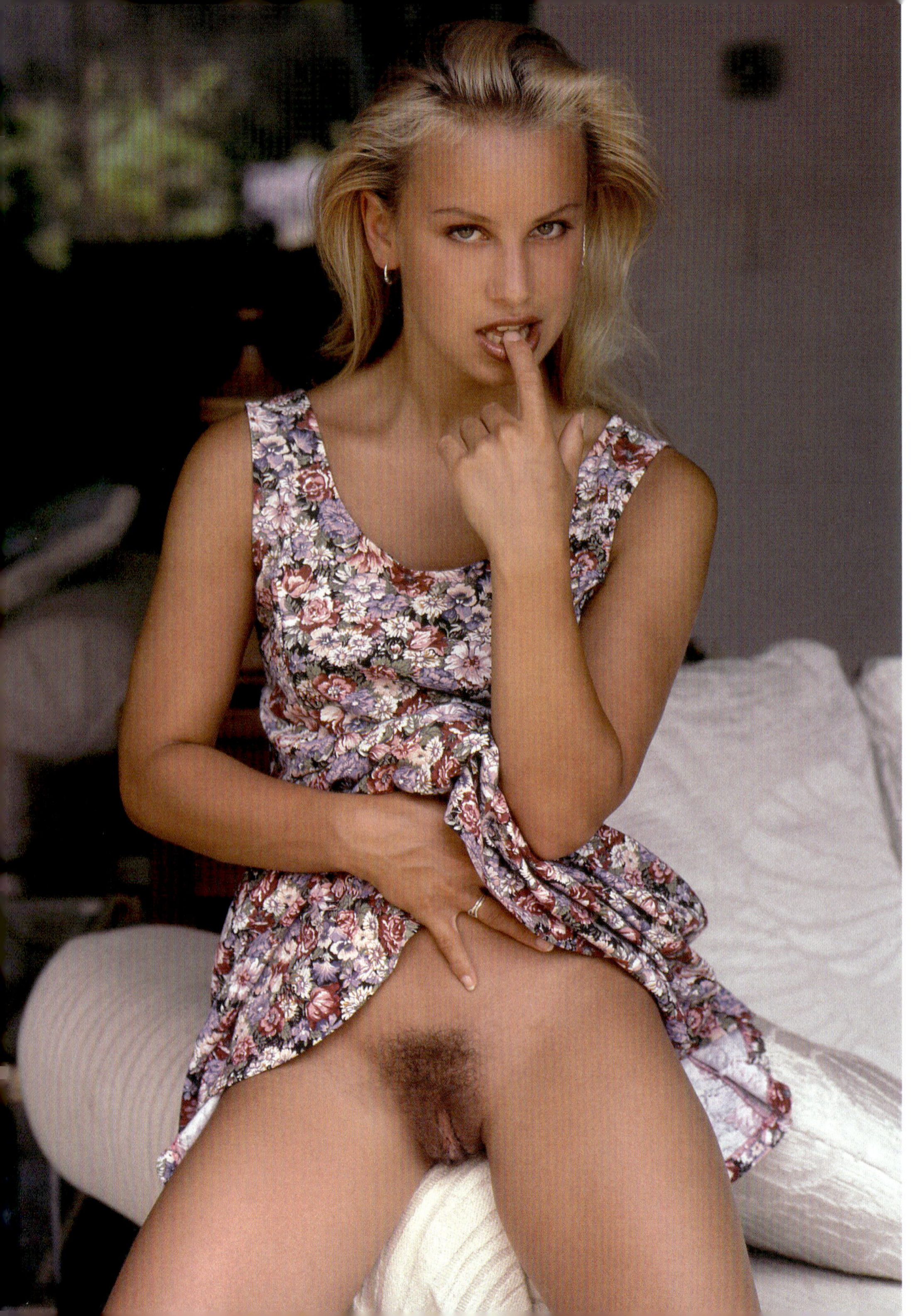

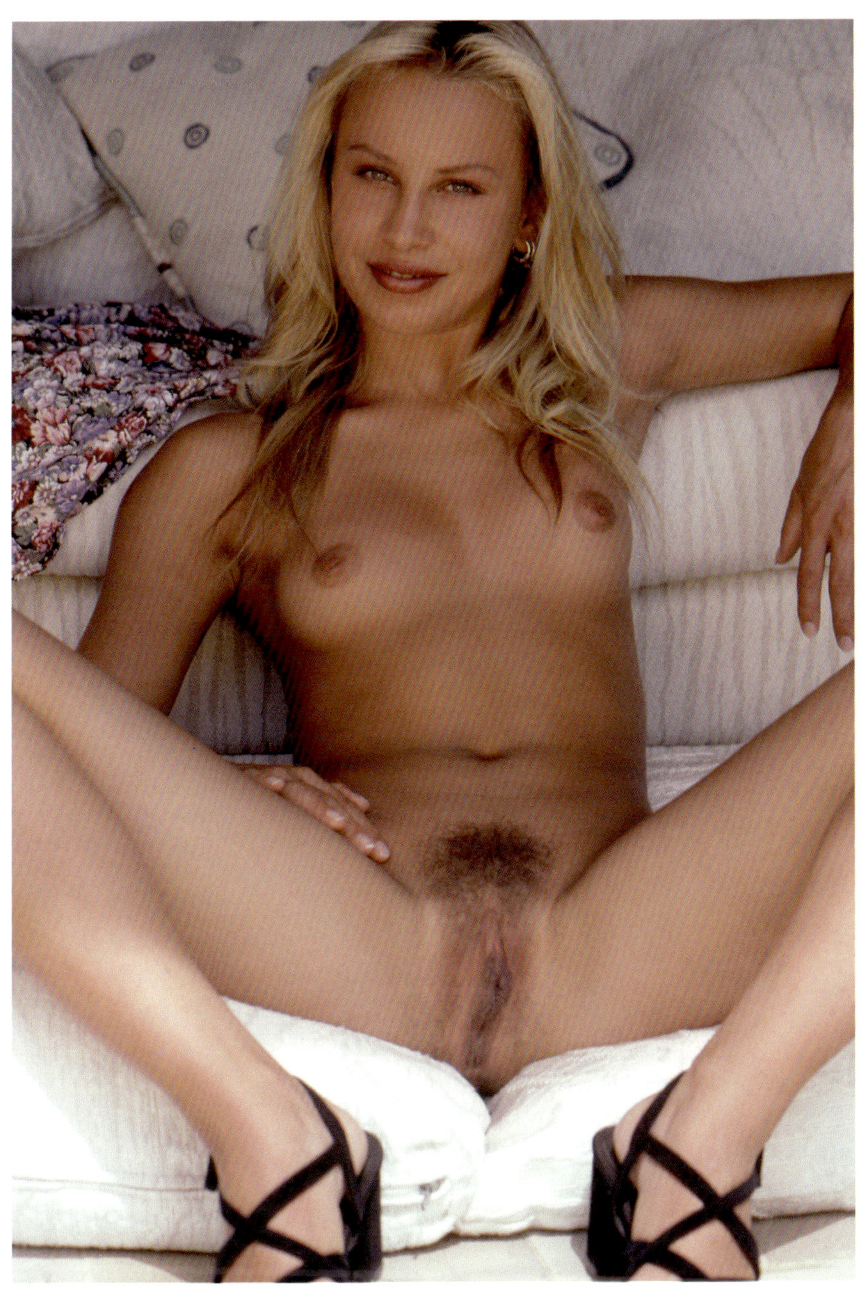

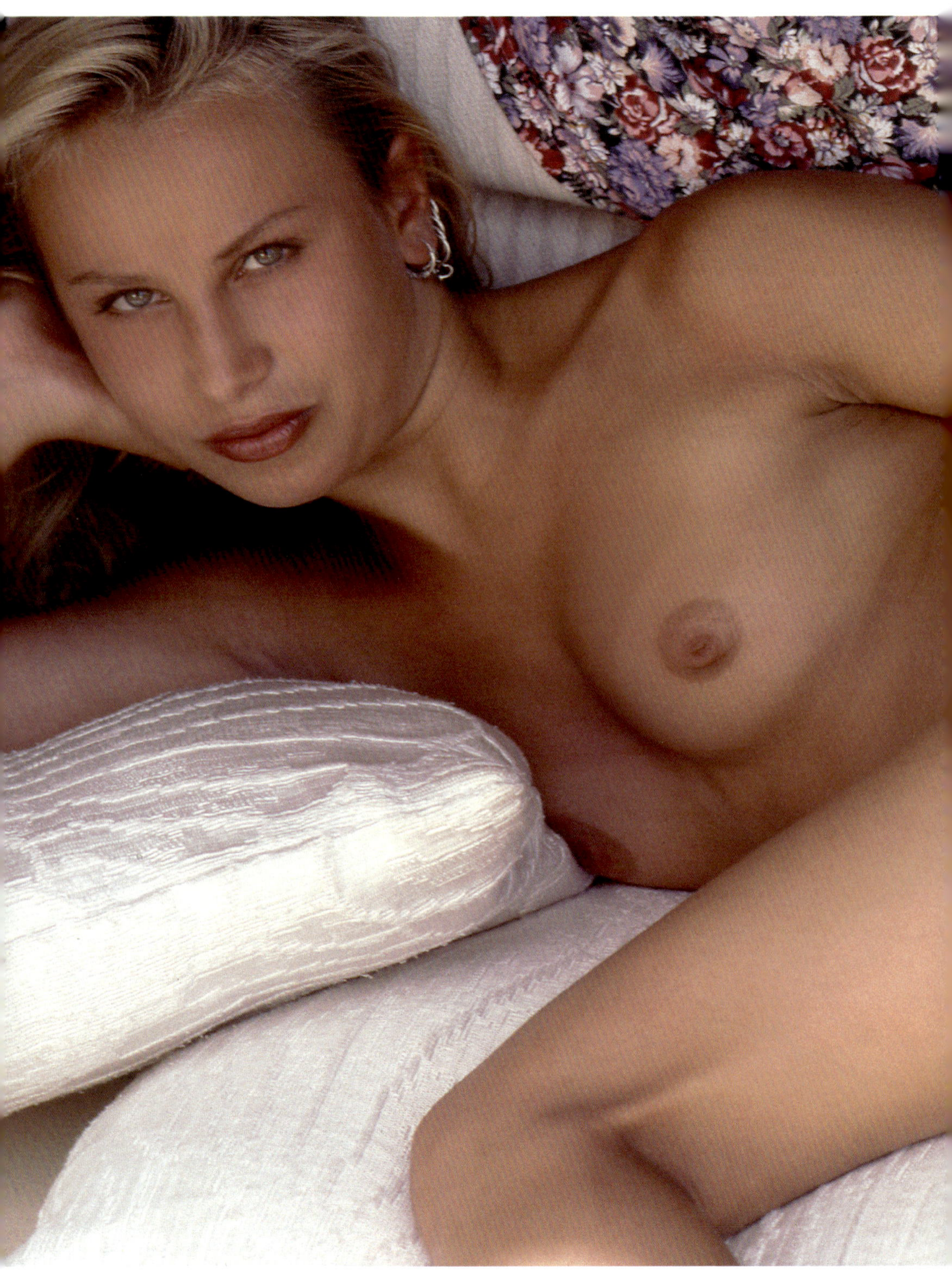

PAOLA

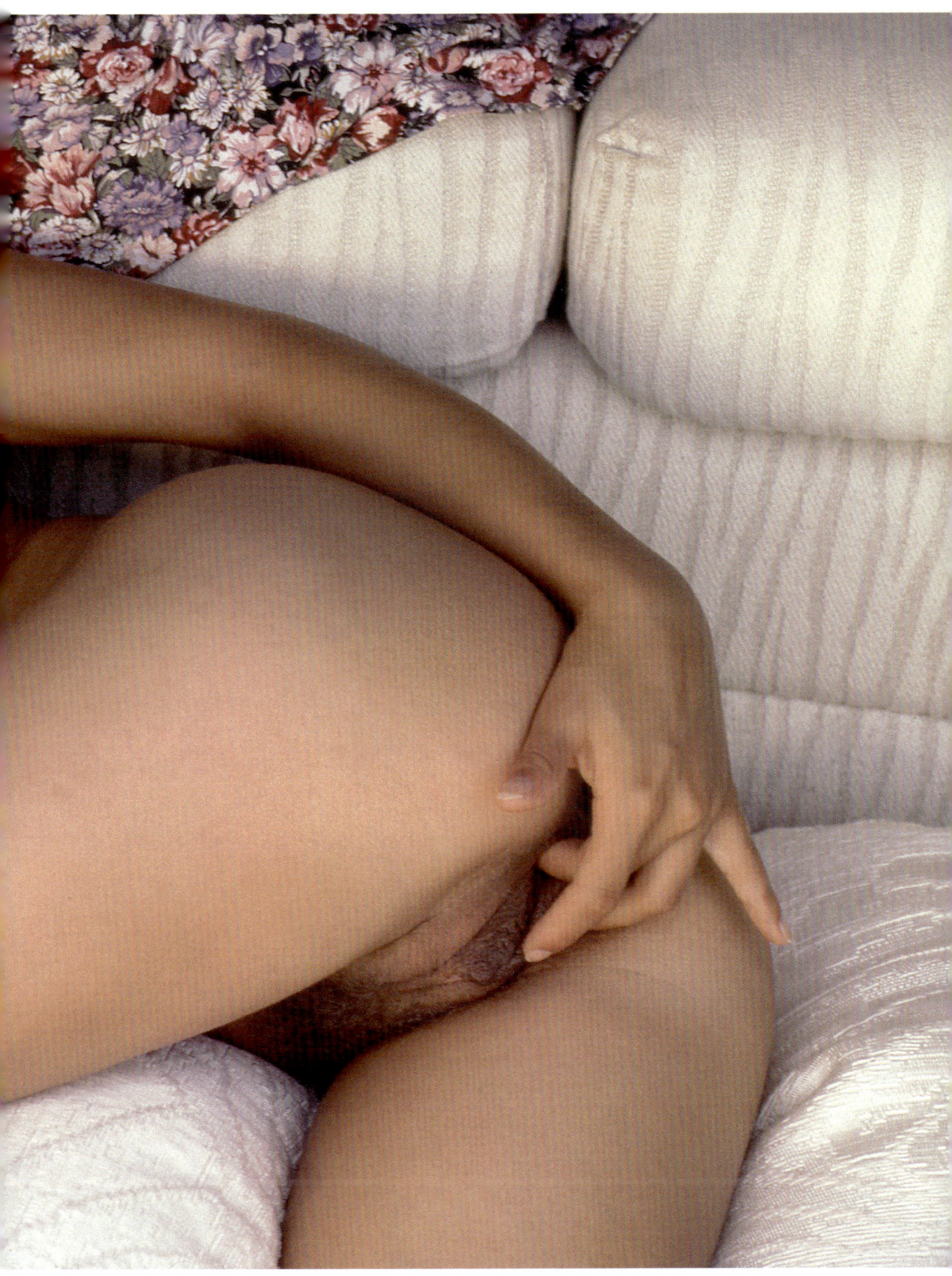

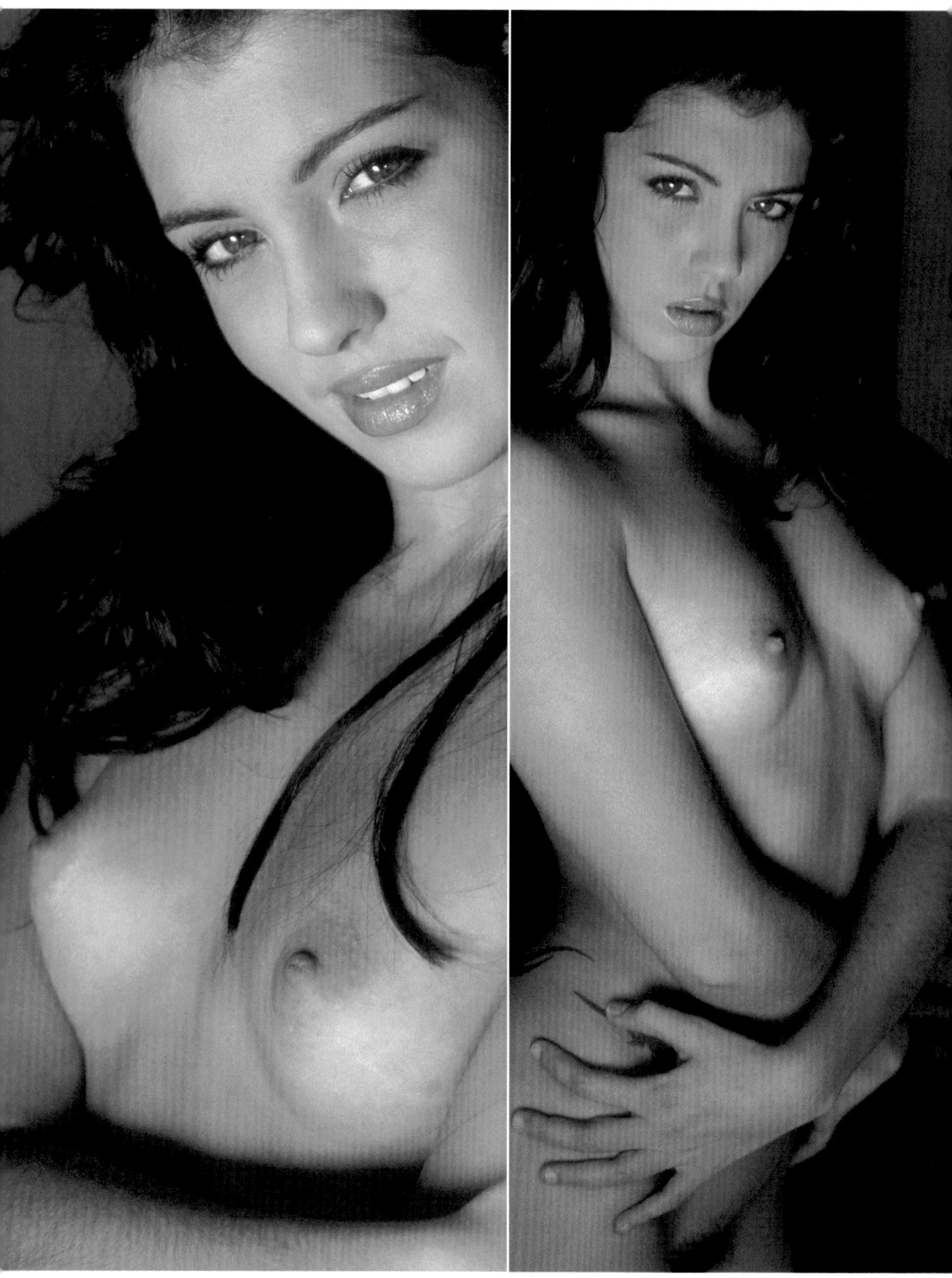

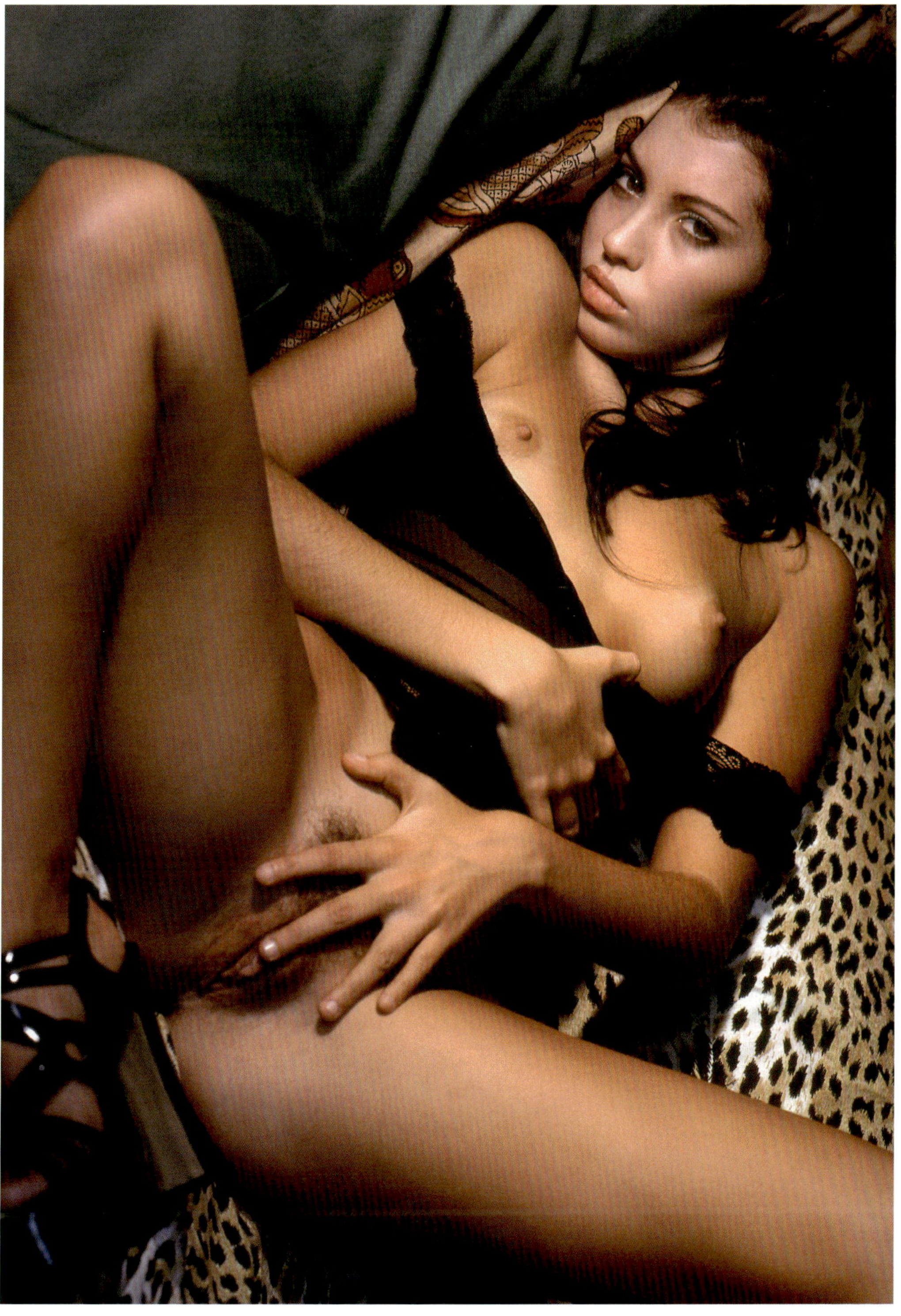

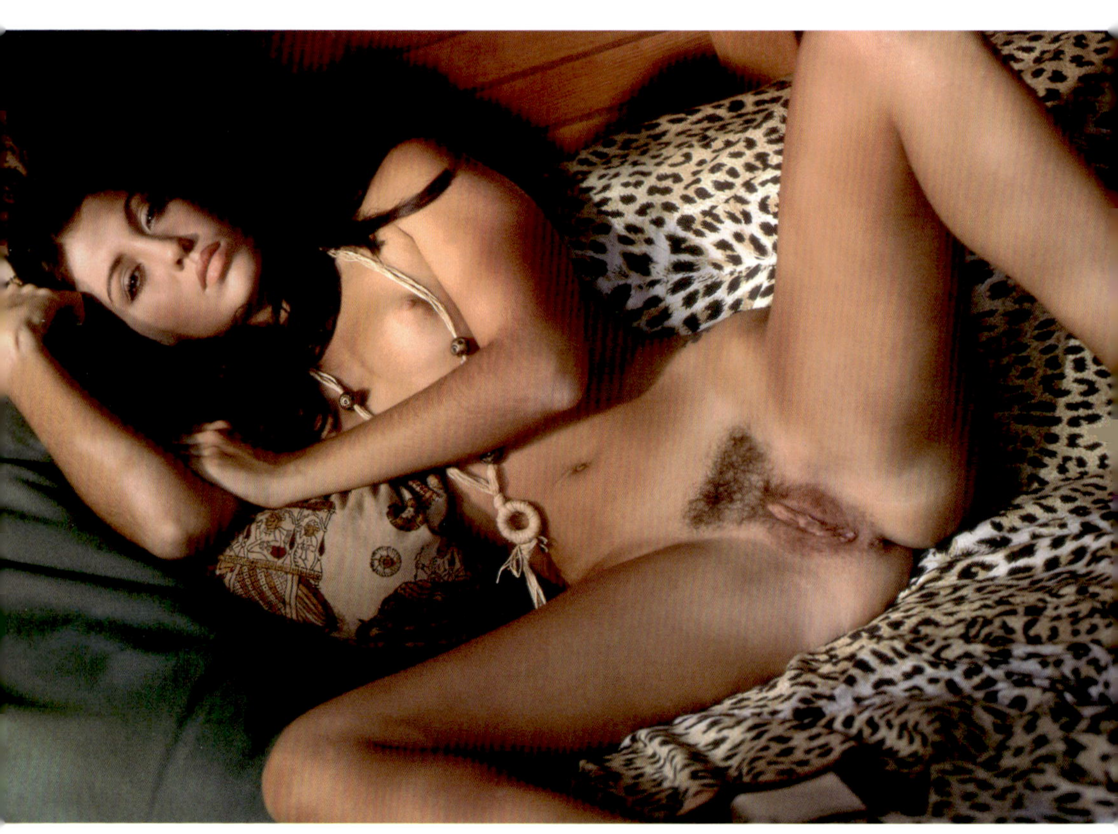

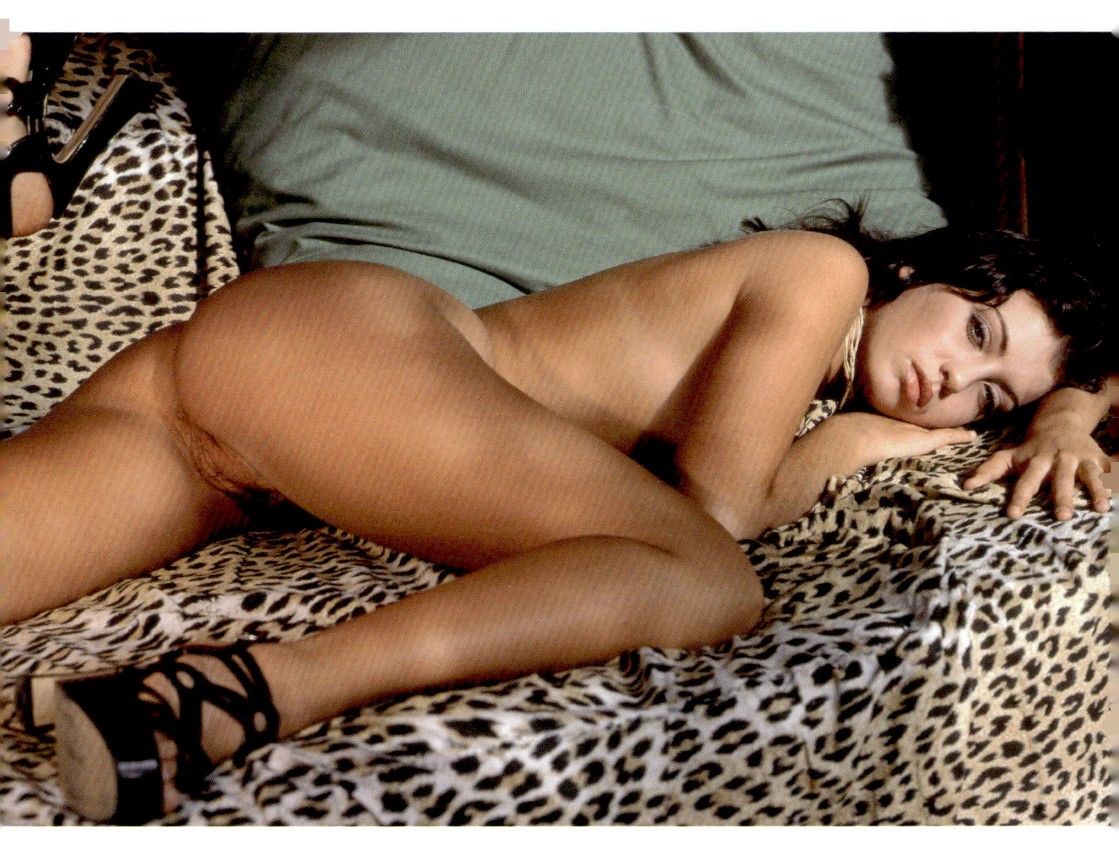

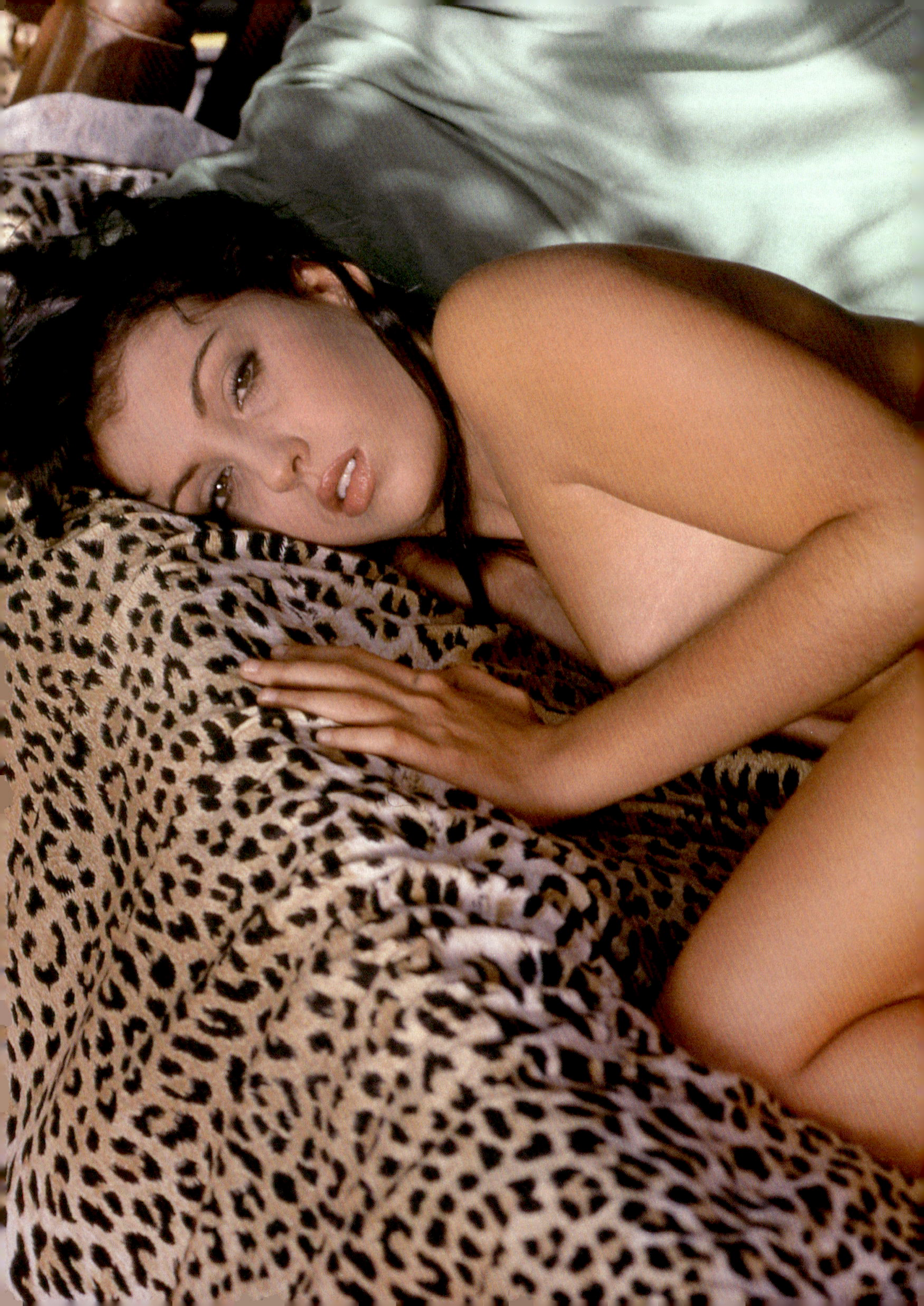

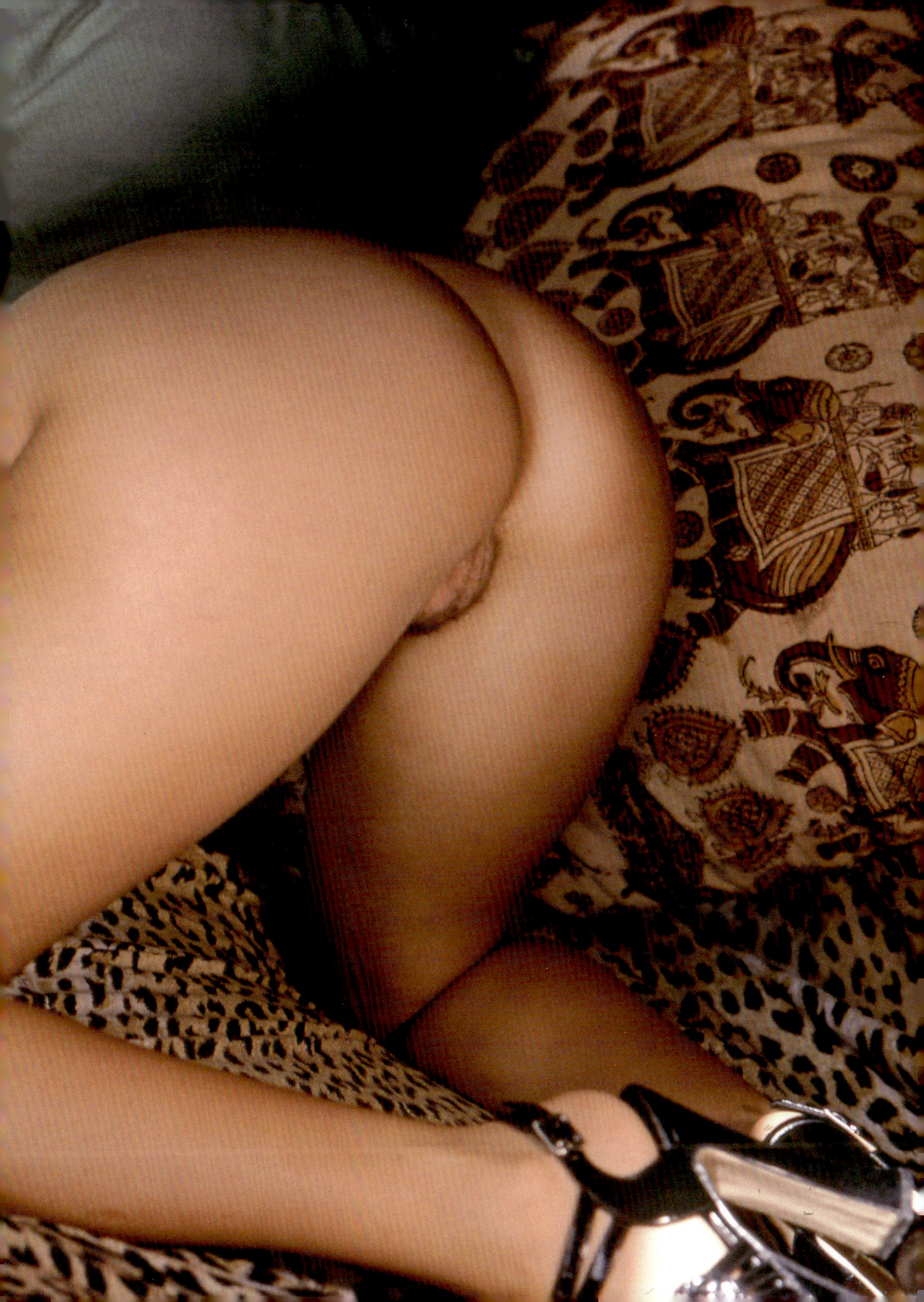

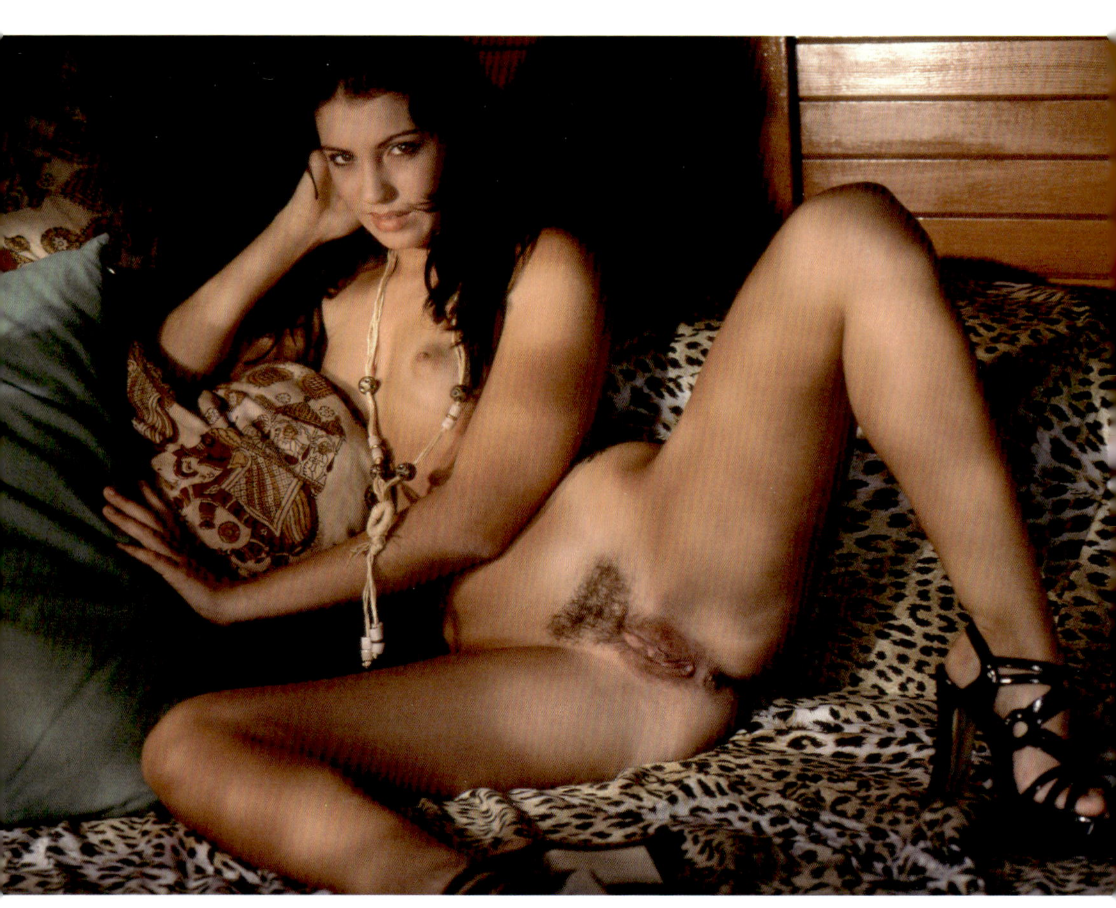

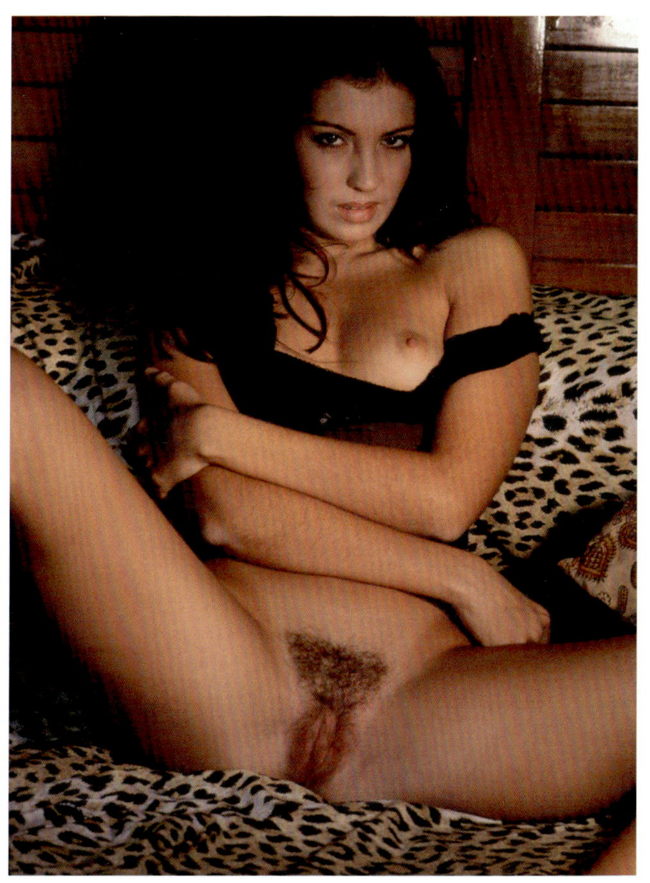

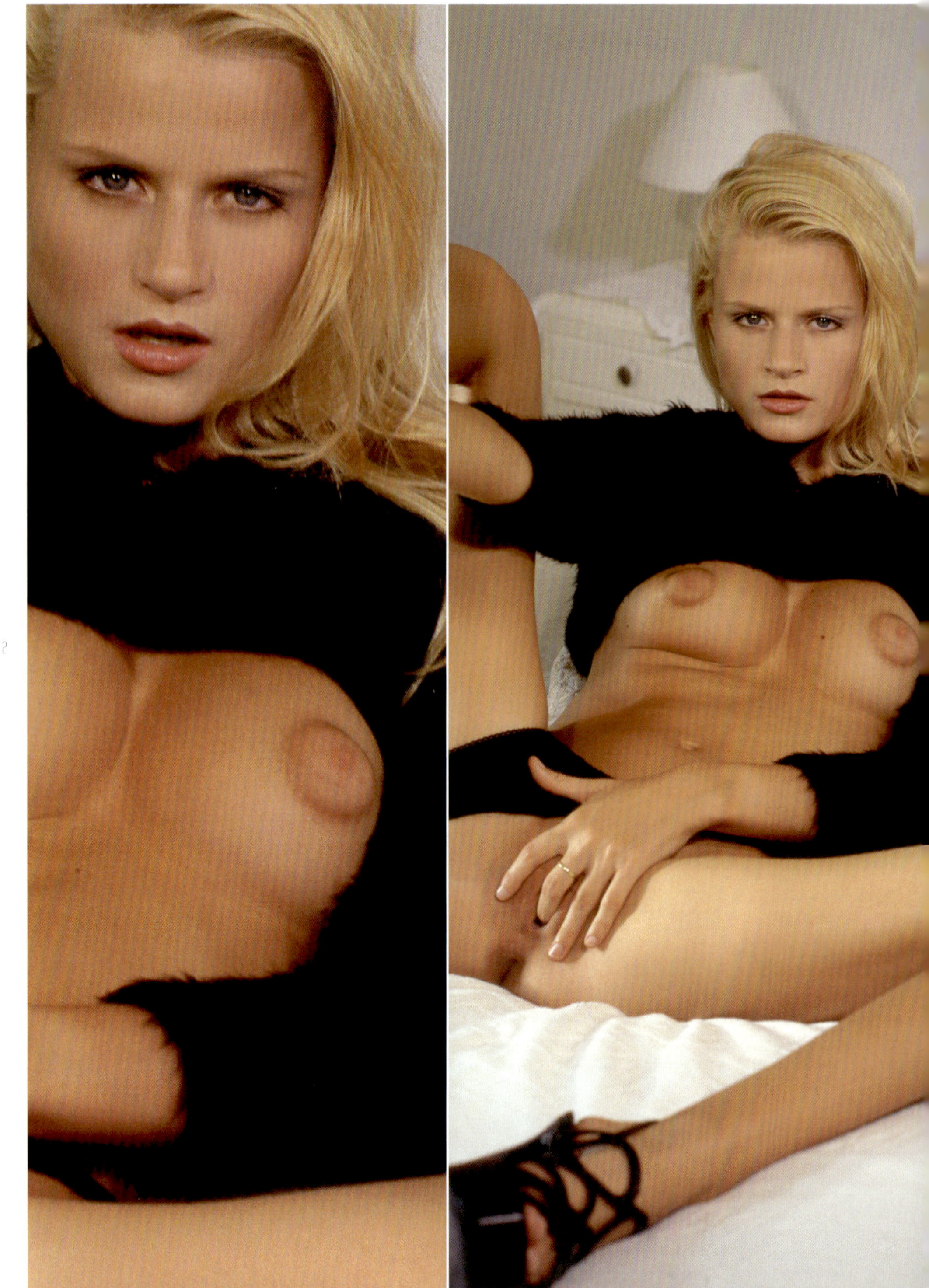

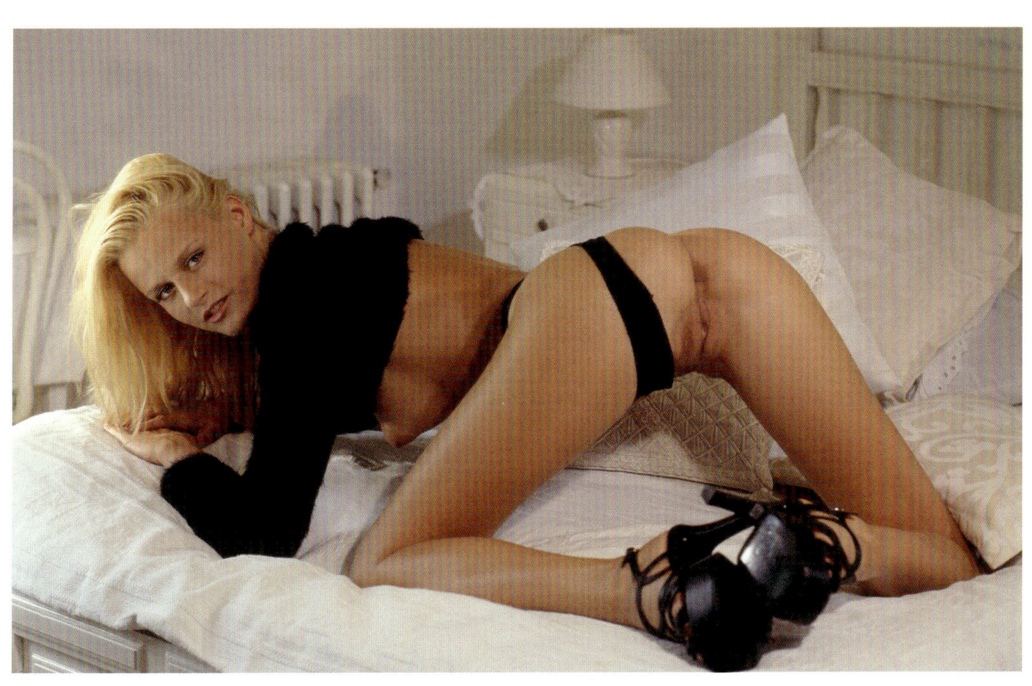

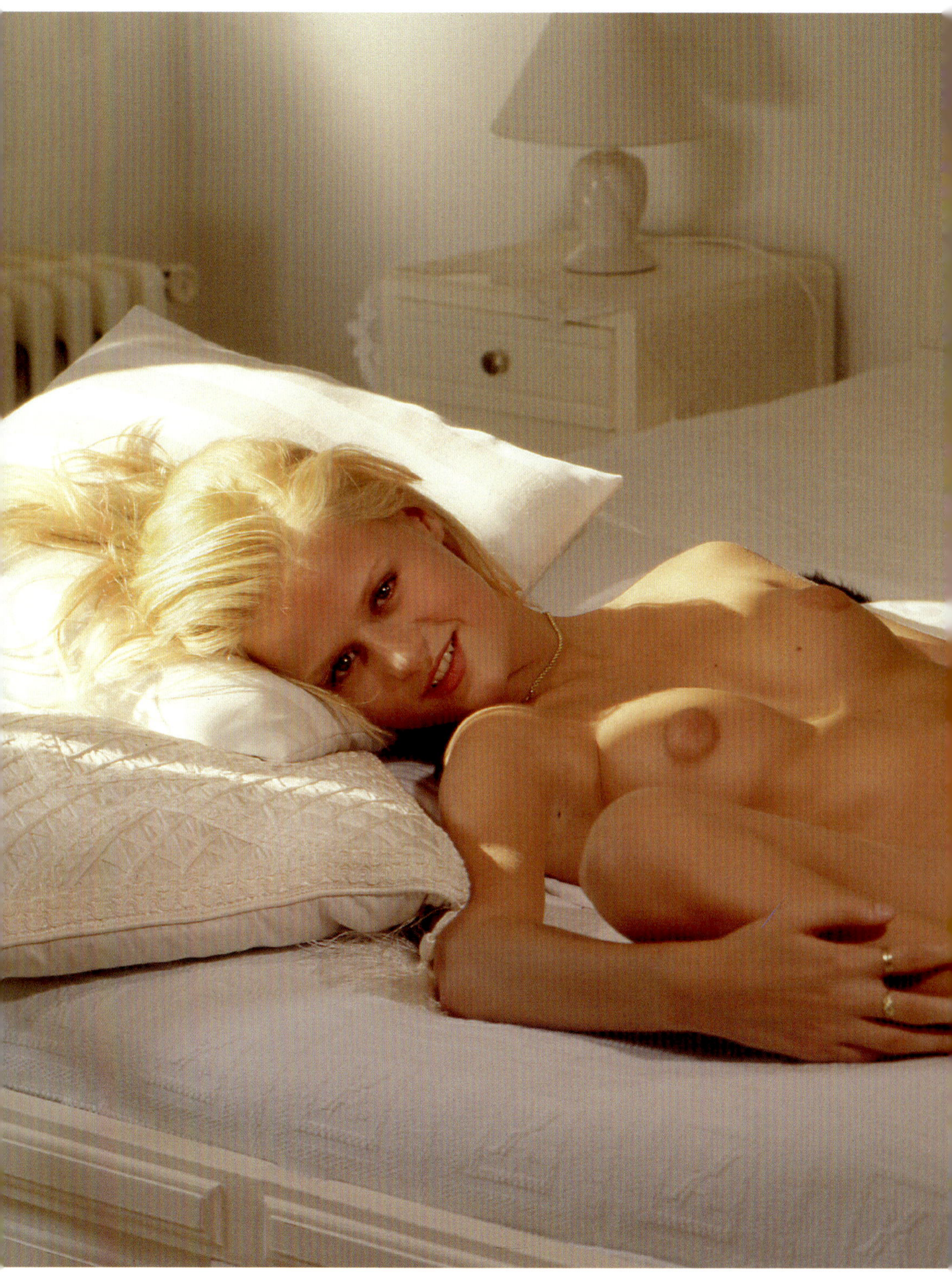

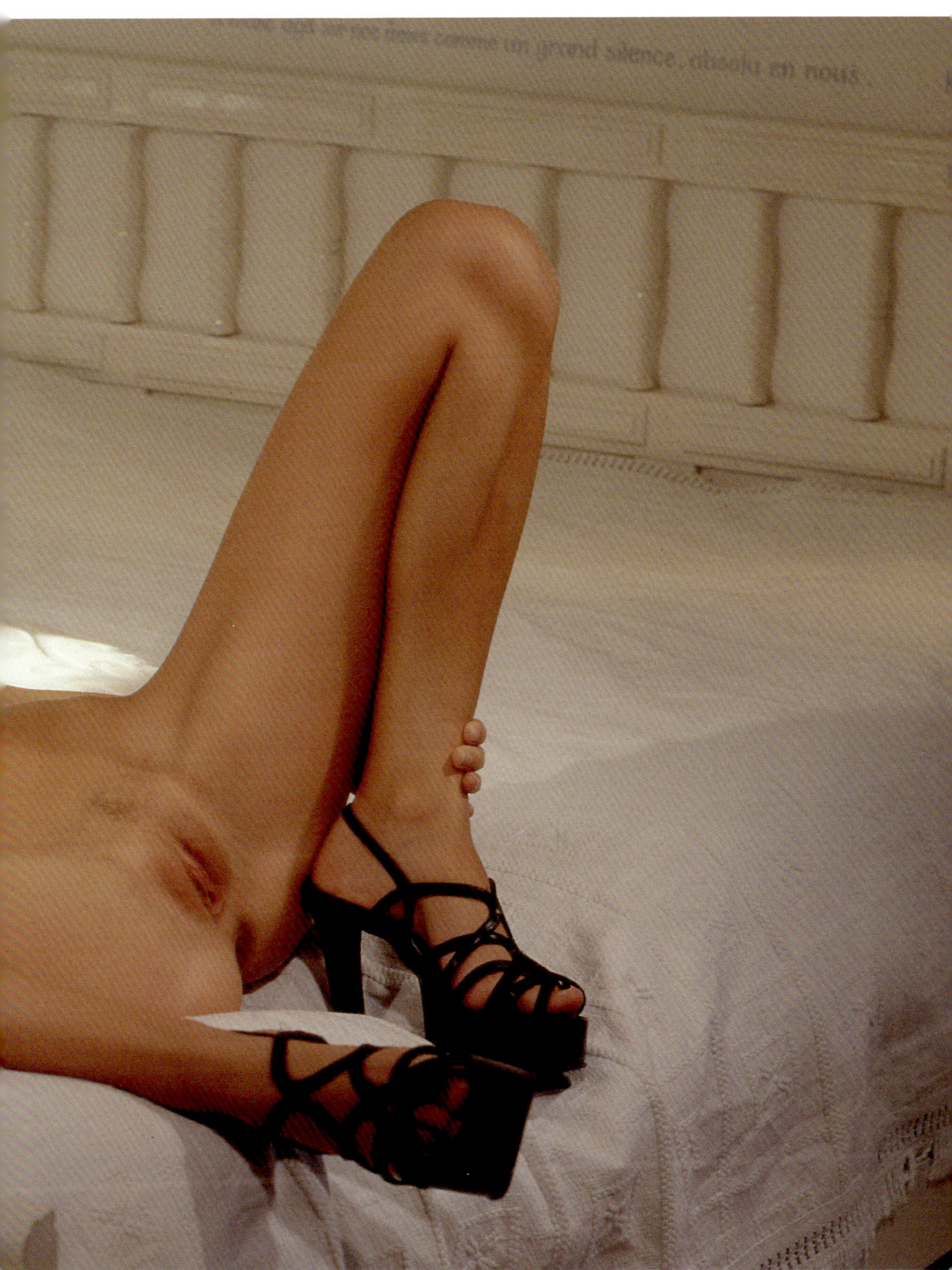
comme un grand silence, absolu en nous.

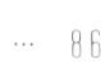

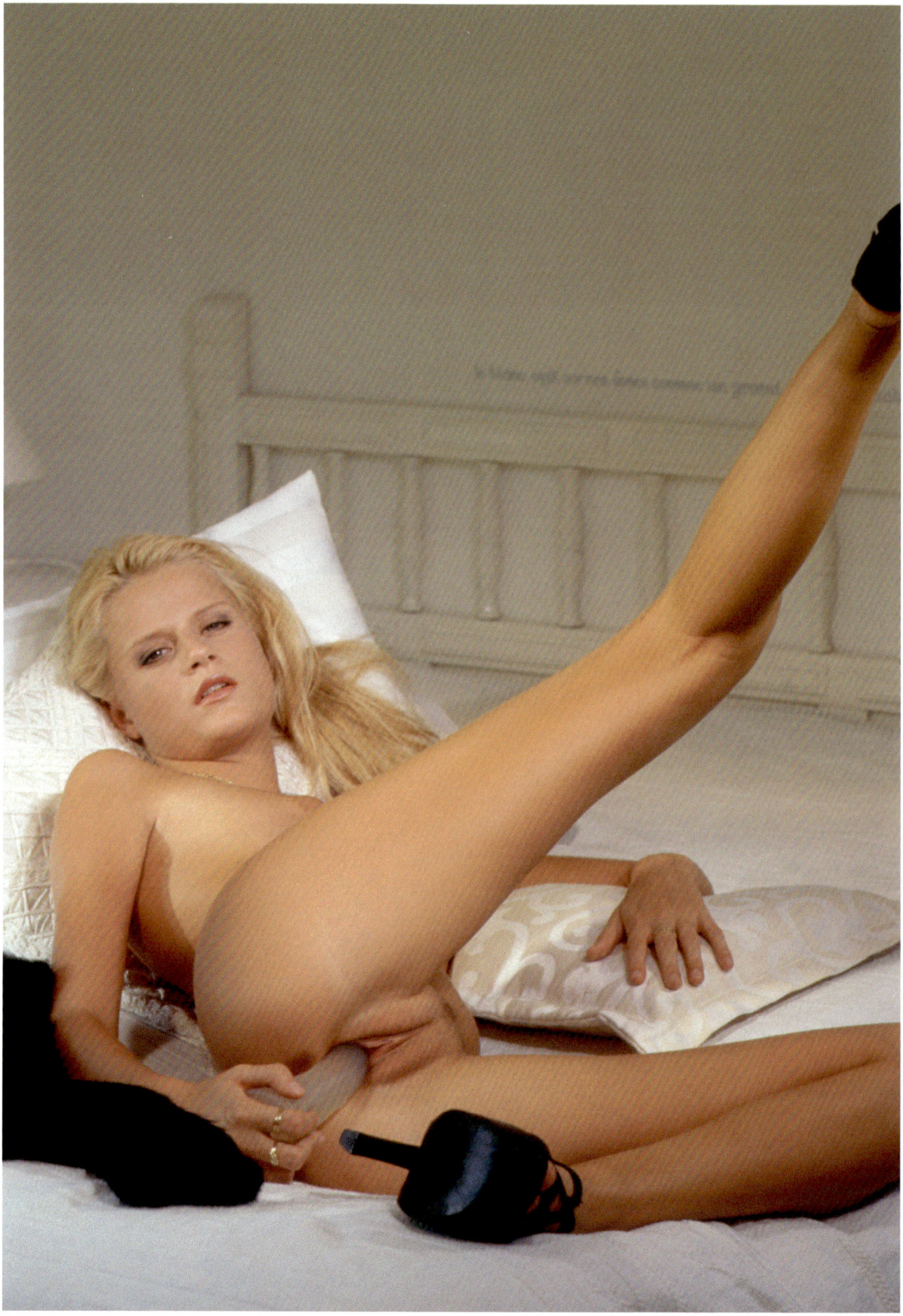

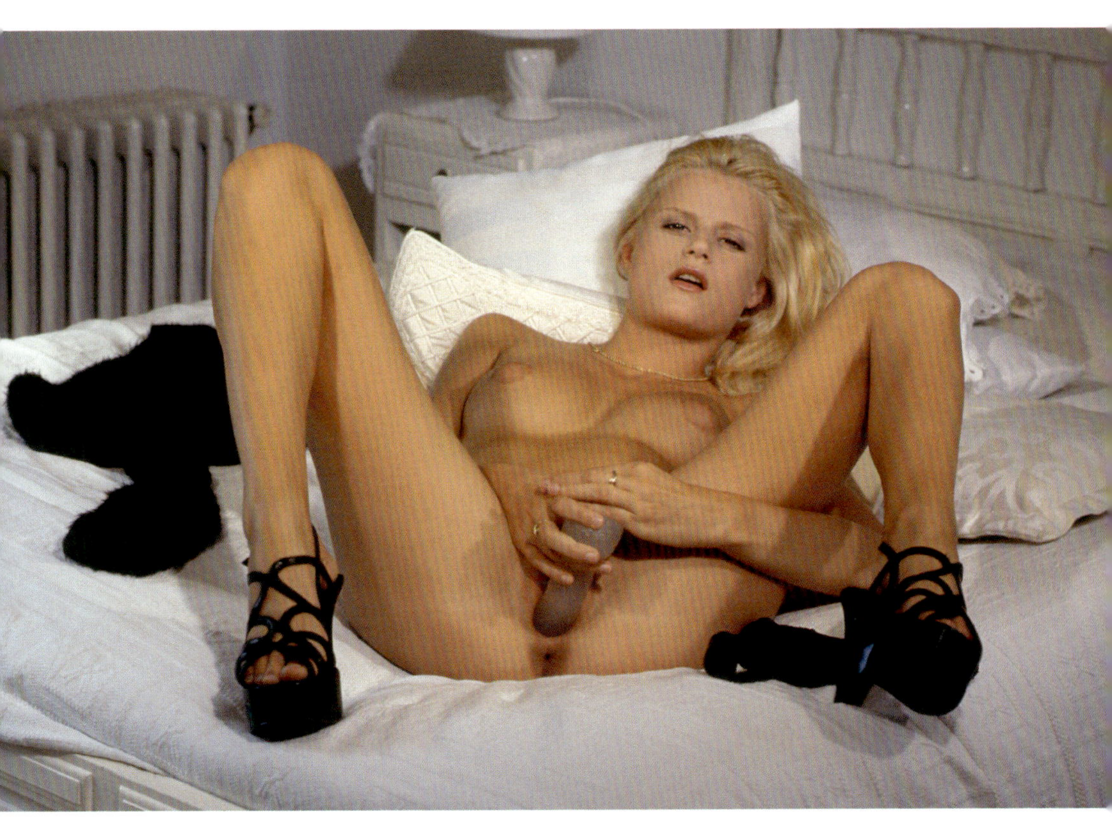

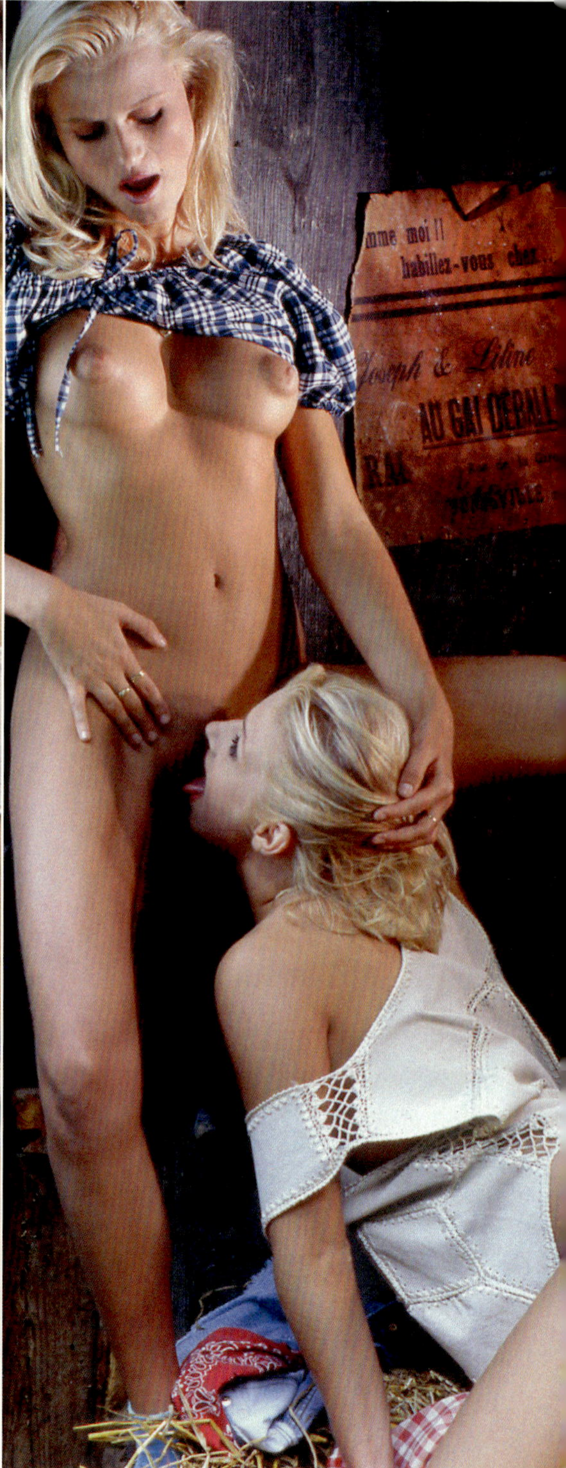

SOFIA AND LINDA

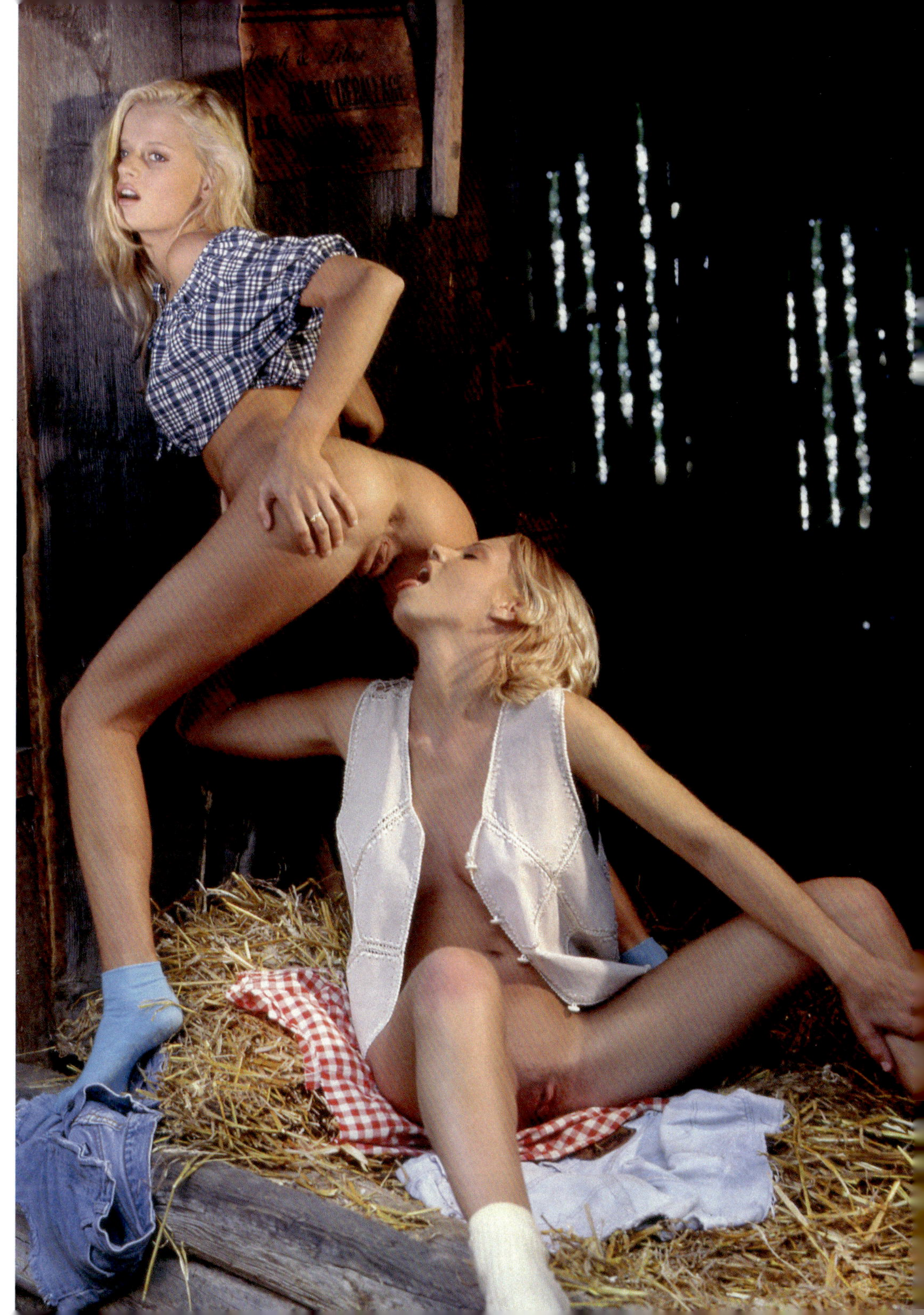

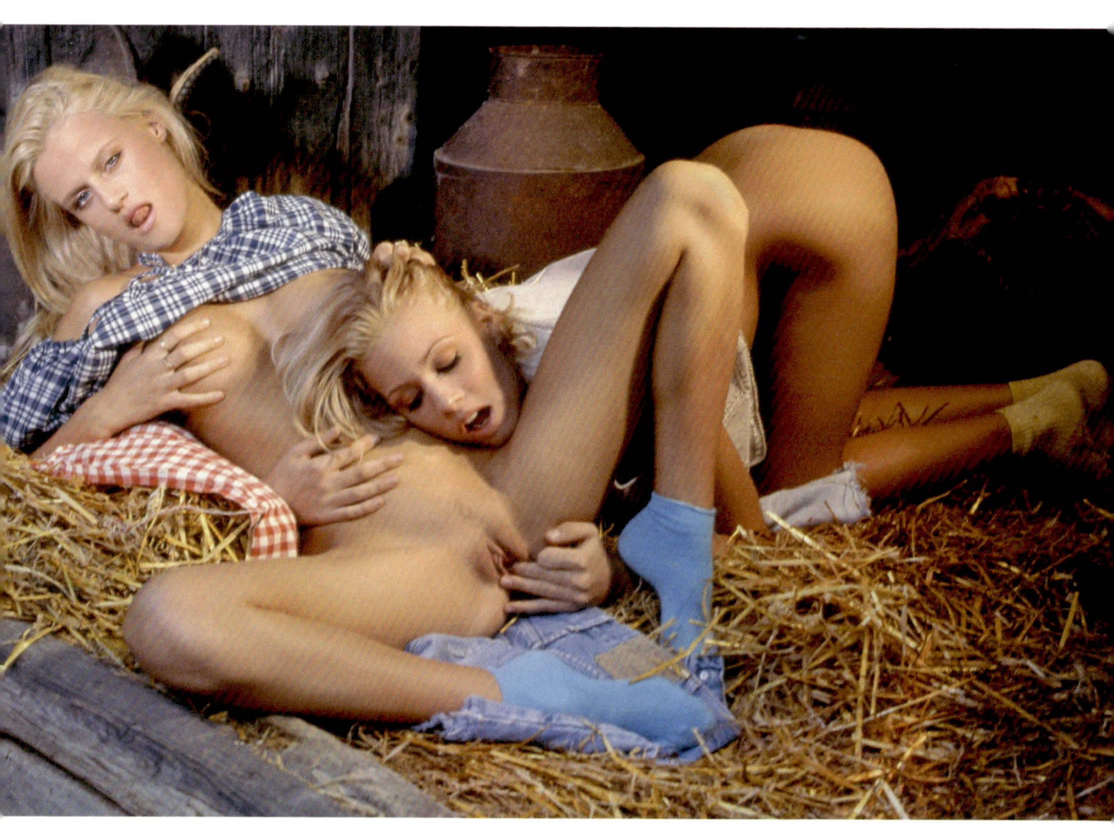

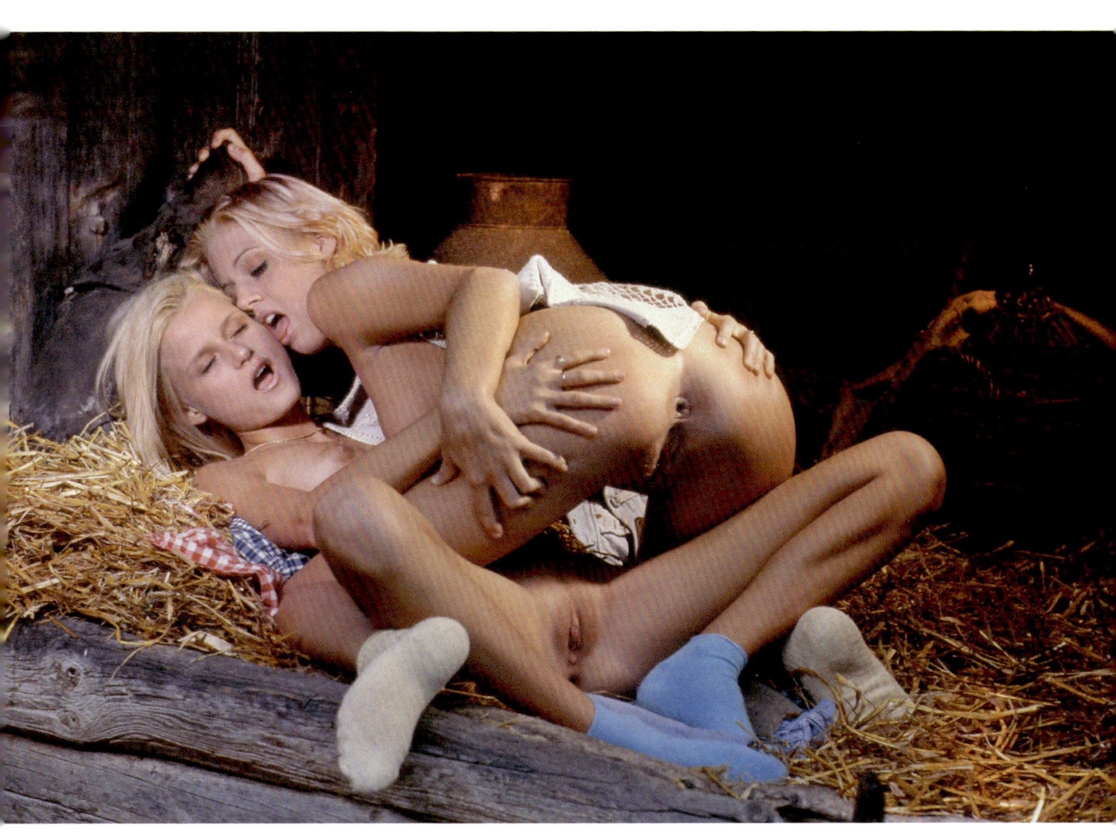

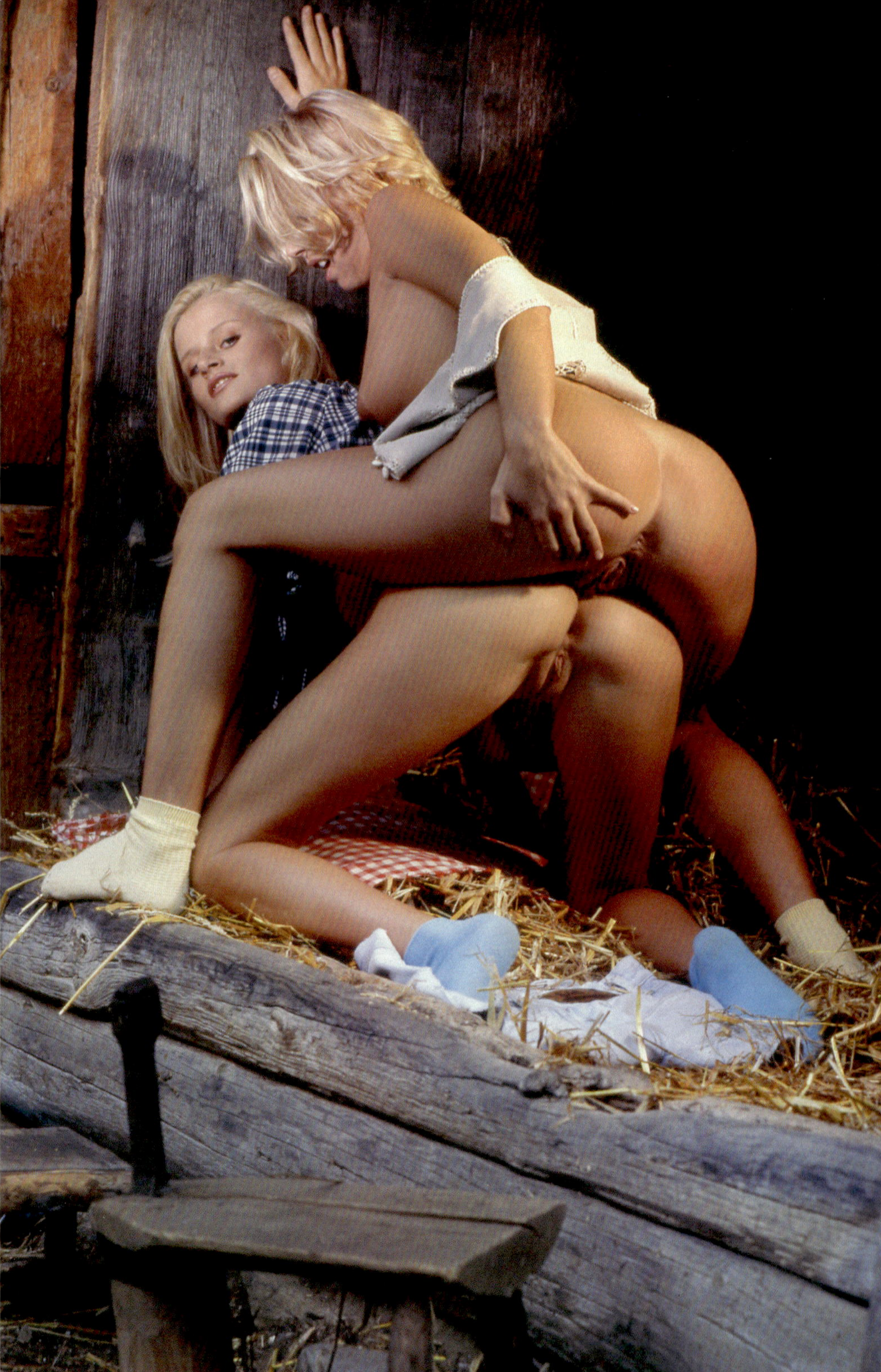

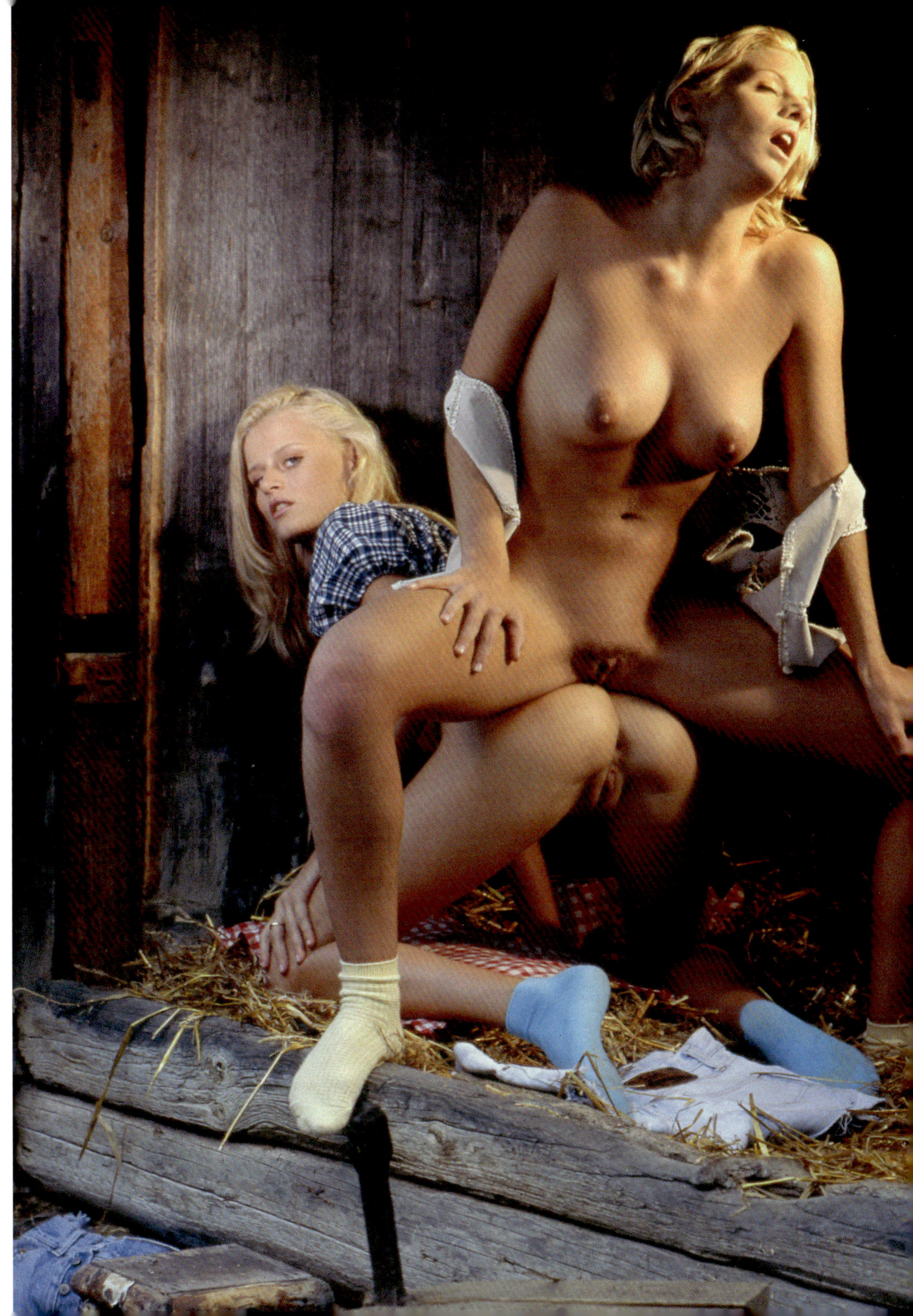

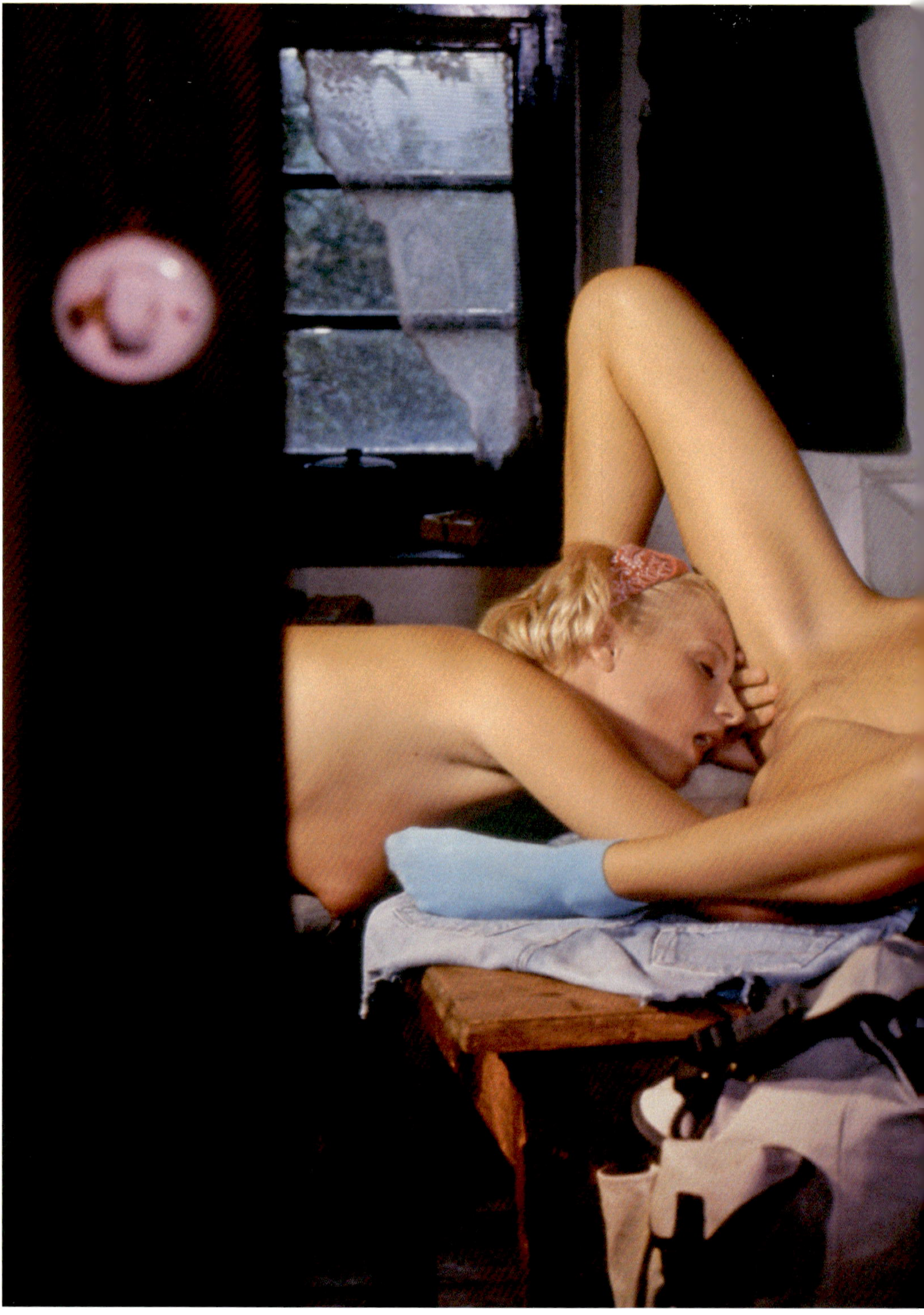

SOFIA AND LINDA

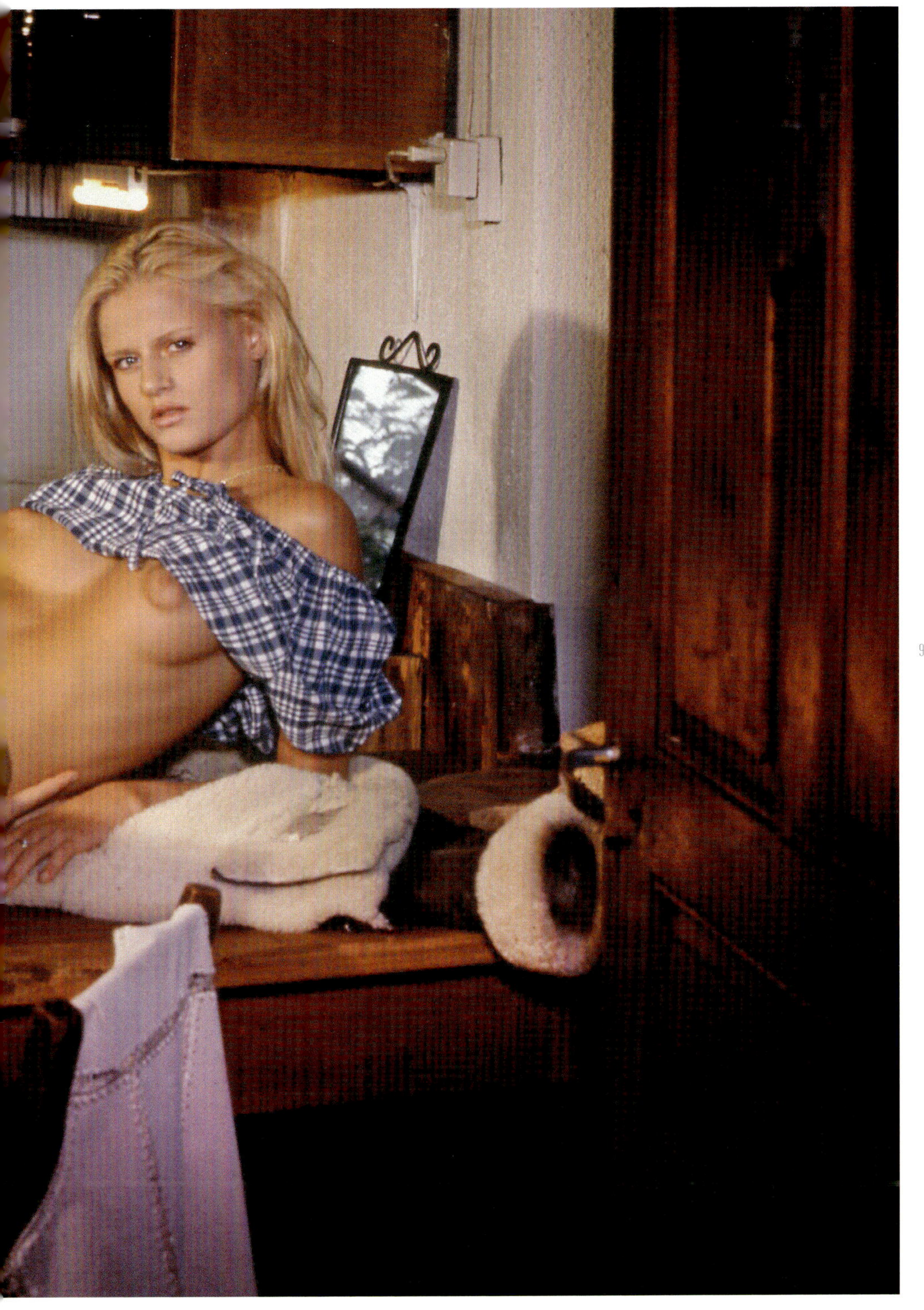

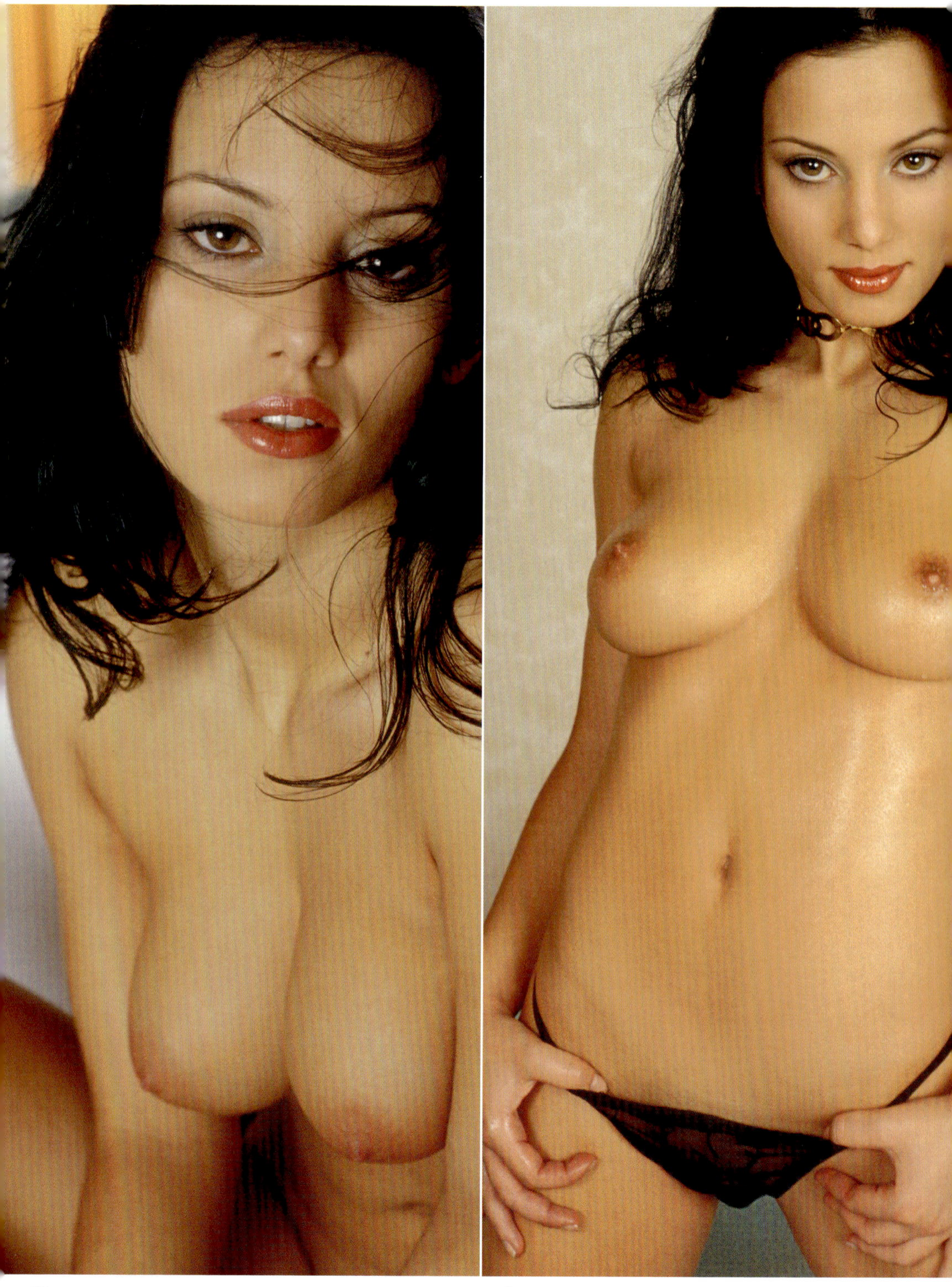

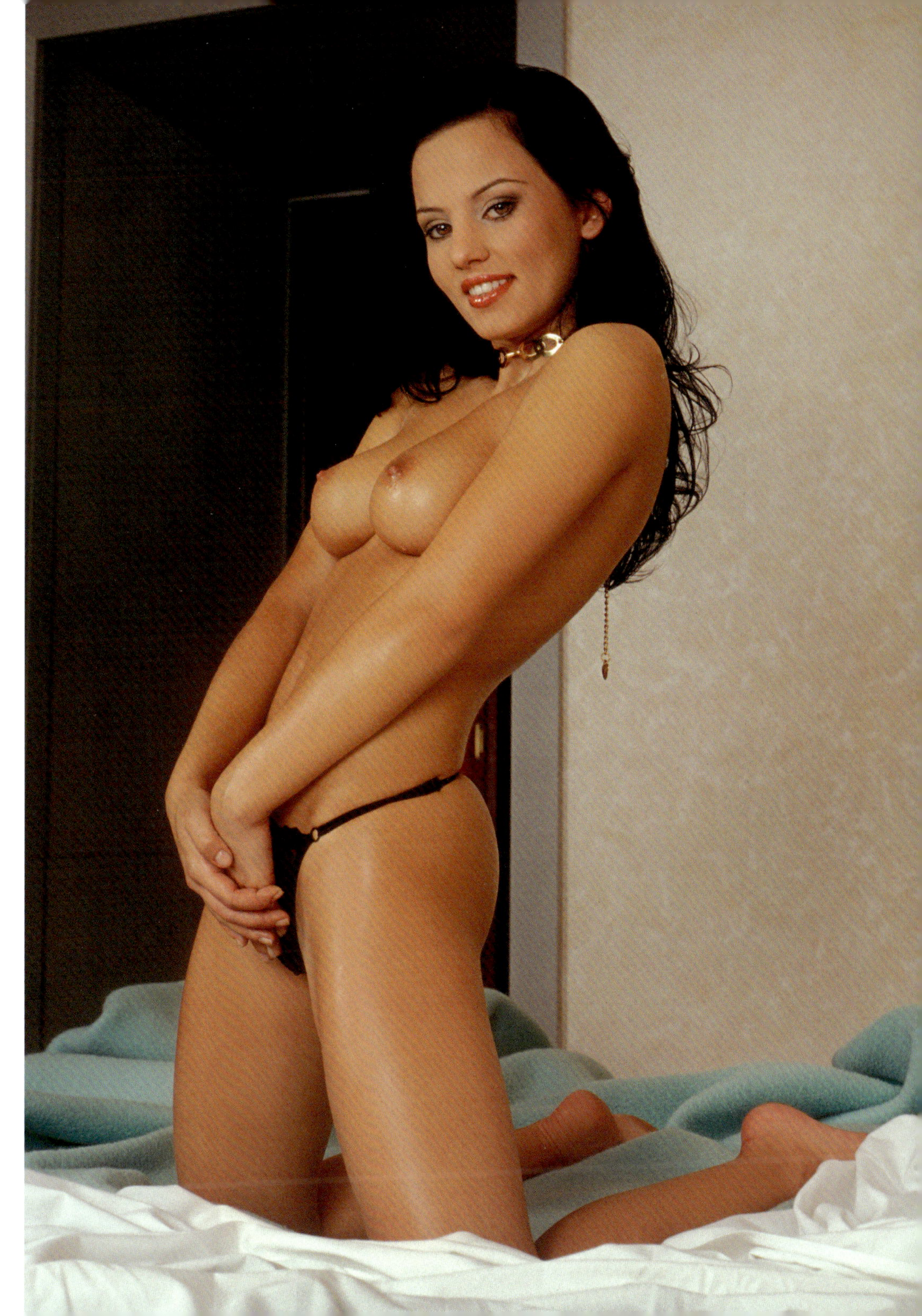

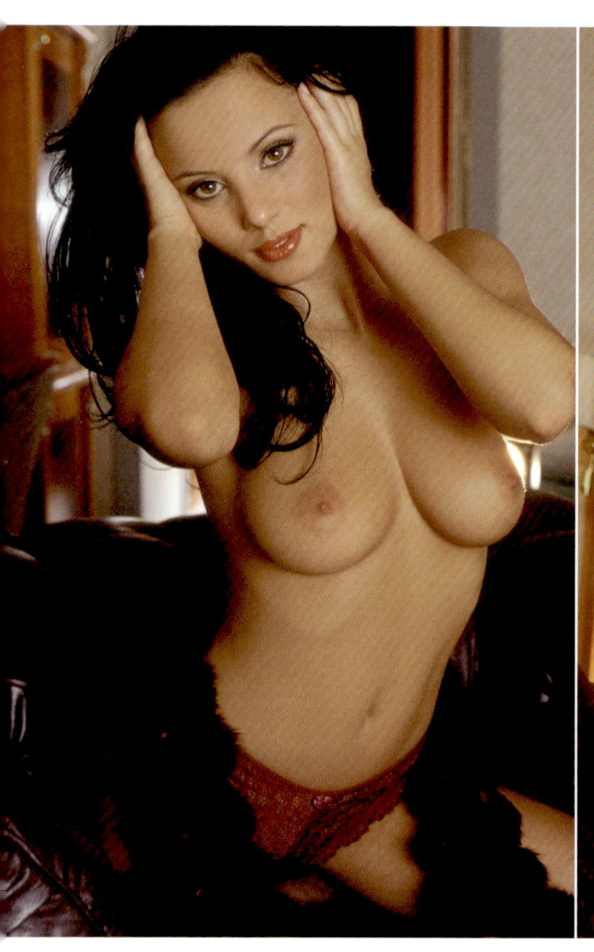

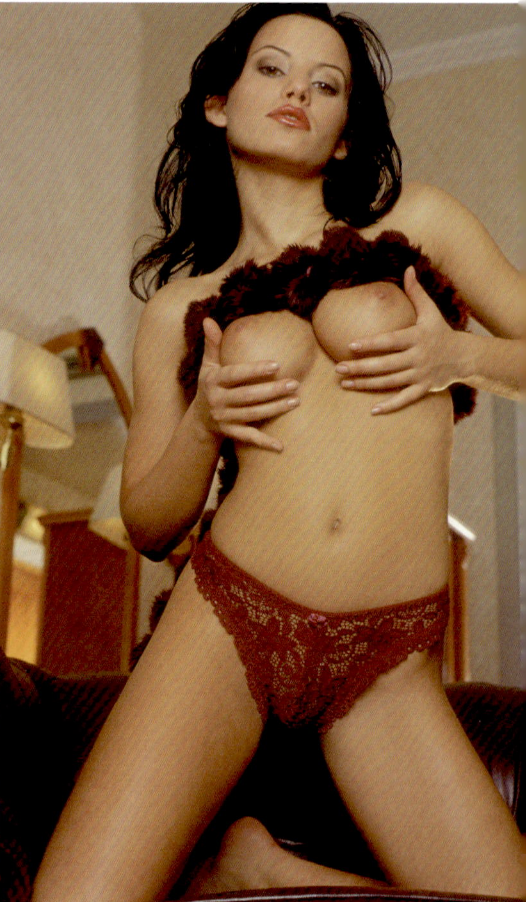

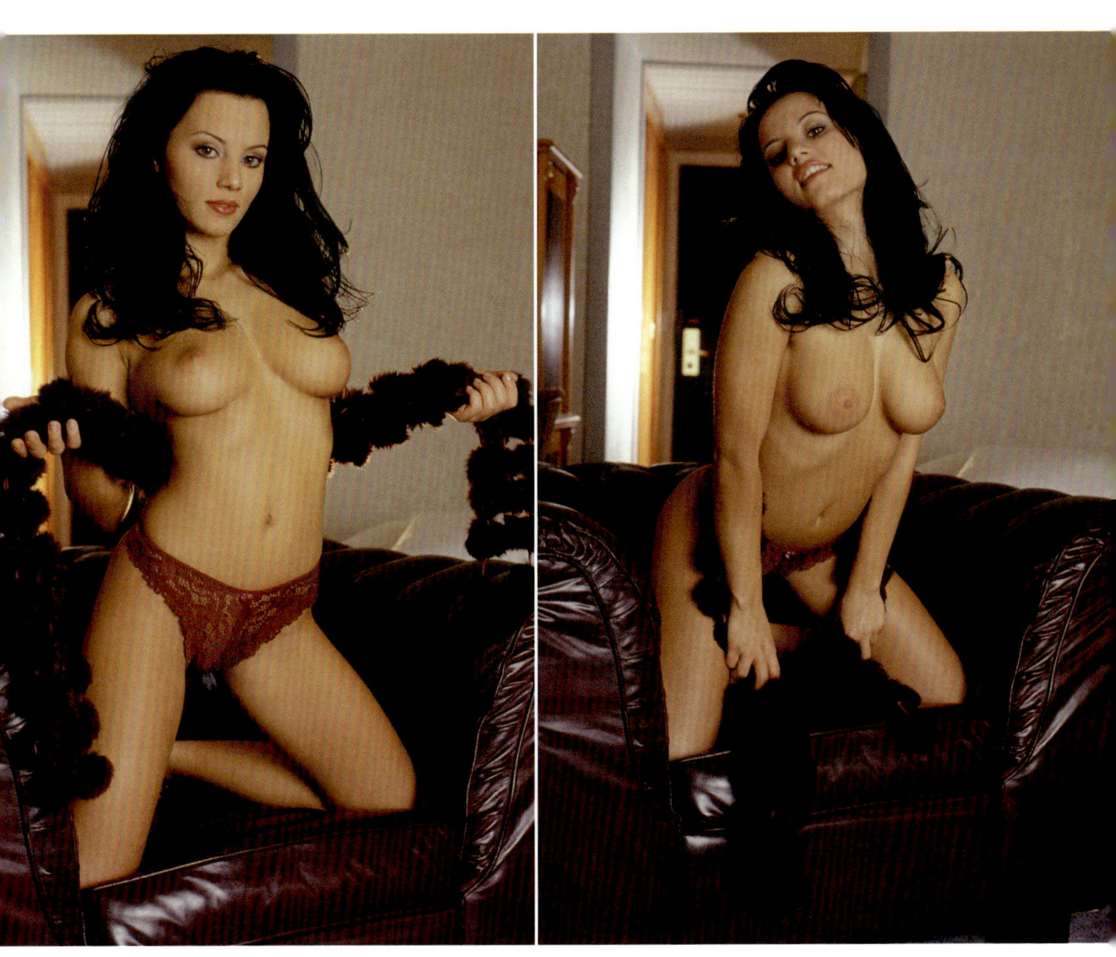

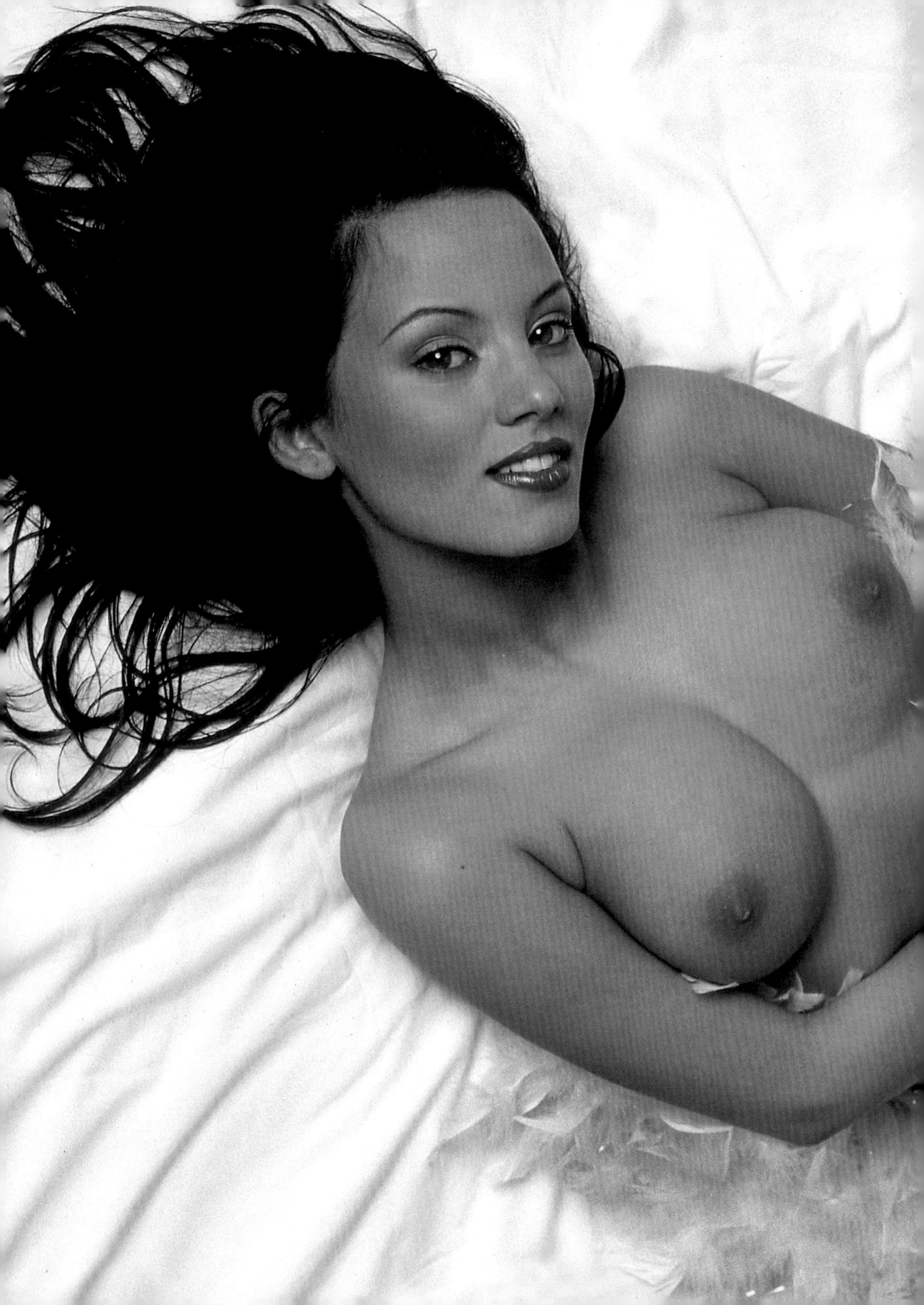

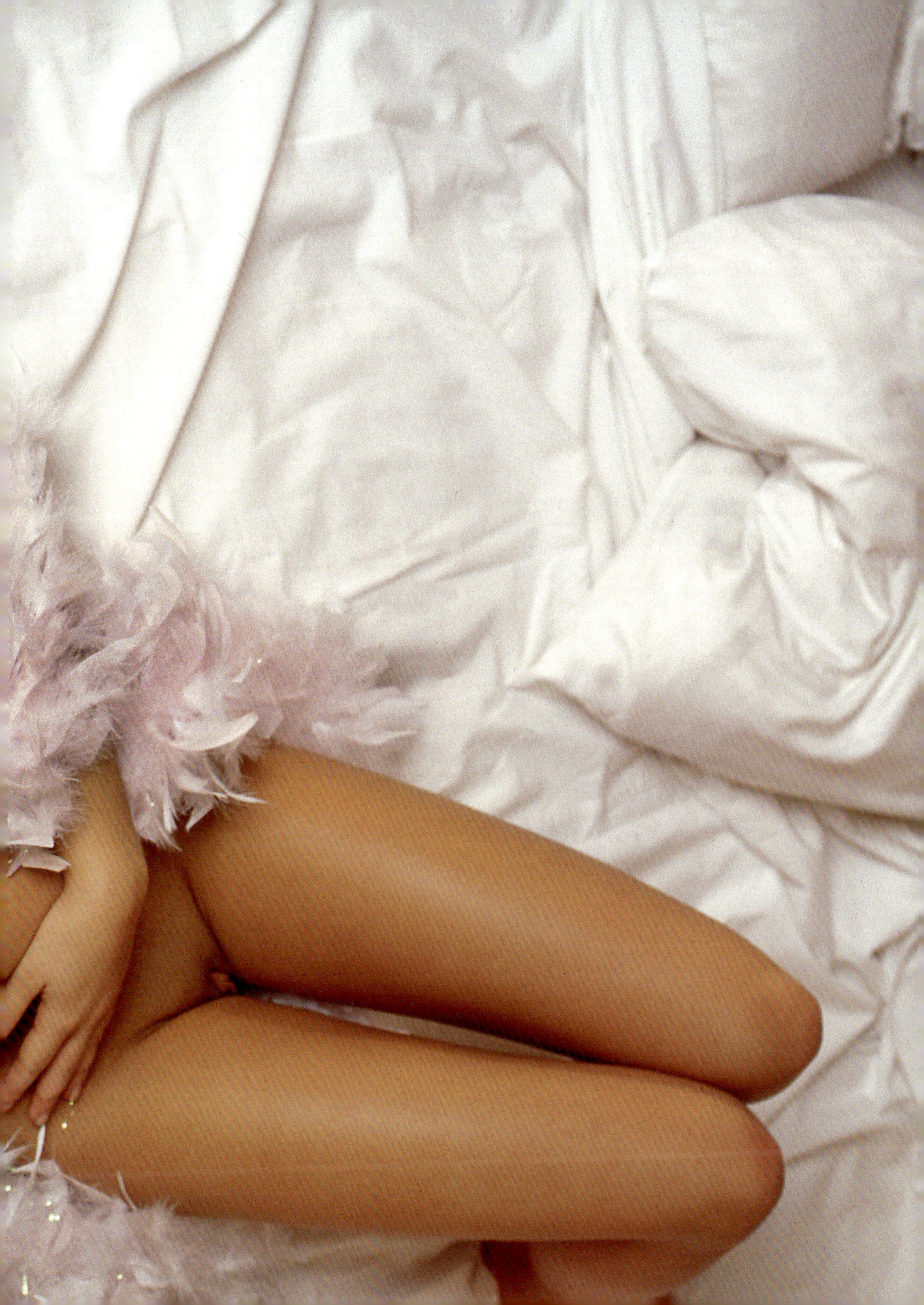

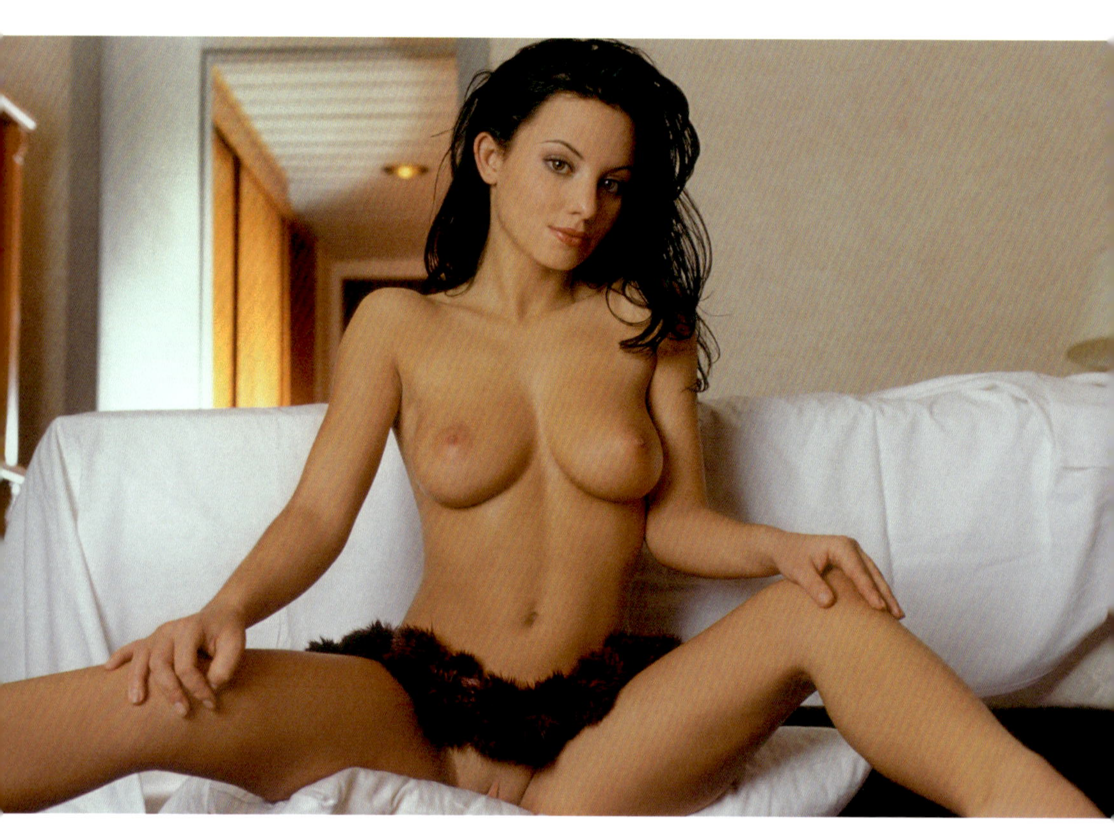

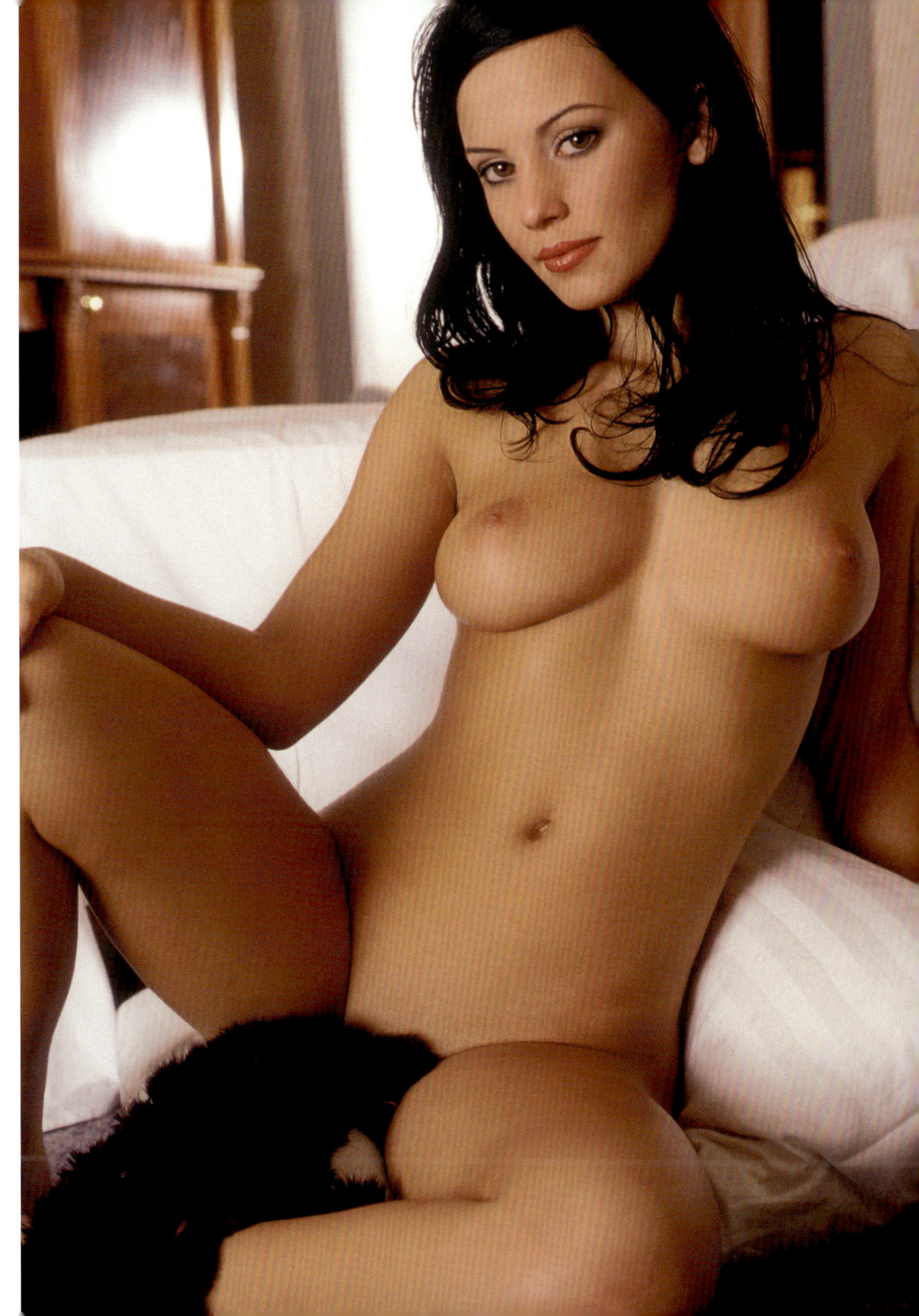

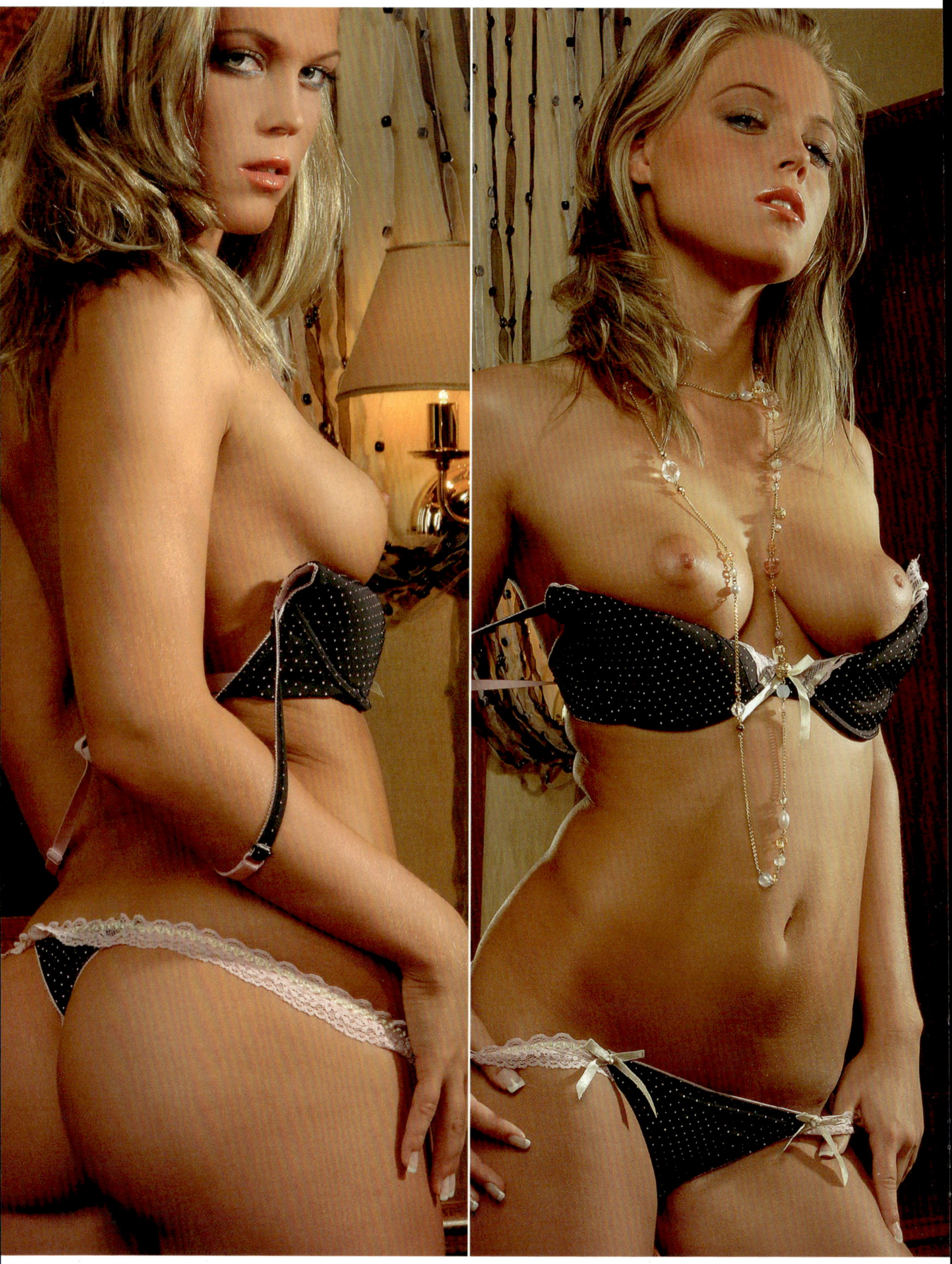

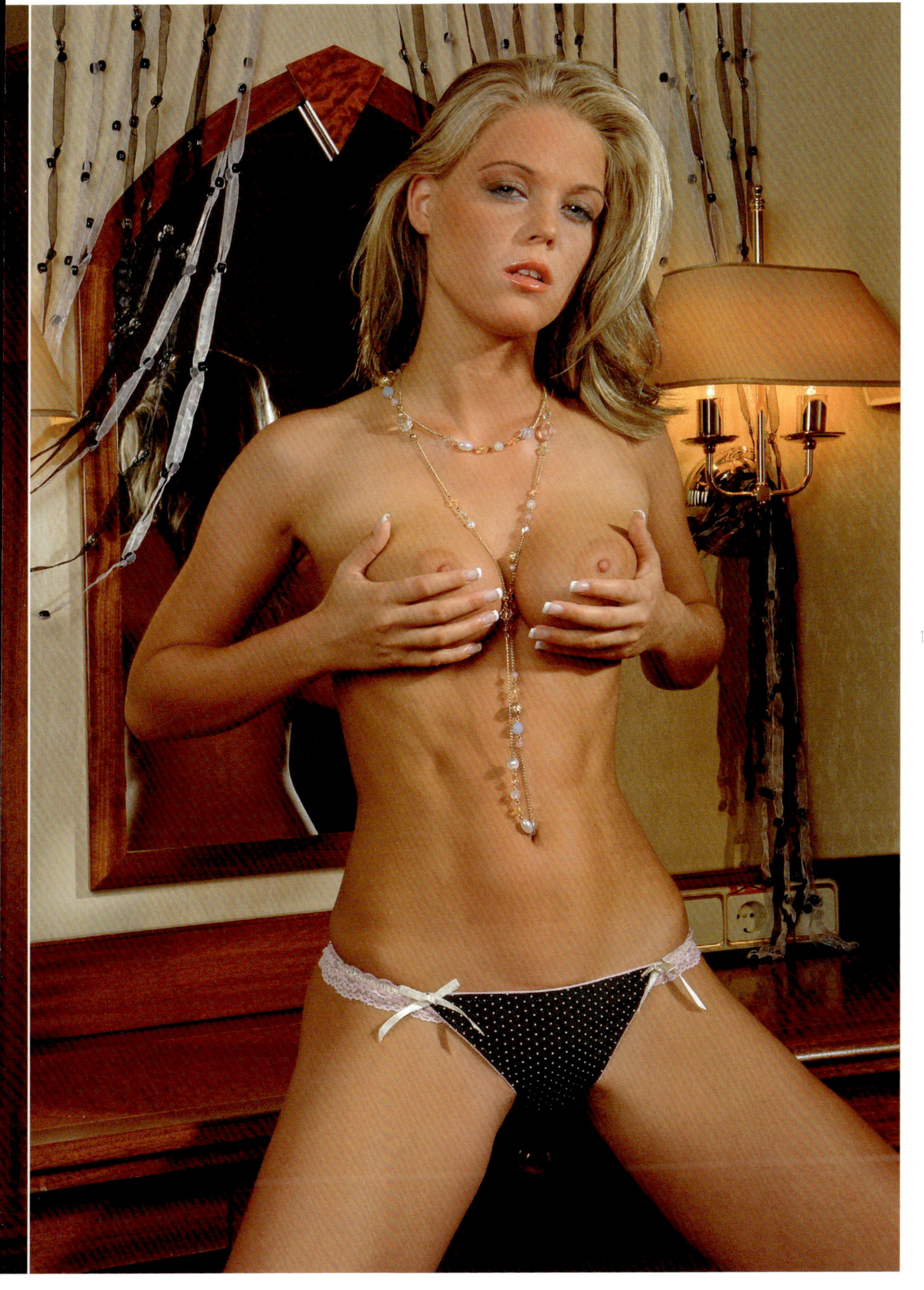

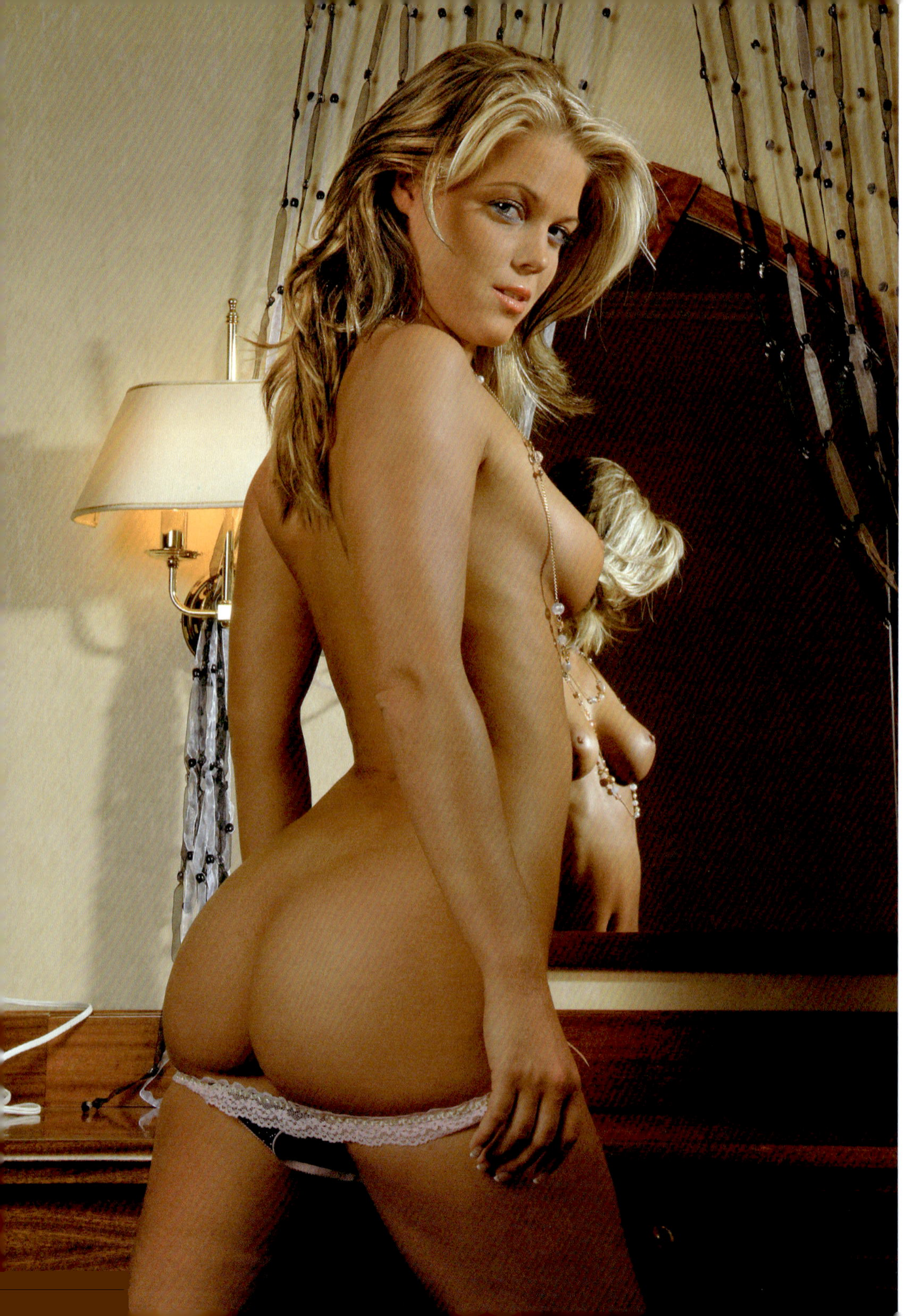

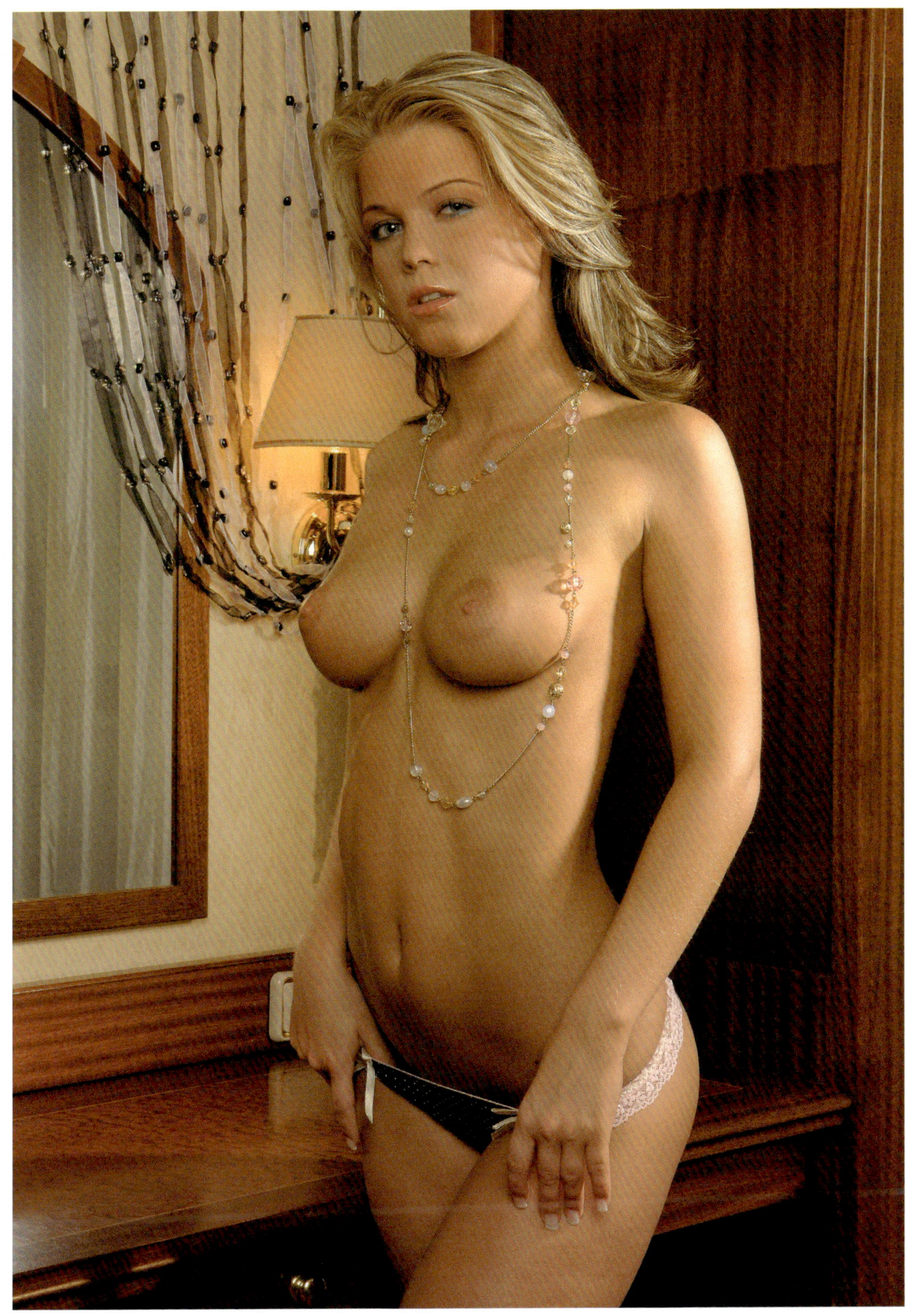

TRiSHa

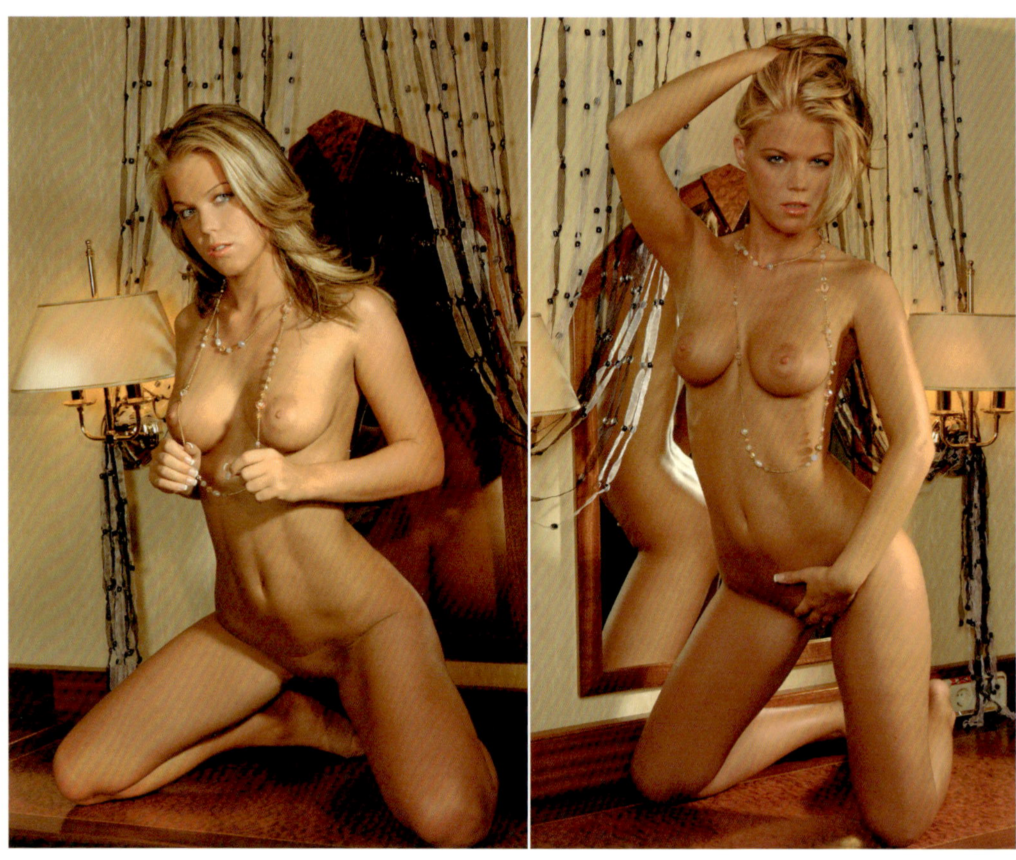

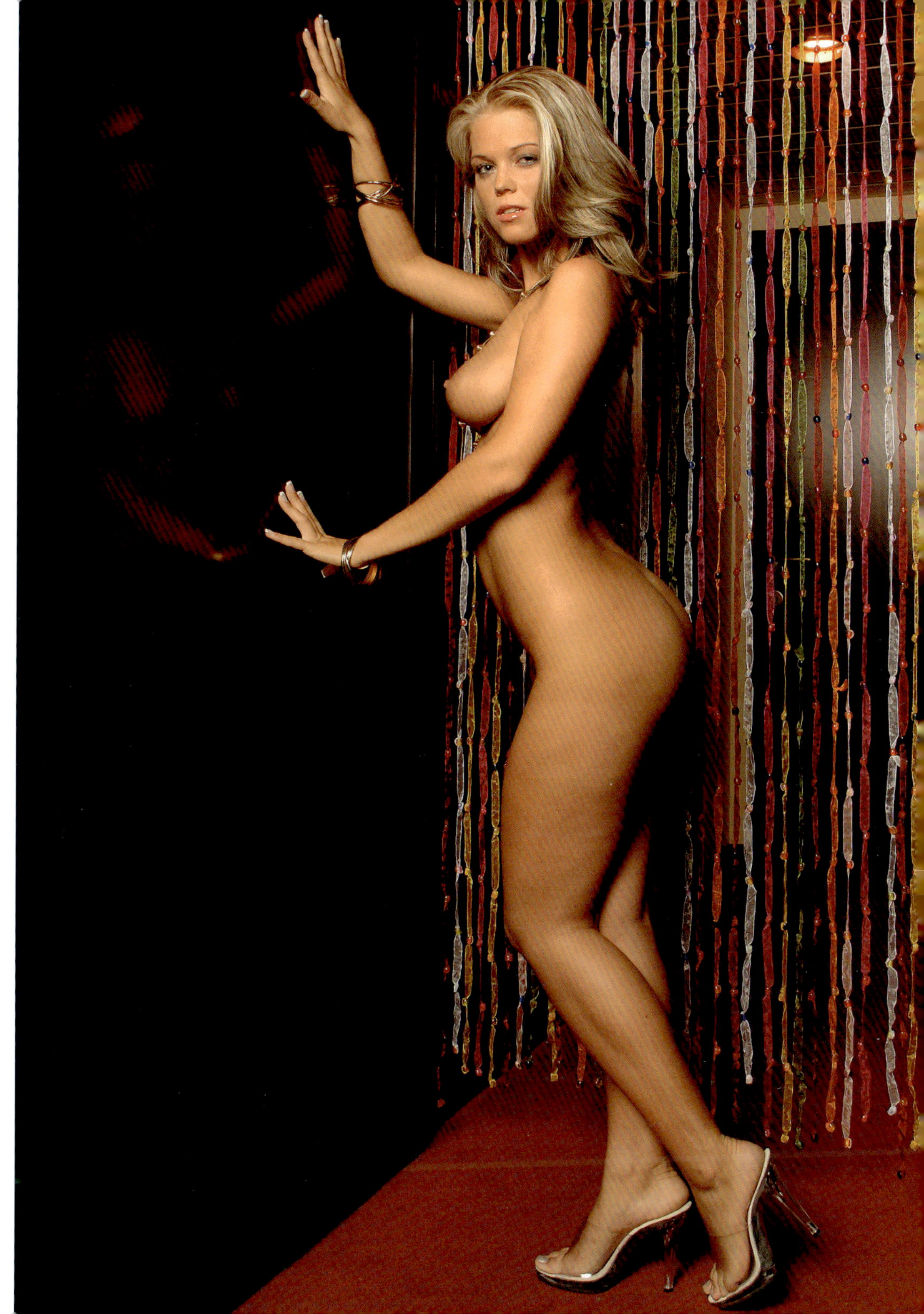

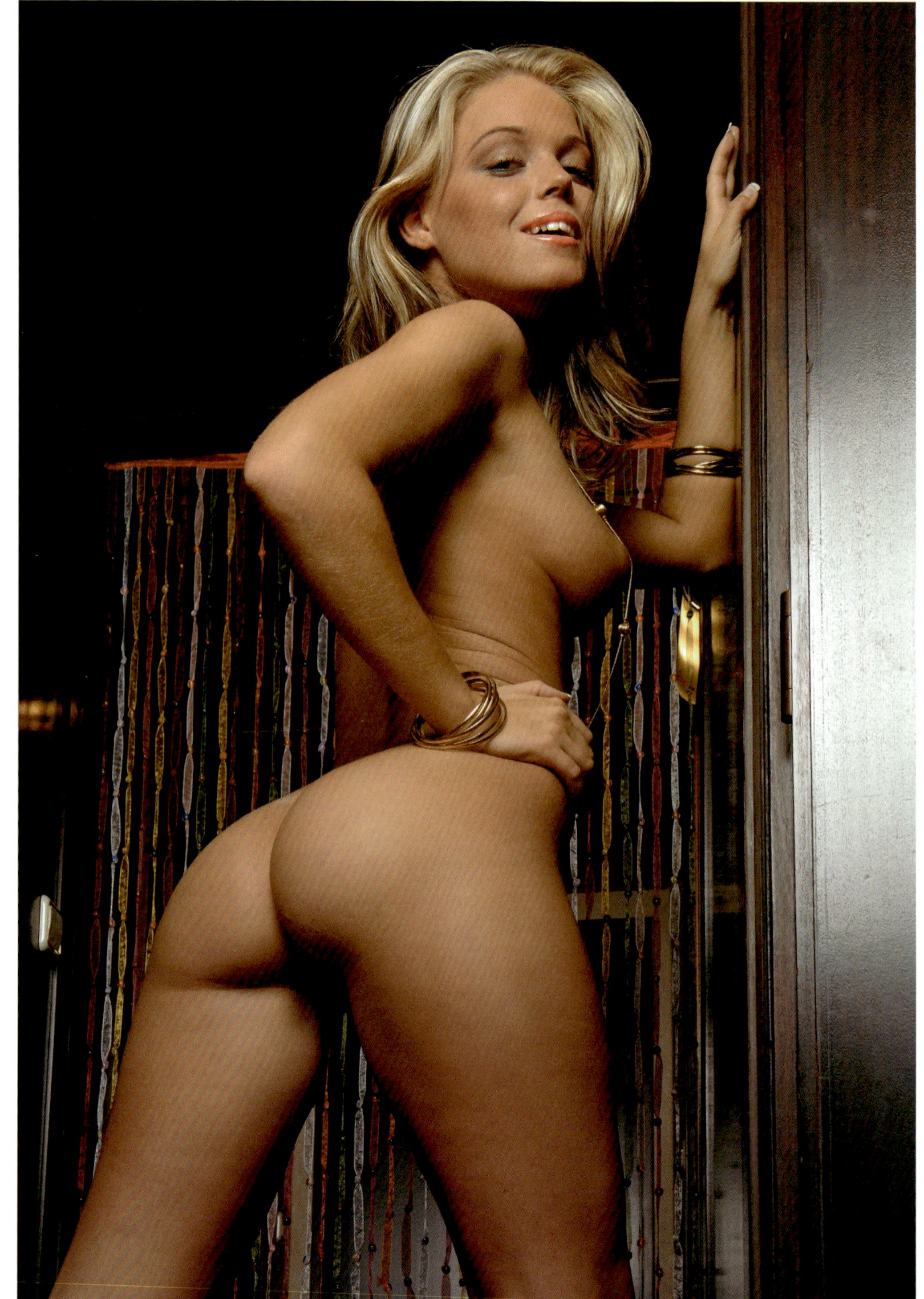

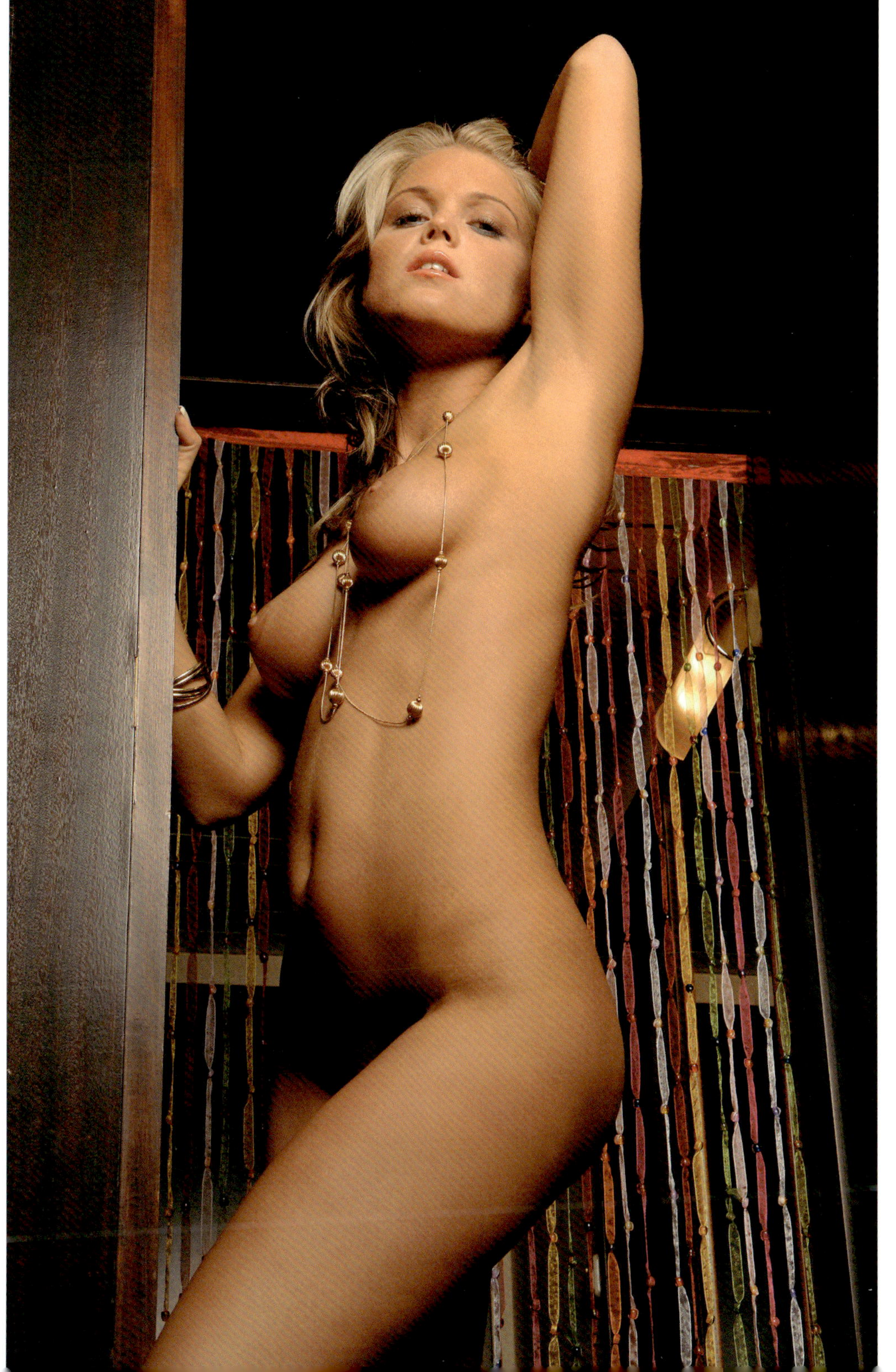

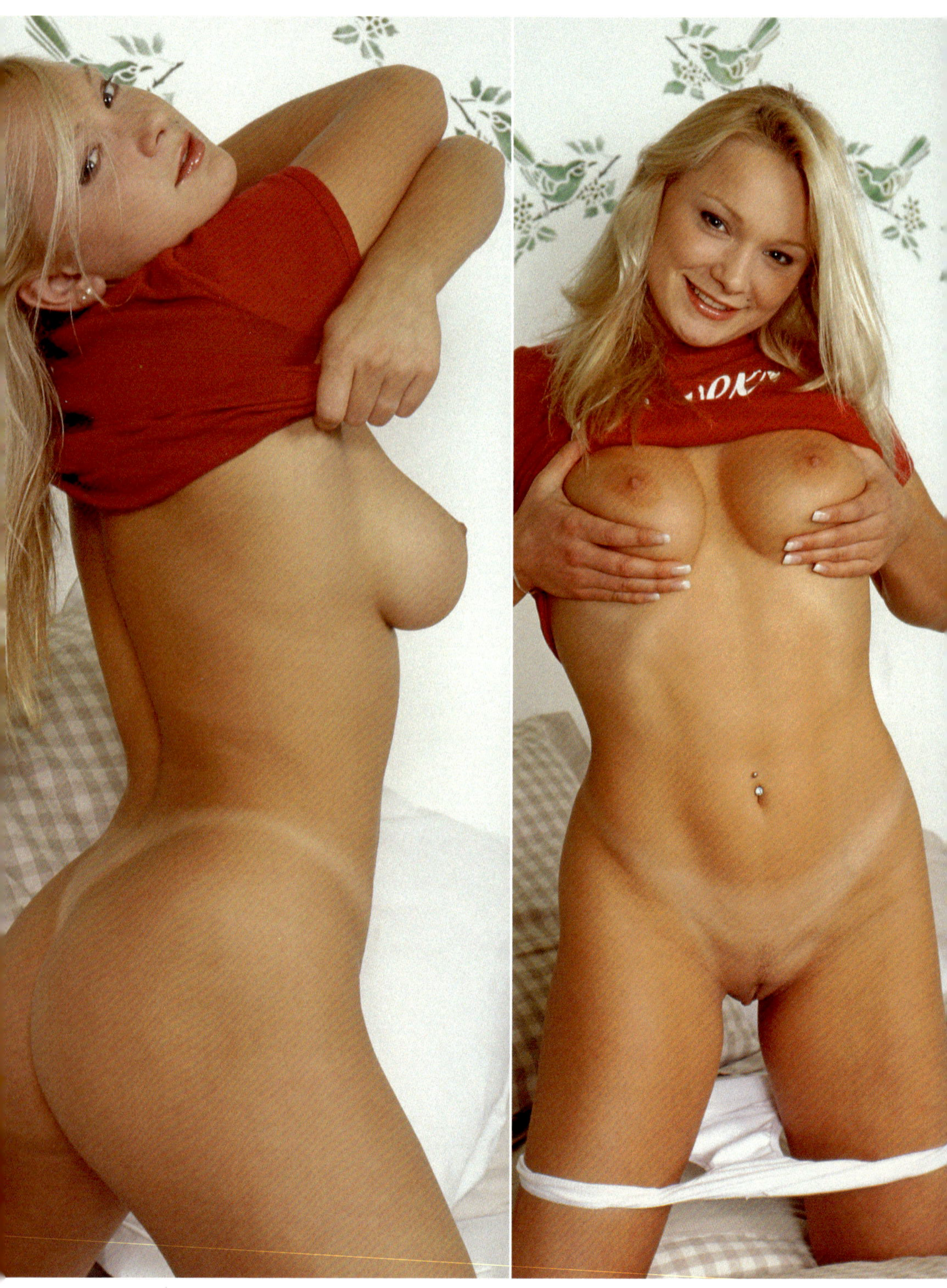

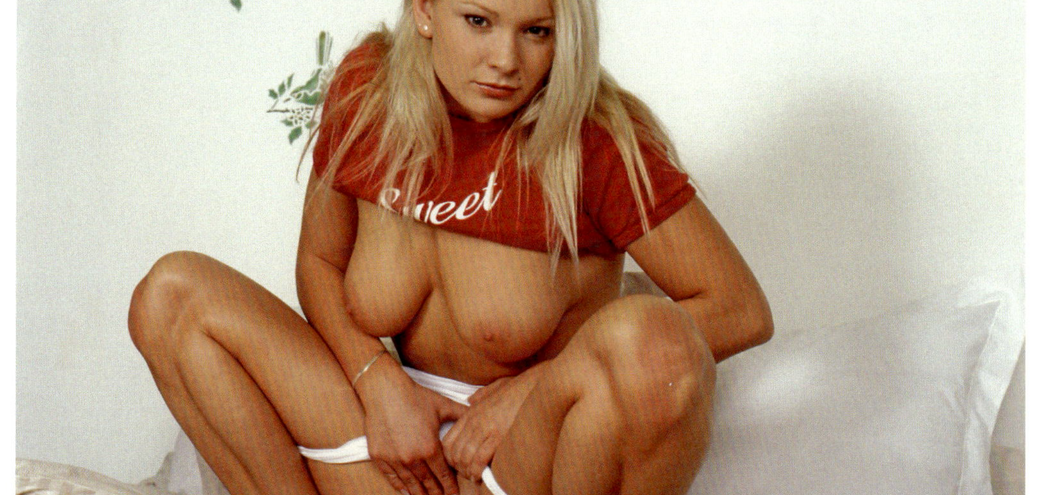
Sweet

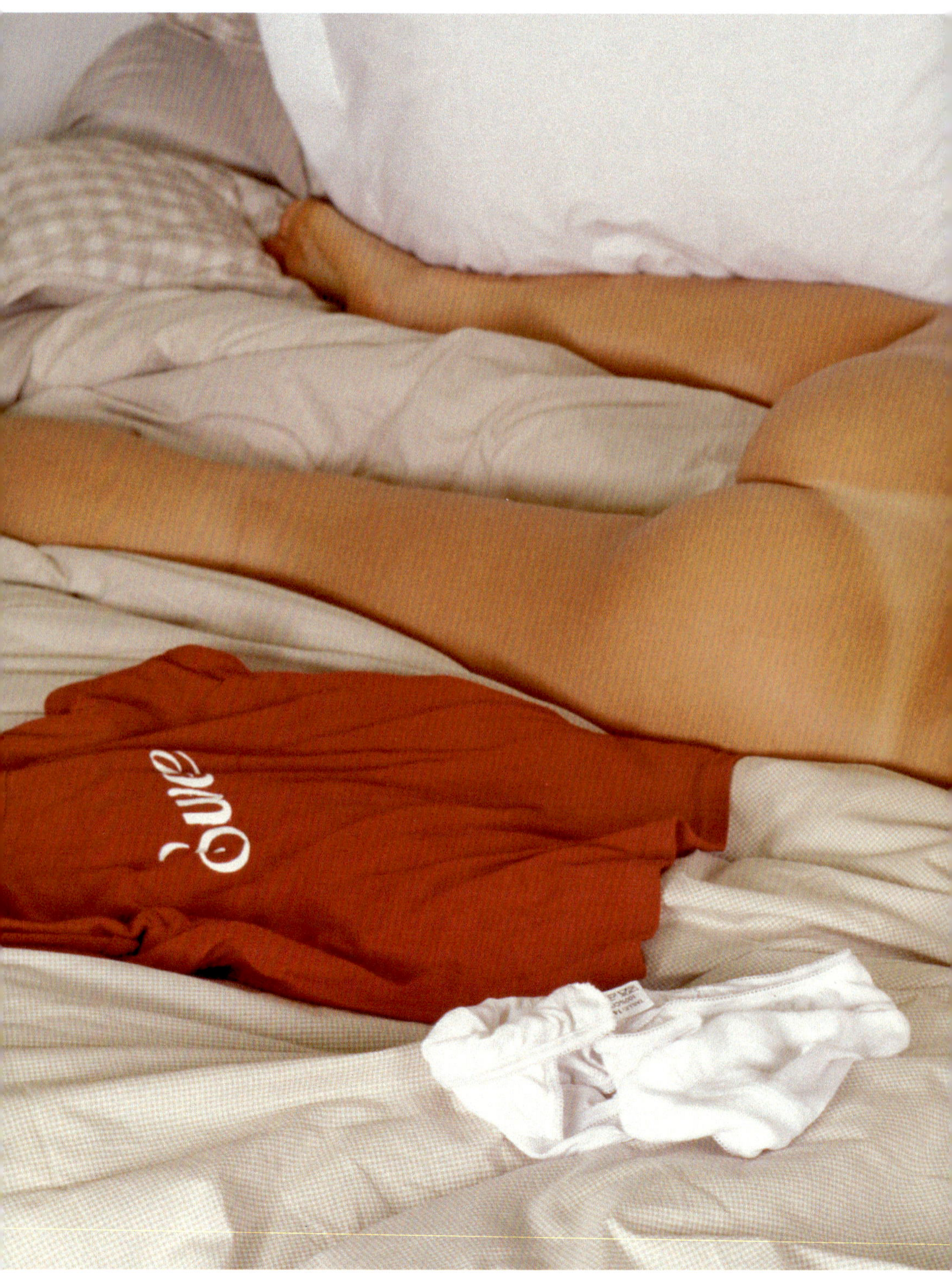

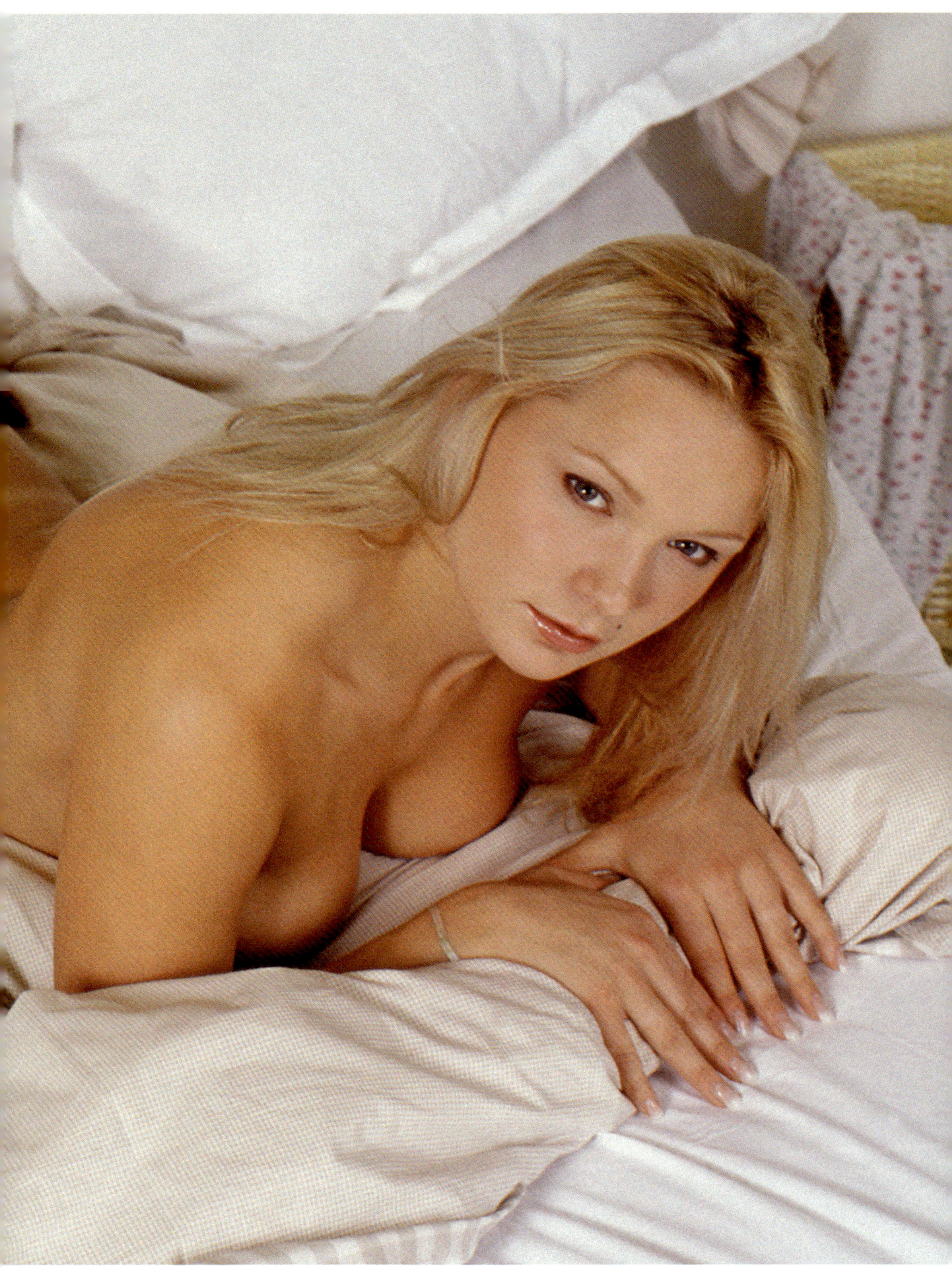

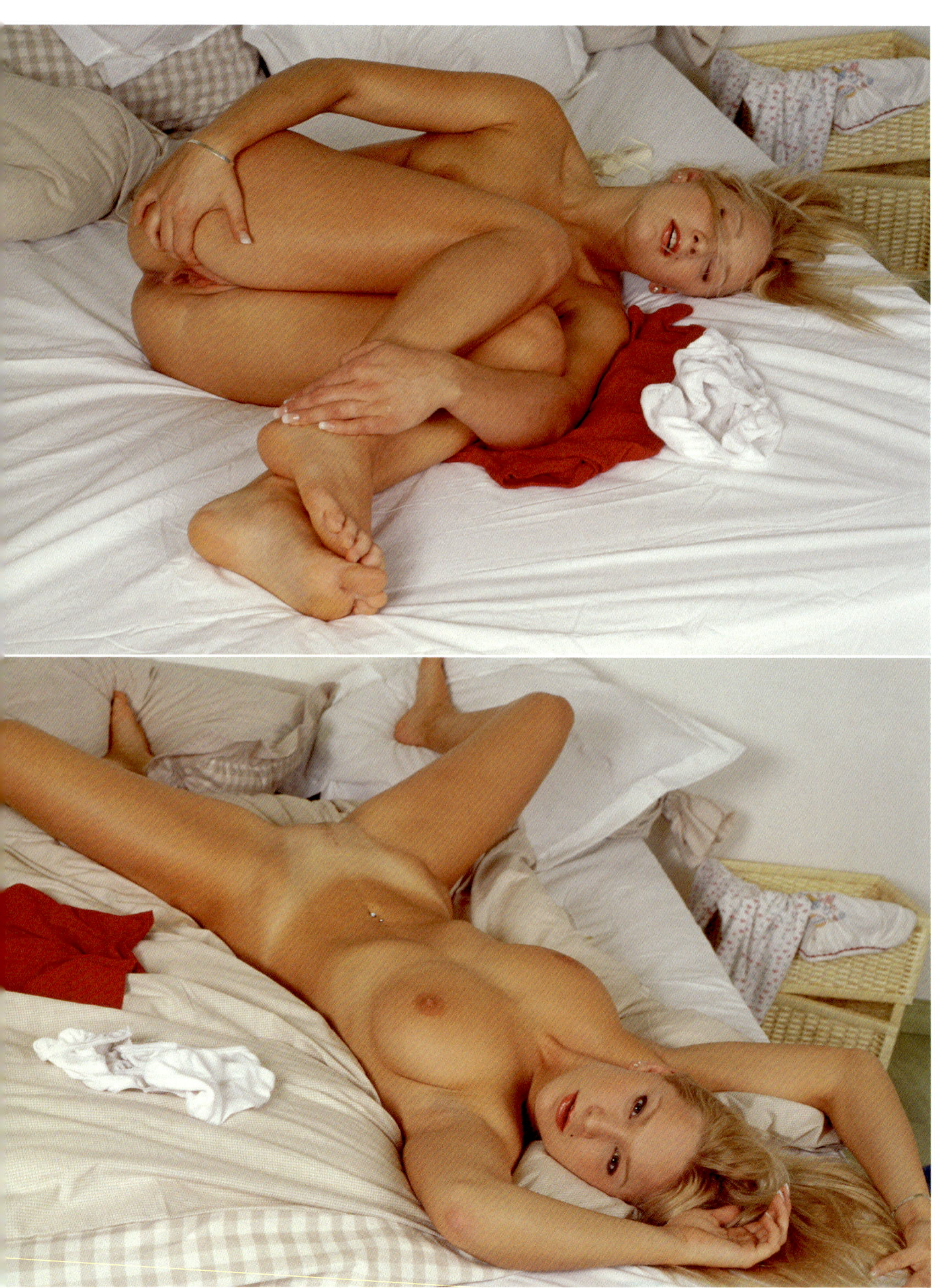

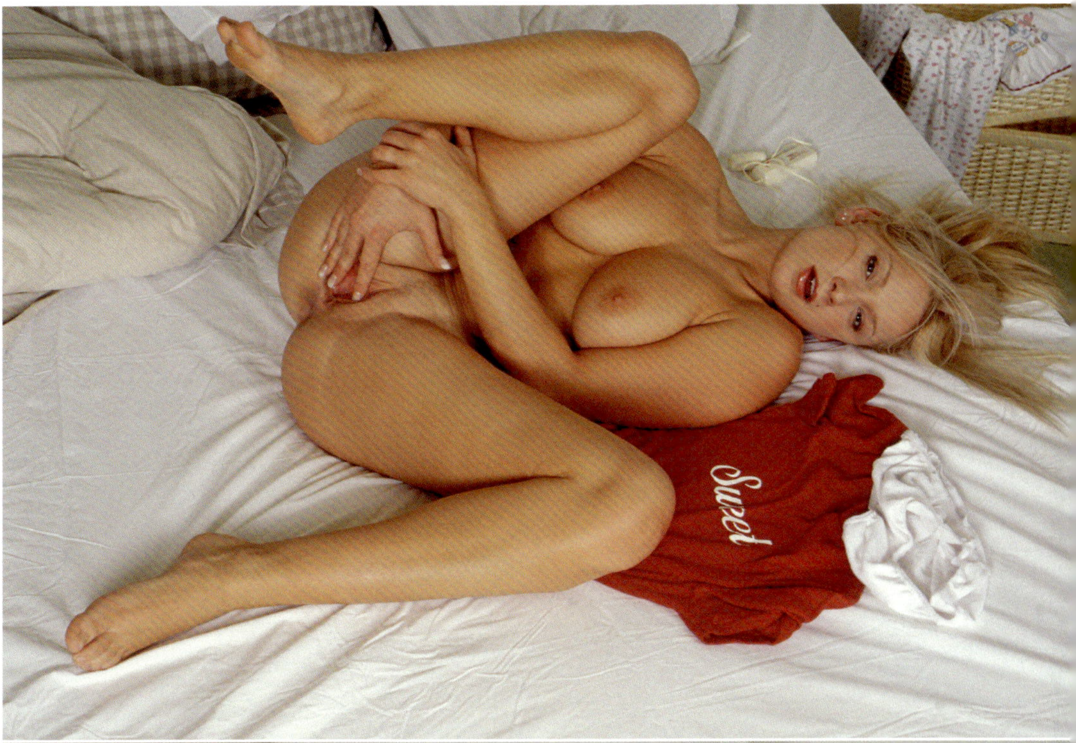

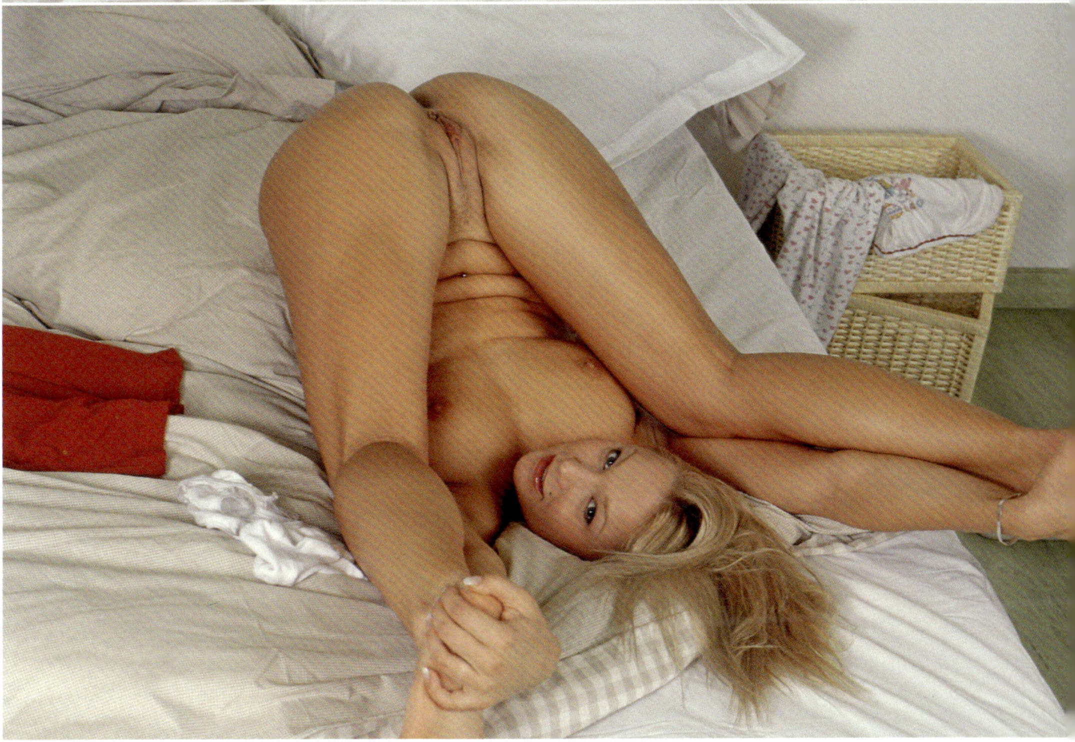

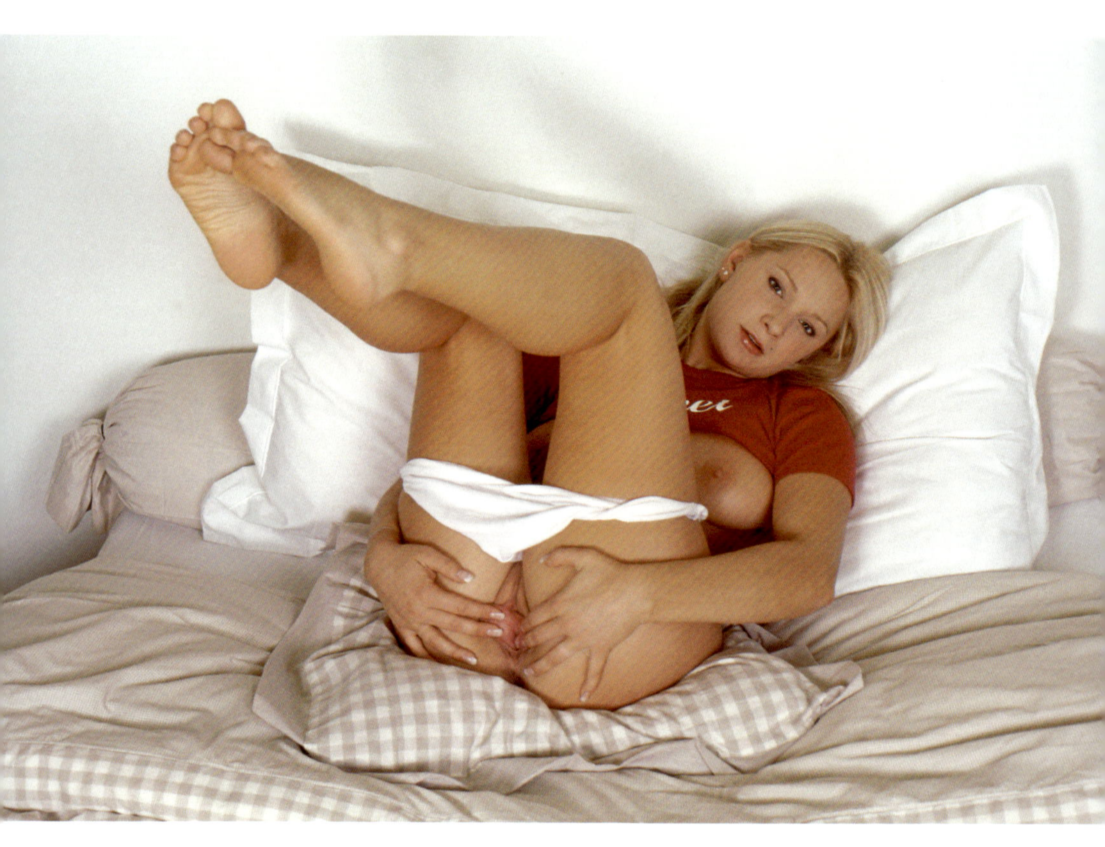

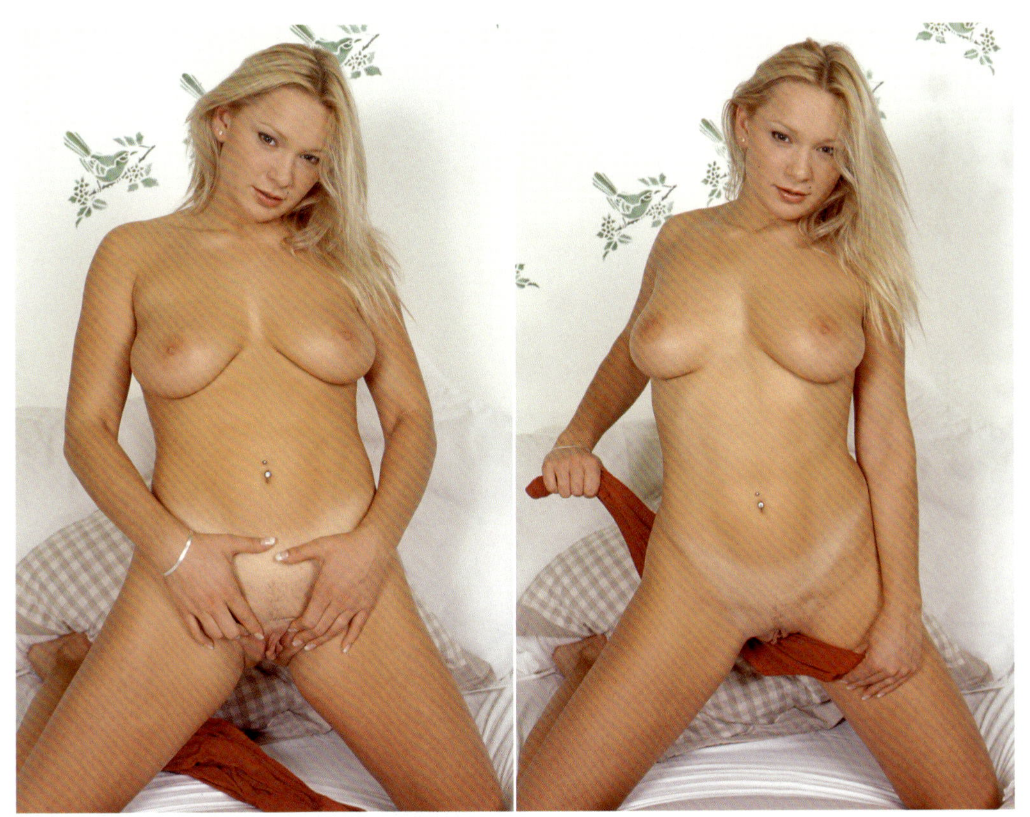

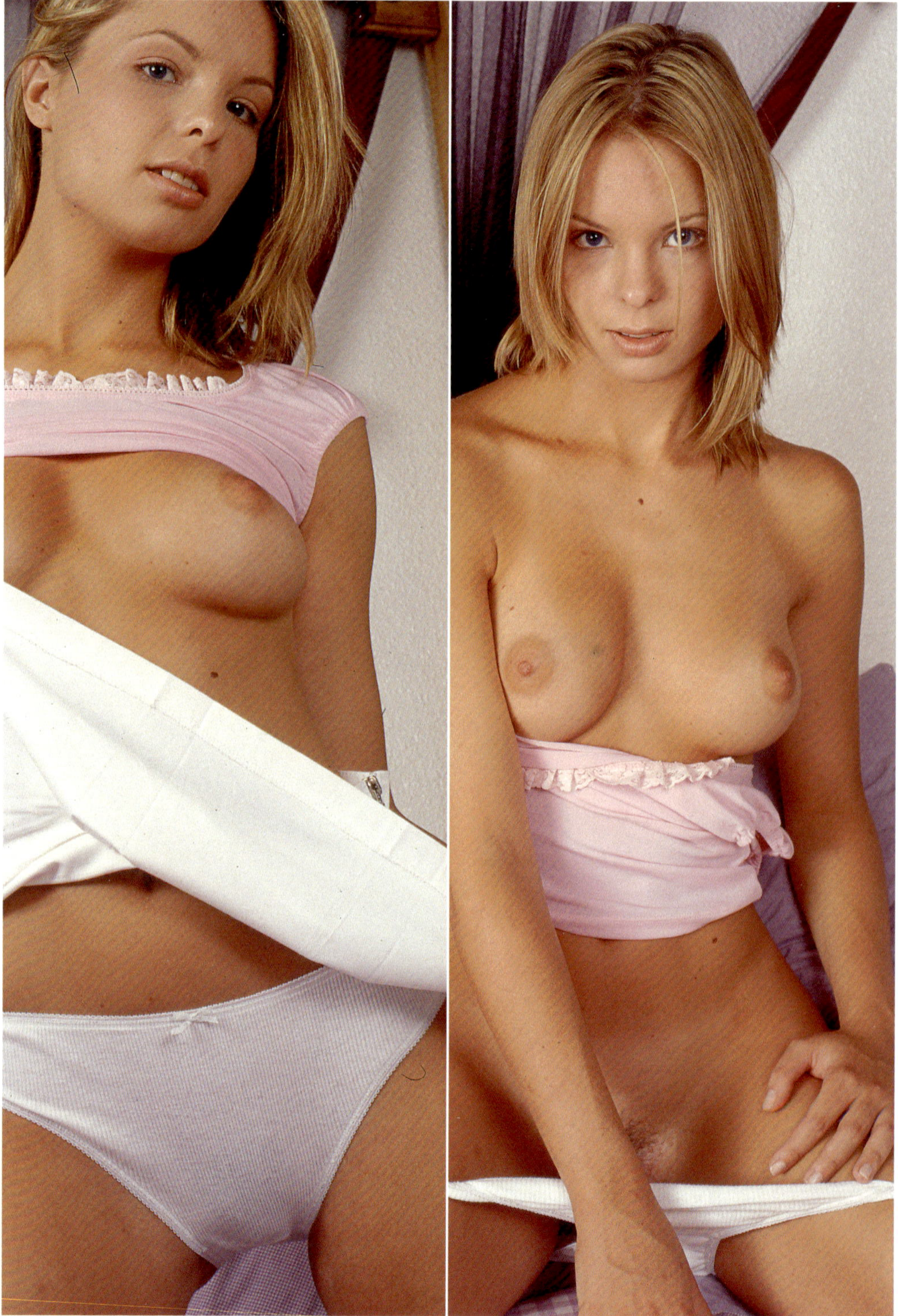

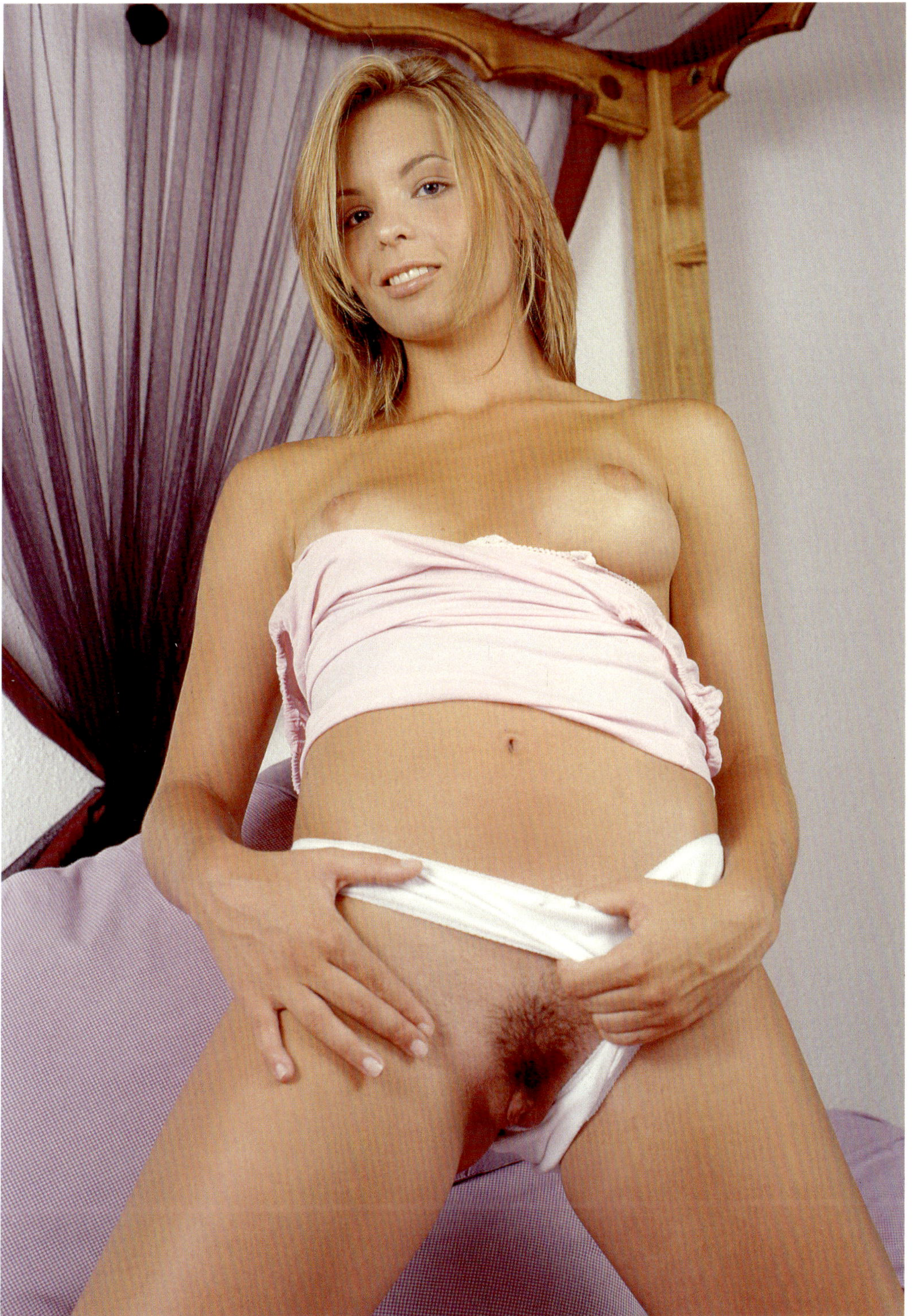

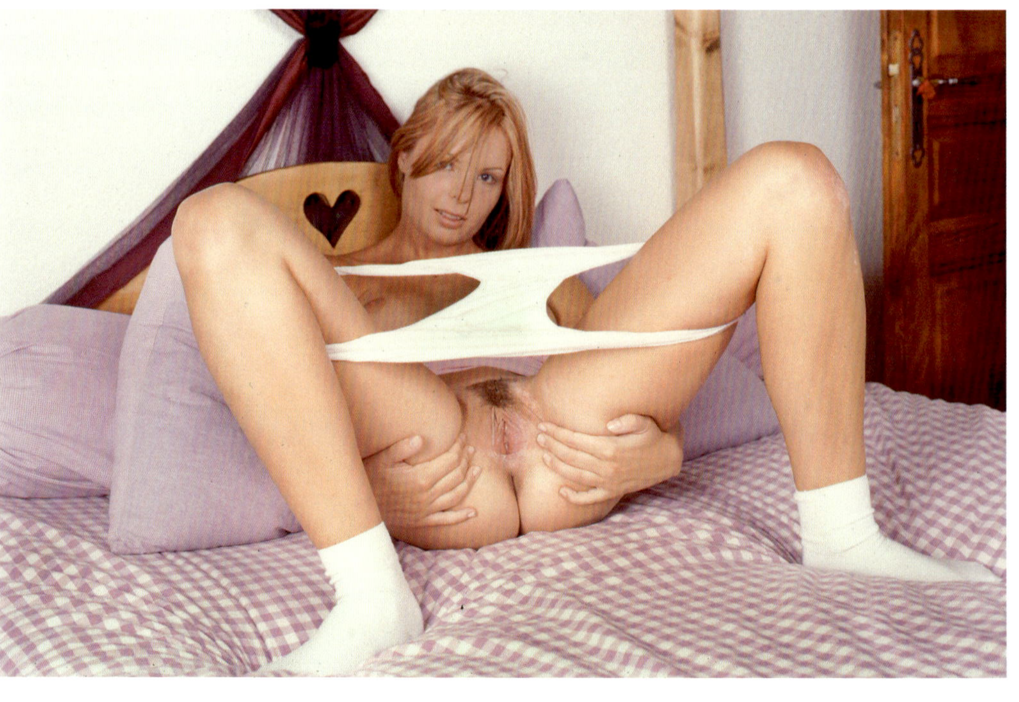

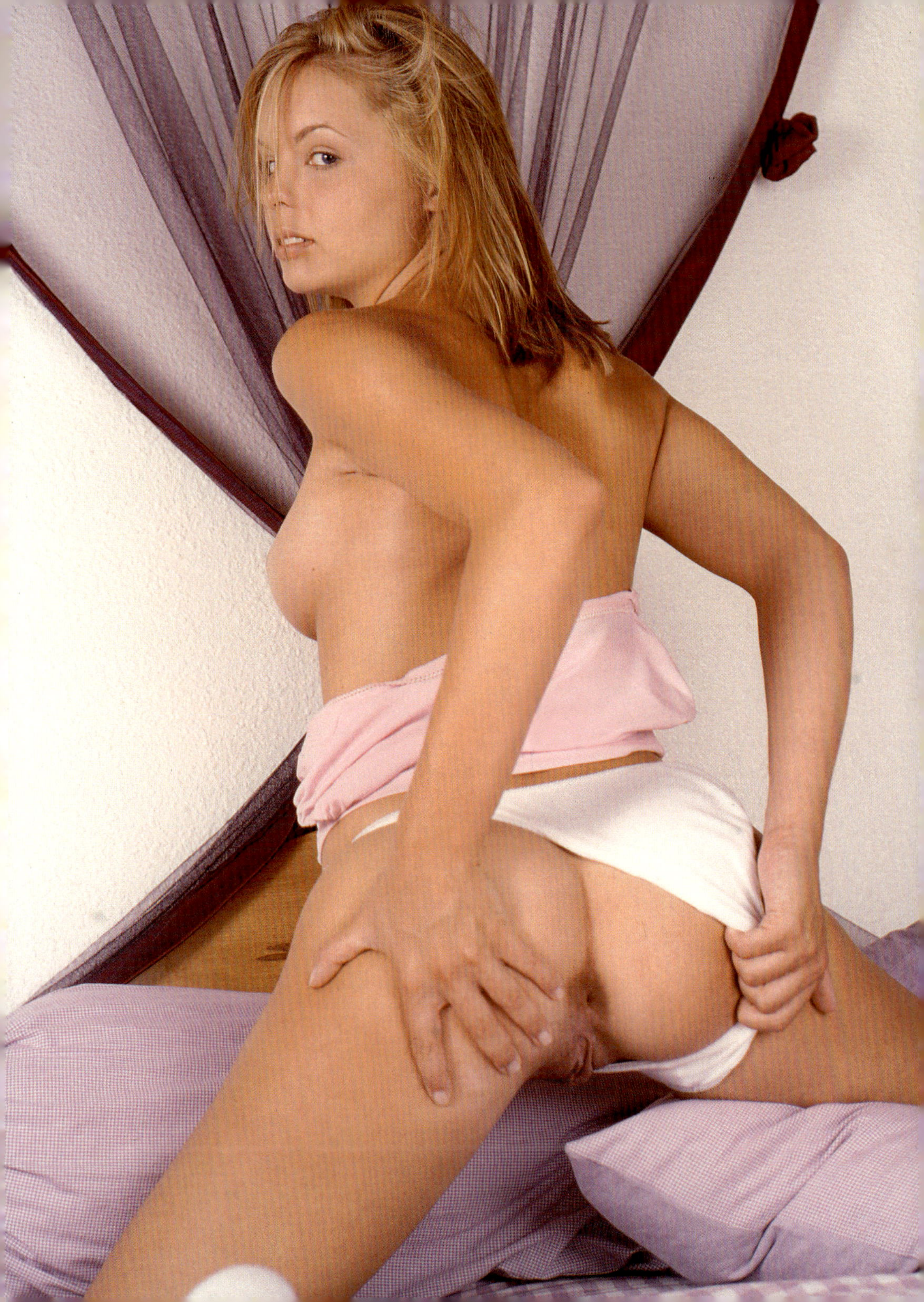

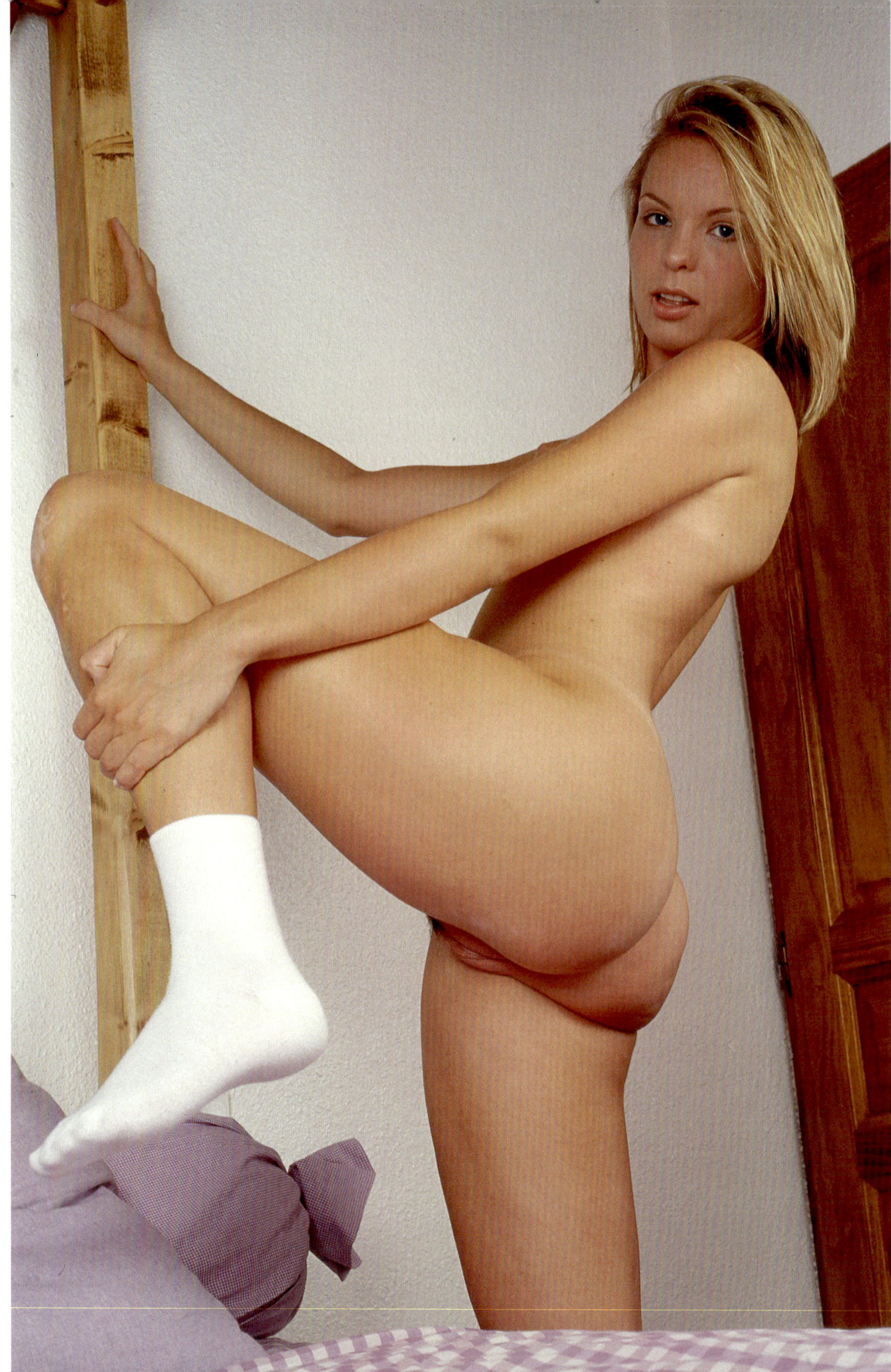

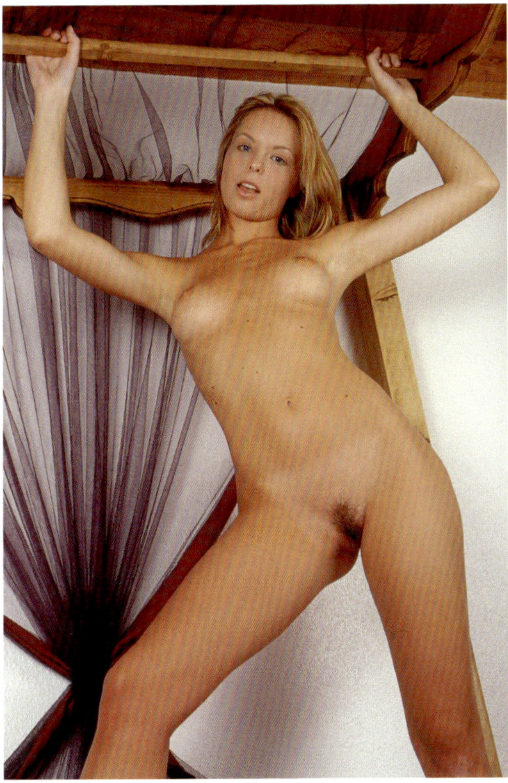

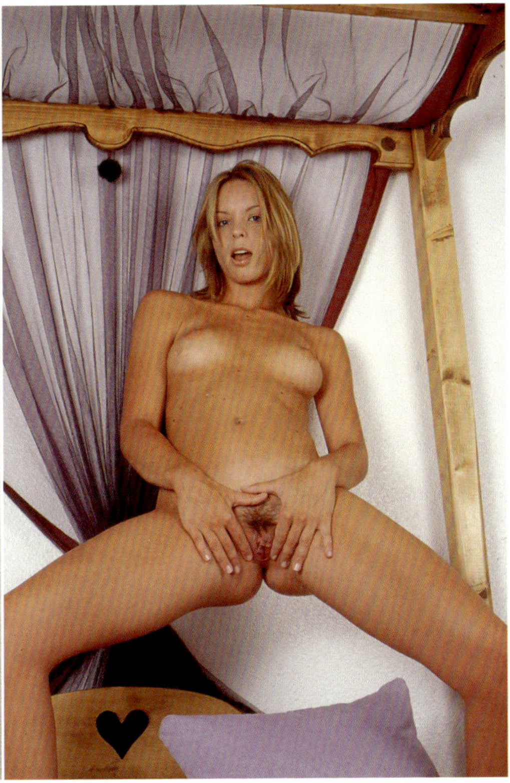

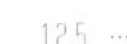

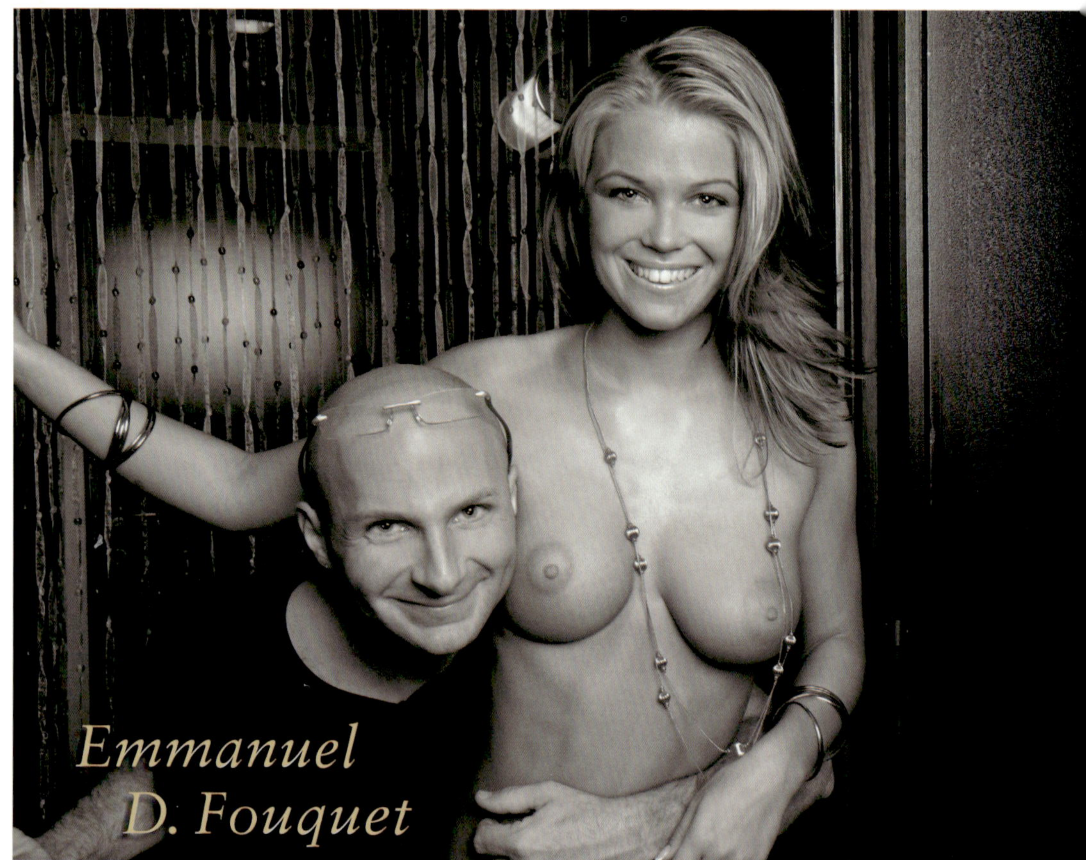

Emmanuel D. Fouquet

wanted to learn a profession in which being surrounded by beautiful women is part and parcel of the job. He left the Savoy Alps in 1991 and travelled to Paris, coming under the wing of Christian Chauveau. This famous man trained Emmanuel in the skills of the make-up artist. Emmanuel's first assignments were tough, low-paid jobs, which came his way via various model agencies. Until, that is, he took the plunge and decided to go to America. Prompted by an invitation from renowned Penthouse photographer Hank Londoner, he soon got to know others in his profession. He also acted as an agent for Londoner, for Suze Randall and Vivian Thomas as well. He used the sessions to watch and learn how the artists worked. Thus began a meteoric career, and today his photos grace the covers of Penthouse, Hustler, Private and other magazines, including many erotic calendars currently circulating Europe. Enjoy the magic of his pictures!

Emmanuel Fouquet wollte einen Beruf erlernen, be
dem er immer von schönen Frauen umgeben ist. S
ging er 1991 nach Paris, um künstlerischer Visagis
zu werden. Zuerst führte ein harter Weg schlech
bezahlter Arbeit durch diverse Model-Agenturer
bis er den Sprung nach Amerika wagte, eingelade
vom renommierten Fotografen Hank Londoner, de
unter anderem für Penthouse arbeitete. In diese
Kreisen lernte er schnell weitere Fotografen kenne
und wurde für einige auch Agent, z.B. für Londone
selbst, aber auch Suze Randall und Vivian Thomas
Er nutzte die Zeit bei den Shootings, um die Künstle
zu beobachten und ihre Arbeitsweisen zu erlerner
Eine steile Karriere begann, heute zieren sein
Bilder die Umschläge von Penthouse, Hustler, Privat
und anderen Magazinen und viele der in Europ
kursierenden erotischen Kalender. Lassen Sie sic
von seinen Fotos bezaubern!